The changing face of ESP in today's classroom and workplace

Edited by
Nalan Kenny,
King's Leadership Academy, UK
Linda Escobar,
Universidad Nacional de Educación a Distancia (UNED), Spain

Series in Education

Copyright © 2021 by the authors.

All rights reserved. No part of this publication may be reproduced, stored in a retrieval system, or transmitted in any form or by any means, electronic, mechanical, photocopying, recording, or otherwise, without the prior permission of Vernon Art and Science Inc.

www.vernonpress.com

In the Americas:
Vernon Press
1000 N West Street,
Suite 1200, Wilmington,
Delaware 19801
United States

In the rest of the world:
Vernon Press
C/Sancti Espiritu 17,
Malaga, 29006
Spain

Series in Education

Library of Congress Control Number: 2020933974

ISBN: 978-1-64889-099-4

Also available: 978-1-62273-911-0 [Hardback]; 978-1-64889-063-5 [PDF, E-Book]

Product and company names mentioned in this work are the trademarks of their respective owners. While every care has been taken in preparing this work, neither the authors nor Vernon Art and Science Inc. may be held responsible for any loss or damage caused or alleged to be caused directly or indirectly by the information contained in it.

Every effort has been made to trace all copyright holders, but if any have been inadvertently overlooked the publisher will be pleased to include any necessary credits in any subsequent reprint or edition.

Table of contents

List of Figures — vii

List of Tables — ix

List of Acronyms — xi

Preface: The changing face of ESP in today's classroom and workplace — xv
Elena Bárcena Madera
Universidad Nacional de Educación a Distancia (UNED)

Section I: ESP in specific fields — 1

Chapter 1 **The Importance of Formulaic Language in Aviation English: A case study** — 3
Tarek Assassi
University of Mohamed Kheider, Algeria

Chapter 2 **Linguistic and code-mixing practices in the linguistic landscape of Jordanian cities: The use of English in advertisements on printed product labels** — 15
Omar I. S. Alomoush
Tafila Technical University, Jordan

Chapter 3 **ESP-Needs Analysis for Khartoum State Vocational Training Centers' English Language Syllabus: An Evaluative Study** — 31
Mohamed Abdelsalam Osman Mohamed Ahmed
Dar Al Uloom Private School, UAE

Chapter 4 **Where is English Needed at Work? Voices from Iranian Business Sectors** — 45
Mohammad Amerian
Allameh Tabataba'i University, Iran

Section II: ESP through technology and culture　　63

Chapter 5　**Transnational Digital Literacy Practices of Two Karen Refugee Female Adolescents: Multimodality and Spaces**　　65
Sonia Sharmin
East West University, Bangladesh

Chapter 6　**ESP and the Beatles: Songs are not only for fun**　　79
Ian Michael Robinson
Univeristy of Calabria, Italy

Chapter 7　**Challenges of E-Learning in Teaching ESP: Prospects and Drawbacks**　　97
Svetlana Rubtsova, Tatiana Dobrova
Saint Petersburg State University, Russia

Chapter 8　**Common Perceptions and Misperceptions about ESP: an overview**　　115
Amina Gaye
Fatima College of Health Sciences, UAE

Section III: ESP and EAP in CLIL and ELT　　125

Chapter 9　**Program implementation without pedagogical standardization: A case of English language program teachers utilizing disparate classroom language policies**　　127
Brian G. Rubrecht
Meiji University, Japan

Chapter 10　**Examining L2 learners' source text reading strategies for an MA module assignment in a UK university**　　149
Takeshi Kamijo
Ritsumeikan University, Japan

| Chapter 11 | **Investigating the system of TRANSITIVITY in passive *that-clauses* of research abstracts** | 163 |

Leonardo Pereira Nunes, Bárbara Malveira Orfanò
Federal University of Minas Gerais, Brazil

| Chapter 12 | **Designing research for academic writing in the field of psychology** | 179 |

Joanna Moraza Erausquin
Universidad Nacional de Educación a Distancia (UNED)

| Chapter 13 | **Lexical hedging and boosting strategies in the abstracts written by undergraduate ELT students** | 195 |

Arzu Ekoç
Yildiz University, Turkey

| Chapter 14 | **Analysing English Dative Alternation in the Interlanguage of students in CLIL context** | 215 |

Ivan Calleja Rituerto
Universidad Nacional de Educación a Distancia (UNED)

| *Contributors* | *235* |
| *Index* | *239* |

List of Figures

Figure 1.1 Complex Relationship with Phraseology and Natural Language (Stephany 2011, p. 26) — 8

Figure 1.2 Aviation English Users (adapted from Mekkaoui 2013, p. 13) — 8

Figure 1.3 Aviation English Users — 11

Figure 2.1 Categorization of proper names on labels on products — 21

Figure 2.2 Example of the trilingual Arabic, English, and RA pattern on two cartons of apple and orange juice — 23

Figure 2.3 Example of the bilingual Arabic-English combination on cleaning and washing products — 25

Figure 2.4 Example of the triangular Arabic-English pattern on a rice sack — 26

Figure 2.5 Example of the trilingual Arabic-English-RA pattern on labels on other products — 27

Figure 3.1 Socio-demographic Profile of Trainers (Teachers) — 37

Figure 7.1 MOOC "English: postgraduate qualified exam" — 109

Figure 7.2 Online Additional Educational Programme "Translation and Interpreting in the Sphere of Professional Communication" — 110

Figure 8.1 ESP classification by professional area (Dudley-Evans & St. John, 1998, p. 6) — 117

Figure 11.1 The grammar of experience: types of process in English — 166

Figure 11.2 CQL used in both corpora — 170

Figure 11.3 Set of concordance lines for passive *that*-clauses in the *CorIFA* — 171

Figure 11.4 Set of concordance lines for the passive *that*-clauses in the English *Lingua Franca* corpus — 172

Figure 11.5 Types of processes realized by verbs in passive that-clauses in the *CorIFA* — 173

Figure 11.6 Types of processes realized by verbs in passive that-clauses in the English *Lingua Franca* corpus — 174

Figure 12.1 Quantitative questionnaires results (Professional Field) — 188

Figure 12.2 Quantitative questionnaires results (Academic Field)   188
Figure 12.3 Quantitative questionnaire (Results Collapsed)   189
Figure 12.4 Difficulties found with academic writing   190
Figure 14.1 Global Correct Response (Pretest)   225
Figure 14.2 Correct Response (DA condition, Explicit Teaching)   226
Figure 14.3 Correct Response (DA condition, Implicit Teaching)   228
Figure 14.4 Development line per group   228

List of Tables

Table 2.1 Summary of languages used on labels on products	21
Table 2.2 Percentages of languages used on mobile water bottles and soft drinks	22
Table 2.3 Percentages of languages used on mobile washing and cleaning product packaging	24
Table 2.4 Percentages of languages used on rice and sugar products	25
Table 2.5 Percentages of languages used on other products	26
Table 3.1 Trainees' Age Description	36
Table 3.2 Chi-Square Test Results for Trainees' questionnaire	38
Table 3.3 Chi-Square Test Results for Trainers' questionnaire	39
Table 4.1 The Profile of Business Sectors	49
Table 4.2 Demographic Profile of The Managers (MGT: management, Eco.: economics, B: bank, Ins.: insurance, SE: stock exchange, Ind.: industry, Com.: commerce, T: tourism)	50
Table 4.3 Demographic Profile of The Staff (MGT: management, Eco.: economics, Acc.: accounting, B: bank, Ins.: insurance, SE: stock exchange, Ind.: industry, Com.: commerce, T: tourism)	51
Table 4.4 Results of EFA for the Questionnaire	53
Table 4.5 Emerged Themes in Response to Open-ended Questions of the Questionnaire	56
Table 4.6 Summary of the Managers' Interview	57
Table 5.1 Ming's Digital Literacy Practices	69
Table 5.2 Saw's Literacy Practices	69
Table 6.1 Statements to agree or disagree with	90
Table 7.1 SPbU e-learning environment in teaching ESP/EAP	106
Table 10.1 Coding Categories for Data Analysis	154
Table 11.1 Representational meaning within the clause [adapted from Halliday and Matthiessen (2014, p. 83)]	165
Table 11.2 Examples of grammatical realizations within the system of TRANSITIVITY (adapted from Halliday and Matthiessen (2014, p. 225)	165

Table 11.3 Types of processes in instances taken from the English *Lingua Franca* corpus in several domains of knowledge	167
Table 11.4 Academic genres in CorIFA	169
Table 11.5 Verbs realizing processes in passive *that*-clauses in *CorIFA*	173
Table 11.6 Verbs realizing processes in passive *that*-clauses in the English *Lingua Franca* corpus	175
Table 12.1 Qualitative questionnaire (University teachers' answers)	183
Table 12.2 Qualitative questionnaire (Students and professionals' answers)	185
Table 13.1 Undergraduate Students' Use of Lexical Hedges	202
Table 13.2 Undergraduate Students' Use of Boosting Hedges	205
Table 14.1 Pre-test Score (All subjects)	224
Table 14.2 Explicit Teaching Group	226
Table 14.3 Implicit Teaching Group	227
Table 14.4 Correct response: Both groups collapsed	228

List of Acronyms

AE	Arabicised English
APA	the American Psychological Association
ATCs	air traffic controllers
BA	Bachelor of Arts
BELF	English as a Business lingua franca;
CBI	content-based instruction
CBT	competency based training
CEFR	Common European Framework of Reference
CFA	confirmatory factor analysis
CLIL	Content and Language Integrated Learning
CLP	classroom language policy
CMC	computer-mediated communication
CorIFA	corpus of academic English
CQL	Corpus Query Tool
DA	Dative Alternation
DEAP	action plan for digital education
EAOP	English for Academic and Occupational Purposes
EAP	English for Academic Purposes
EALTS	English for Aviation Language Testing System\
EBP	English for business programs
EGP	English for general purposes
ELT	English Language Teaching
EMI	English as a Medium of Instruction
EOP	English for Occupational Purposes
EFA	exploratory factor analysis
EFL	English as a foreign language
ESAP	English for specific academic purposes
EU	European Union

FSES	Federal State Educational Standards of the Russian Federation
GE	general English
GEP	general English proficiency
HR	human resources
HRA	Human Resources Assessment
ICAO	International Civil Aviation Organisation
IDPs	the internally displaced people
IKCO	Iran-Khordo Co.
ILO	International Labor Organization
IMO	Industrial Management Organization
ICT	Information and communication technologies
ISCO	International Standard Classification of Occupations
KDD	KiD Drink
LL	linguistic landscape
LSP	language for specific purposes
MA	Master of Arts
MBC	Maximum Bacterial Control
MEC	Spanish Ministry of Education
MGT	management
MOOC	massive open online courses
MM	methodological methods
NEIs	native English instructor(s)
NICICO	National Iranian Copper Industry Company
NIOC	Iranian National Oil Company
NISCO	National Iranian Steel Company
NNS	non-native speaker
NS	native speaker
OECD	The Organisation for Economic Co-operation and Development
OOC	Open online courses
PP	pedagogical practices
RA	Romanised Arabic
RF	Russian Federation

SFL	Systemic Functional Linguistics
SOCEC	School of Commerce English Concentration
SPbU	Saint Petersburg State University
SPSS	Statistics package for social science
TSA	Target Situation Analysis
UNIDO	United Nations Organization for Industrial Development
UFMG	Federal University of Minas Gerais
UNESCO	The United Nations Educational, Scientific and Cultural Organisation

Preface:
The changing face of ESP in today's classroom and workplace

Elena Bárcena Madera

Universidad Nacional de Educación a Distancia (UNED)

English for Specific Purposes (henceforth, ESP) is a subset of English as a second or foreign language which usually refers to teaching the English language to undergraduate and postgraduate students, training students of professional modules, and people already in employment. Its history is directly linked to the history of the twentieth century. After the British Empire and World War II, the economic, scientific and technological leadership and expansion of the U.S.A. caused professionals all over the world to adopt the official language of this country as a vehicle of international communication. Since its appearance in the 1960s, ESP has occupied the attention of the academic and research communities. Its central focus has been progressively diversified from English for science and technology in academic contexts, which occupied the earliest studies. Attention was diverted subsequently to studies on teacher training and interlanguage, genre, corpus and innovative methodologies and technologies. The underlying interest for the field was related not only for learning/teaching processes, but also to other types of applications, such as automatic text generation, question-answering systems and machine translation. The perspective here was rather mathematical and related to features like lexical closure and grammatical systematicity. Didactics, the main research application within ESP, is today largely determined by the enormous variety of specialized knowledge communities, genres and text types, businesses, academic disciplines and human activity in general.

The changing face of ESP in today's classroom and workplace is a valuable contribution to the research literature in ESP from several perspectives. Firstly, this international volume is illustrative of the research on ESP that is taking place in four continents (Africa, America, Asia, and Europe), fourteen countries (Algeria, Bangladesh, Brazil, Iran, Italy, Japan, Jordan, Russia, Spain, Sudan, Turkey, and United Arab Emirates), and fourteen higher educational institutions (including face-to-face and distance learning modalities). Secondly, this volume comprises an unusual selection of studies and, in that sense, it offers a rare panoramic account of ESP research. Thus, the book is divided into three major sections: (1) ESP in specific fields, (2) ESP through technology and culture, and (3) ESP and EAP (English for Academic Purposes) in CLIL (Content and Language Integrated Learning) and ELT (English Language Teaching). This structure allows the reader to be informed about recent research that has been undertaken in different areas of the world on the field of ESP from three well-defined perspectives: domains of application, technology, and pedagogy. The domains of study are varied, such as aviation, shopping bags, and psychology. The most common one is business and economy, although there are several studies with other goals, which cut across different domains. Both the written and the oral modalities are covered in the chapters, although the former receives more attention, as expected in ESP research. There is a range of genres covered, the most common being abstracts, which cut through many professional and academic written text types. The common underlying goal of all the pieces of research presented in the chapters is the improvement of aspects of the ESP instruction, such as technical vocabulary and phraseology. Since ESP is one of the learner-centered modalities within the field of English as a Second/Foreign Language, there is a recurrent concern, usually present in mainstream ESP research, regarding the adequacy of academic syllabi to students' real needs, which largely align with the communicative requirements of their future professional niches.

The first section of this volume starts with a chapter authored by Assassi and entitled "The Importance of Formulaic Language in Aviation English: A case study". As inferred by the title, aeronautics is the first specific field of application of this section. This is not a fortuitous fact since, as Assassi explains, English is the international language of aviation and is, therefore, mandatory for Algerian people working in this growing industry to master this linguistic variant, so that they can operate on aviation internationally. This goal is not devoid of challenges, especially in the case of Algeria, where other more widespread languages are seen to interfere with English and there are no specialized academic programmes for this language. This chapter presents research that highlights the affordances of developing listening comprehension skills and fluency in non-routine flying scenarios. The proposed specialised language programme includes aviation phraseology as a type of lexical approach since it is claimed that it helps reach native-like proficiency that can be crucial in ensuring safety in critical situations.

Chapter 2 focusses on a case study in Jordan, in which Alomoush assesses linguistic and code-mixing practice with reference to the use of English in adverts on printed product labels. The domain of study is "shopping bags". Discursive representations of economic globalisation and implicit English-centred policies are analysed in a heterogeneous corpus of language samples. The premise of the research is related to potential differences in terms of monolingual and multilingual practices and the study reveals that economic activity has a direct impact on the use of English only and, conversely, of code-mixing practices (i.e. Arabicised English and Romanised Arabic), reflecting a melding of local and global identities. Therefore, this study establishes a relation between language choice and the luxurious vs. ordinary socioeconomic and cultural associations involving the type of products. The chapter, in summary, reveals aspects of the sociolinguistic landscape of Jordan and the attached social prestige of the English language in this country.

Ahmed assesses the needs analysis for Khartoum State's vocational training Centres in Chapter 3. Based on a number of hypotheses, firstly, it analyses the extent to which trainees' English language needs in the Sudanese vocational training centres are met by the corresponding academic syllabi. Secondly, the level of satisfaction of the teaching staff at the training centres with the English language syllabi is analysed. Following an analytical methodological approach, the findings of the study reveal the convenience of meeting the expectations and increasing the motivation of the trainees through courses focused on technical vocabulary. The chapter concludes that further ESP needs analyses should be undertaken by the expert community and that the trainers and trainees' views and experiences about academic syllabi should be taken into consideration when judging the effectiveness of ESP courses.

In Chapter 4 Amerian focuses on occupational English for university graduates in today's Iranian business sectors from a professionals' perspective. The research presented is related to the practical dimension of EAP across various disciplines, and how learners must be effectively prepared for the real use of English that they will eventually need to use at work. The study undertaken involves Iranian human resource managers and employed graduated students as stakeholders. It focuses on various sectors within the fields of business and economics. Among the findings, employers consider productive English skills to be more important for employees than receptive ones and there is a discrepancy between the academic evaluation of Professional English and managers' views in the practical working environment. This chapter, and with it the whole section, finish with a reflection about the need for reconsidering the pedagogy of EAP courses in business, including not only the teaching methodology but also the contents and the learning activities in light of students' future occupational demands.

After this mosaic-like view of research concerns in various key domains of application, the second section of this volume deals with four more chapters on ESP concerning technology and culture. Chapter 5, entitled "Transnational Digital Literacy Practices of Two Karen Refugee Female Adolescents:

Multimodality and Spaces", is authored by Sharmin, who undertakes a study of the literacies of two Karen refugee adolescents living in the Southeastern United States. Scholarship is identified to be lacking in this type of ethnolinguistic population. However, this study also finds that their digital lives outside school abound with rich literacy practices that can be incorporated into their academic literacy practices. More interestingly, although not all of them help these people develop as learners, those activities that connect them with their own community emotionally have a remarkable cognitive impact. The experience reported in this chapter shows that if teachers are informed about the digital literacy practices of displaced learners from media-impoverished backgrounds and incorporate them in their instructional design, they can become proficient technology-supported ESP learners.

Chapter 6 outlines an extensive experiment conducted by Robinson in which students of Social Work and Social Policy were provided with Beatles songs in each lesson for different activities and functions in English learning, with the students appreciating this and finding it an effective use of ESP. Songs, a widely used tool in general English teaching, are not so common in ESP. The use of the songs is reported to be constant throughout the course and target a wide range of linguistic and even soft capabilities. The results from this qualitative research reveal that students view this song-based approach within ESP training not only as being appropriate, but also valid and effective.

E-learning, a key focus for many higher education institutions around the world, is considered by Rubstova and Dobrova in Chapter 7. They focus on goal 4 of the 2030 Agenda for Sustainable Development, as adopted by the United Nations. Goal 4 is concerned with ensuring inclusive and equitable quality education and promoting lifelong learning opportunities for all. The authors claim that not only are digital technologies having a major impact on the educational system, they can also bring goal 4 into effect. This is due to the key role that they can play in distance teaching/learning for disciplines, including ESP. A scenario is then presented involving a wide range of distance learning programmes for ESP developed at the Faculty of Modern Languages of Saint Petersburg State University, even if there is not a great demand for such courses, as can be expected.

Finally, Gaye in Chapter 8 assesses the broader area of perceptions and misconceptions in ESP. She starts with a reflection on the fundamental role of learners' needs in the ESP approach to course design and teaching activity. The author refers back to abundant expert literature to claim that ESP is one of the main learner-centered modalities within English as a Second/Foreign Language. Her theoretical reflections go on to consider common misconceptions about ESP, such as whether it is about the teaching of a given specialized variety of English with divergences from the standard language.

Furthermore, ESP teaching is often limited by English instructors to the teaching of vocabulary, in detriment to other aspects of language use. This chapter attempts to provide useful insights into the teaching/learning process of English in specialized contexts.

The third and last section of this volume is dedicated to pedagogical issues. In Chapter 9, Rubrecht focuses on a programme implementation without pedagogical standardization. By assessing the SOCEC programme at a Japanese university, he considers the debate regarding L1 inclusion. He concludes that CLP (classroom language policy) should happen after student's characteristics, which deals with their prior learning experiences, proficiency levels in the target language and learning goals. Chapter 10, entitled "Examining L2 learners' source text reading strategies for an MA module assignment in a UK university" and authored by Kamijo, who deals with the connections between reading source research texts in content-based courses, understanding intertextuality within that genre, and developing writing skills. The author observes how little research has been undertaken on the reading of source texts by second language learners and the cognitive processes of critical analysis that this activity involves. An experiment applies the cognitive reading framework and presents some learners using think-aloud methods to read self-selected reviews of scholarly literature. Findings indicate a comprehensive representation of the source texts via the adoption of critical and evaluative reading strategies of the learners, such as the elaboration of content, the creation of inferences, awareness of the textual structure, and the use of paraphrased descriptions.

Chapter 11, entitled "Investigating the system of TRANSITIVITY in passive that-clauses of research abstracts" and authored by Nunes and Orfano is grounded in Halliday's Systemic Functional Linguistics theory and corpus linguistics methodologies. As part of this research, verbs are explored within the system of TRANSITIVITY in passive that-clauses retrieved from research abstracts within the Corpus of Academic English, a learner corpus from the Federal University of Minas Gerais in Brazil. They are compared with similar elements from a reference corpus containing abstracts published in high-impact journals across various disciplines. Among the findings, there are higher frequencies of passive that-clauses with verbs realizing mental processes in the former corpus. Investigating how these students use passive constructions in abstracts in comparison to a Lingua Franca corpus can yield interesting insights that have the potential to improve the design of academic writing pedagogical materials for Brazilian graduate and undergraduate students.

Moraza Erausquin is the author of Chapter 12, entitled "Designing research for academic writing in the field of Psychology". The chapter offers a reflection of the prominent role of professional text writing in the training of

ESP, which accounts for the recent high number of apps aimed at this skill. Specifically, different qualitative and quantitative methodologies are used to identify the most challenging texts for Psychology professionals for students to work with real templates. Among the findings are several linguistic features that are inherently difficult for psychologists when writing common texts in their specialized domain. Taking such difficulties into account, students are guided in the writing of professional Psychology texts. The templates created are available in both Spanish and English, so that students of the latter can undertake an effective contrastive approach. The templates can, therefore, be used as learning materials in bilingual Psychology programs.

Ekoç considers in Chapter 13 the phenomenon of hedging and boosting on the writing of abstracts by undergraduate ELT students. It deals with a linguistic topic which is common to the majority of text and discourse types: hedging and boosting, i.e., showing detachment or increase of commitment to the proposition on the part of the speaker/writer, respectively. The author refers to the body of literature on interactional metadiscourse markers and other strategies used by academics and researchers and observes that little attention has been paid to their teaching until now. He focuses on abstracts given their relevance in the submission process for conference presentations, articles, book chapters, etc. An experiment is then presented, which consists of a number of students of ELT writing abstracts that summarize their presentations as part of an oral expression and public speaking course. The number of occurrences of lexical and grammatical hedging and boosting reveals some use of these strategies and also the need to include interactional metadiscourse markers in undergraduate writing classes to tone down or strengthen their statements as appropriate.

Calleja Rituerto presents a pilot study on a specific grammatical phenomenon as part of an ESP course in the field of Catering undertaken by Spanish young adult learners in Chapter 14. The course follows a CLIL methodology. The focus of the study is the learners' interlanguage during the acquisition of English dative alternation in the process of addressing personal relations and as part of the commercial or professional interchange. There are two groups of learners in the study, one that receives explicit instruction on the linguistic structure and another that receives no feedback, following a strict communicative approach. The experiment reveals difficulties with both methodological perspectives and suggests that instruction should not only focus on cross-linguistic contrasts but also prioritize complex interface integration.

The plethora of topics and studies covered offers a valuable modern insight into the main concerns of the ESP stakeholders, namely university teachers, professional instructors, postgraduate and undergraduate students, and researchers. Each piece of work presented in this volume has its own motivations and perspectives on this field, but they all have in common a contemporary applied approach, beyond old clichés like that of the supremacy of the English language due to the leading role of certain native speaking countries, or the existence of specialized variants as abstract subsystems that contrastively exhibit common, reduced and divergent features with respect to the standard variants of the language.

In this volume, the reader will find an updated illustration of ESP research that is taking place internationally. The learner-centredness that characterizes the field of ESP is presented in its rich socioeconomic and cultural varieties, which includes displaced people (and their peculiar linguistic realities). Similarly, the socioeconomic scenario behind ESP instruction covers relevant sustainability issues, as defined by the United Nations. This book reflects not only the complex reality of the professional and academic worlds of reference, but also the maturity of the field of ESP at the time of its publishing, which builds on its identity as an international vehicle of verbal communication used mainly in occupational domains or areas of reality. The work presented is generally well-grounded on some of the latest theoretical principles of linguistics and/or learning. The chapters often seek to innovate the practical methodology of teaching ESP (via CLIL, EMI [English as a Medium of Instruction], etc.) and explore its strategic use at both national and international levels. This collection of chapters will undoubtedly help the reader understand the significance of ESP in society, particularly in professional and academic domains, and the need to respond to their evolution using learner-centered instructional design and materials and technological resources and tools, as they become available.

Section I:
ESP in specific fields

Chapter 1

The Importance of Formulaic Language in Aviation English: A case study

Tarek Assassi

University of Mohamed Kheider, Algeria

Abstract: Aviation is one of the fastest-growing industries in today's world. As English is the international language of aviation, it is imperative for non-native speakers who are interested in aeronautics to master the English language to operate properly on the international level. Algeria as any other country is setting goals on different fields to join the new globalised world. However, Algerian aeronautics professionals, namely pilots and air traffic controllers (ATCs), are facing difficulties mastering the English language and more accurately speaking fluently because of several reasons such as mother tongue interference, lack of specialised EFL and ESP programmes, and using French within the specialty teaching/learning context. Fluency is highly required by the International Civil Aviation Organisation (ICAO) to operate internationally especially on non-routine situations such as incidents and accidents, which 80% of them are caused by the breakdown of communication on radiotelephony. These unusual circumstances necessitate the use of plain English and an improved listening comprehension skill giving the speech time limitation, which is a critical factor in aviation. As a certified assessor by Bournemouth University Aviation Experts-UK, the researcher has conducted an observation and assessment process (two years), interviews with aviation professionals, and questionnaires to novice pilots/ATCs, subject specialists, and the ESP teacher at Aures Aviation Academy-Algeria. The data analysed show that Algerian aeronautics professionals need a specialised language programme that takes into consideration teaching formulaic sequences and pre-fabricated chunks of language as the researcher proposes. The main reasons behind these recommendations are linked to novice pilots' and ATCs' educational background, the specialised language they learn (aviation phraseology) and its similarity to teaching formulaic sequences adopting the lexical approach, and finally the major role such sequences and situation-bound utterances play in improving listening comprehension and fluency; which, again, are highly required by the ICAO. To sum up, the researcher recommends chunking and teaching formulaic sequences because of their noticeable importance to reaching a native-like proficiency and more importantly, to ensure flights' safety and avoid any breakdown of communication.

Keywords: Aviation English, ESP, communication

***

1. Introduction

The aviation business is one of the most developing fields in today's economy. Algeria, similar to several other countries, and according to the Royal Melbourne University of Australia's English Language Testing for Aviation, a study conducted by experts for the sake of testing Algerian aviation professionals' English language proficiency, is developing its aeronautical system on a rate of 12% per year. The development is concerned mainly with the international flights and creating new destinations with developing the size of national companies' fleets. Since English is the international language of aviation, Algeria is taking serious steps to develop aviation professionals' English language proficiency through extensive instruction and assessment. However, the efforts made up until now are not sufficient and more researchers need to investigate this area of study in the country.

2. Background of the Study

Aviation English is a broad field of study, research, and practice. It is in accordance as a subdivision of the broader set of aviation. Nowadays, this vast field consists of aviation phraseology, plain English, and general English. Each has a different degree of strictness and specialisation. The phraseology is a very strict and limited set of lexical items. It is used exclusively and solely to operate within the routine aeronautical situation. However, plain English is more flexible and it may include more general English expression to serve several language functions to provide more information for the receiver. Finally, General English occurs when both former sets of language fail to fulfil communicative functions most notably in non-routine situations such as incidents and accidents.

Even though we mostly focus on pilots and ATC communication, aviation English concerns other professionals in the field as stated earlier to perform a number of communicative functions. For example, the speech used by pilots for briefings, and flight deck communication; speech used by maintenance technicians (engineers/mechanics), flight attendants/stewards, dispatchers, announcements, or managers and officials within the aviation industry. All of these language functions and specifications require a specific teaching method, content, and arrangements.

Mackay and Mountford (1978) state that:

> "The language of international air-traffic control could be regarded as "special", in the sense that the repertoire required by the controller is strictly limited and can be accurately determined situationally, as might be the linguistic need s of a dining room waiter or air hostess. However, such restricted repertoires are not languages, just as a tourist phrase book is not grammar. Knowing a restricted "language" would not allow the speaker to communicate effectively in a novel situation, or in con texts outside the vocational environment." (pp. 4–5)

On the same breath, and according to the former scholars' statement, Aviation English can evidently be a subset of ESP, equally ranked as English for Science and Technology, English for Business and Economics, and English for Social Sciences (Aiguo 2008).

Douglas (2000 cited in Mekkaoui 2013, p. 10) stipulates that English for International Aviation is not English for general purposes or English for international purposes. Aviation English is a language for specific purposes. Thus, this promises that aviation English is a subset of ESP because of its vast lexical selections that serve different purposes in specific contexts and target situations that require an endorsed teaching content and methodology.

3. The Linguistic Requirements in Aeronautics Communication

The need for proficient language learners and users in the Algerian aeronautical system comes as a result of the ICAO (The International Civil Aviation Organisation) language requirements. Pilots and air traffic controllers need to be proficient to fulfil the ICAO language requirements and at the same time to avoid any breakdown of communication that may lead to catastrophes. The aviation phraseology, which is a highly technical encoded system of communication, does not pose communicative difficulties for aeronautics professionals in Algeria or all over the world.

Nevertheless, plain English, which is considered more natural and creative than the strict aviation phraseology is needed as well. One may ask about the reason for plain English if there is phraseology to use for communication; simply put, phraseology does not serve and fulfil all communicative needs in radiotelephony communication between pilots and air traffic controllers.

To elaborate, plain English is highly required in non-routine situations; in other words, incidents, pans, and unusual circumstances are all considered non-routine situations where phraseology is not sufficient to find solutions for these issues. Thus, plain English is the only option left for radiotelephony communication. Professionals here must be proficient and fluent to avoid any misunderstanding bearing in mind that the timing on radiotelephony is a critical factor and our aviation professionals must react accurately and have a developed listening comprehension and oral language production.

4. Phraseology and Plain English in Aviation

In the 1950s, phraseology in general is used to refer to structural patterns; nowadays, and according to Ellis (2012), it refers to "constructions" and "phraseologisms". He defines the first as a term used in cognitive-linguistic circles as form-meaning mappings, setting as conventionalised speech in the community and embedded in the learner's mind as language knowledge (*ibid*). In other words, it is the relation of the morphological, syntactic, and lexical form, to the semantic, pragmatic, and discourse functions (Croft 2001; Goldberg 1995, 2003, 2006).

On the other hand, the term "Phraseologisms" is from a corpus linguistics perspective. Based on the work of Gries (in press) and Howarth (1998a); Ellis et al. (2008) believes that in addition to the properties stated earlier for "constructions"; phraseologism holds a statistical nature as "the co-occurrence of a lexical item and one or more additional linguistic elements. Which they function as one semantic unit in a clause or a sentence and whose frequency of co-occurrence is larger than expected on the basis of chance" (p. 2). In our case, Phraseologism is just one element or portion of formulaic language as explained below, phraseology is a set of fixed lexical items that are memorised and retrieved as wholes at the time of use, i.e. Formulaic sequences.

4.1. Phraseology

Aviation phraseology is characterised as a rigid subset of the English language. It is highly specialised, structured, and constricted. Aeronautics professionals use Aviation phraseology to meet a limited set of communicative functions that are in a direct link to common, concrete, and work-related topics for routine situations only. Here are some definitions of phraseology according to subject specialists and language specialists as well. Hazrati (2015) explains that the language used for air communication among both Air Traffic Controllers and Pilots is not a standard variety of English Language and has a highly specialised syntax, which we call 'Phraseology'.

However, Li (2016) adds, "Phraseology is used in routine situations by both native and non-native speakers with the goal of clarity and comprehension by very, and is regarded as English for Special Purpose" (p. 11). Both of these definitions show the importance of phraseology in limitation as to help interlocutors communicate effectively is short periods. However, Phraseology is a limited part of language that serves specific functions only. Basturkmen (2006) asserts that phraseology in aviation is "meant to cover all routine situations. It is an example of a language for specific purposes (LSP); in other words, a language that is used in constrained and predictable ways for a limited range of communicative events" (cited in Mekkaoui 2013, p. 10).

Also, Stephany (2012) alongside Shawcross (2011) both believe that phraseology covers only the most common routine situations encountered in air navigation. As a result, aviation phraseology is highly limited and cannot fulfil all communicative needs in aviation communication; thus, plain English comes as both a requirement and a solution to communicate effectively most notably in non-routine situations.

4.2. Plain English

Since aviation phraseology does not suffice for total successful and safe message delivery and reception, plain English came to the existence not only in the form of a recommendation but also as a linguistic requirement for flights' safety by the ICAO. ICAO (2004) is defined as:

> *Spontaneous, creative and no coded use of a given natural language, although constrained by the functions and topics (aviation and non-aviation) that are required by aeronautical radiotelephony communications, as well as by specific safety-critical requirements for intelligibility, directness, appropriacy, non-ambiguity and concision. (p. 14)*

Plain English cannot replace phraseology; to be more specific, Morrow et al (1994) and Howard (2008) claim that when a problem occurs in a communication and there is a chance for communication breakdown, plain English is favoured by addressers and addressees to confirm what they understand, and/or if they are understood perfectly. Therefore, they use plain English when it can cover the situation and fulfil the communicative function properly, but cannot replace phraseology. The following figure represents the relationship between phraseology and natural language, in addition to where plain English stands.

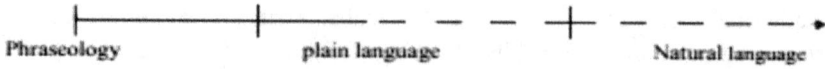

Figure 1.1 Complex Relationship with Phraseology and Natural Language (Stephany 2011, p. 26)

On the other hand, the use of plain English can create communicative issues just as phraseology does. Morrow et al. (1994) elaborate, "because of their tendency to use 'more complex syntax, vague or non-standard terminology' plain English, in other words, is not very plain" (pp. 253-254).

As stated earlier concerning creativity as one of the characteristics of plain English, it should be borne in mind that even if plain English is less constrained than phraseology, it is still not that natural like everyday speech. Stephany (2011) confirms "plain English is less restricted than phraseology but not as natural as everyday speech" (p. 26).

Figure 1.2 Aviation English Users (adapted from Mekkaoui 2013, p. 13)

As the figure shows, the focus of most aviation English researches is on radiotelephony communication using phraseology and plain English between pilots and Air Traffic Controllers. However, Aiguo (2008) relates that aviation English is not restricted to controller and pilot communications. Aviation English can also include the use of English relating to any other aspect of aviation: the language needed by pilot s for briefings, announcements, and flight deck communication; language used by maintenance technicians, flight attendants, dispatchers, or managers and officials within the aviation industry. Aviation English includes but must not be limited to International Civil Aviation Organization (ICAO) phraseology and can require the use of general English at times. (p. 23)

Thus, the researcher must state that there are other participants concerned with aviation English in general such as cabin crew (airhostesses), engineers, and maintenance crew... etc. To sum up, Campbell-Laird (2004) states and in reference to Avianca flight catastrophe (1990, victims: 75), that plain English plays a major role in avoiding such fatal accidents. While Prinzo and Hendrix (2008) insist on the ICAO language requirements and that both phraseology and plain English are necessary for ensuring flights' safety and avoid any communication-related catastrophes.

5. English for Ensuring Flight Safety

Aviation English is the language used for any aeronautical communication between field professionals who do not share the same linguistic background. This language occurs in both routine/ day-by-day aviation operations and for unusual circumstances like incidents and accidents.

Borowska (2016) believes that "communication is one of the cornerstones of air traffic system. Aviation personnel's communication errors are very often a cause of many incidents and accidents" (p. 61). In other words, a successful communication and avoiding any kind of breakdown of communication is compulsory for the safety of every flight. Stewart (1989) describes the "human errors", communication errors included, describes them as a result of bad habits that had been formed over time (p. 38). Both researchers focused on their studies on the fact that these human factors, worth notably communication errors, can be behaviour of not only (NNS) non-native speakers, but native speakers of English as well.

Since we have cleared the idea of communication as a basic element in ensuring flight safety, it is urgent to not only discuss the matter but also to find solutions and avoid any critical mishaps in the near future. Borowska (2016) offers a set of strategies to help ensure a safer flight as far as communication is concerned, to make native speaker aeronautical professionals to familiarise themselves with the challenges faced by NNS. She refers to the following:

- Learning strategies to improve cross-cultural communications

- Refraining from the use of idioms, colloquialisms, and other jargon

- Modulating the rate of delivery

- Making sure there is not too much information in a single transmission. (Rees, 2013, p. 102 cited in Borowska, 2016, p. 63).

Apart from the modulation of the rate of message delivery and the amount of information in a single delivery, which we discuss repeatedly, the use of formulaic expressions that hold a situation bound, contextually related, and culturally characterised has not been given enough research and discussion. Borowska is trying to refrain the use formulaicity (idioms, collocations...) by native speakers.

The researcher believes that it is quite a challenge for the simple fact that, in non-routine situations such as incidents and accidents, aviation professionals and especially pilots cannot always keep calm. Moreover, the nature of the critical situation in addition to the feelings related to the situation (anxiety, confusion...) cannot help pilots refrain from using formulaic sequences in their plain English. However, Borowska believes that her study and our research can have a meeting point and reach a consensus by working from both sides (NS and NNS), to raise the awareness of the first and improve the language training of the second in order to guarantee, to a certain degree, the safety of flights.

In the same vein, and as English has developed to be the language used in NNS-NNS interactions and be called a "lingua franca communication" (House, 2010, p. 363); the researcher believes that the deductions stated in this section apply on both advanced NNS and NS. This is a result of what the researcher noticed while providing tests for pilots and analysing test records of Algerian pilots, who sat for the test in this period. A few number of advanced test-takers noticed by the investigator, one in particular who lives in Canada, had a good control over language in both aviation phraseology and plain English. However, and since this test encourages discussion between both test-takers (EALTS "English for Aviation Language Testing System" paired tests), the second was not a competent language user, and the comfortable use and even (the show off) of the competent test taker reflected negatively on the second candidate. Thus, the researcher opts to shed light on this matter for the same reasons he did for native speakers.

To sum up, only 25% of aviation professionals are native speakers; and this, stresses the fact that aviation English is firstly and an international language and NS are just a minority (Borowska, 2016). As a result, the researcher believes that both researches on both sides are complementary and all aviation and language professionals should cope to come up with solutions and ensure safety in international flights.

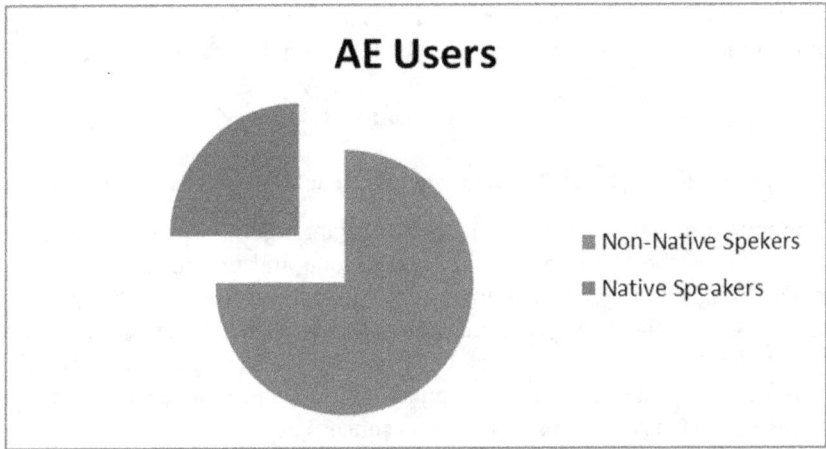

Figure 1.3 Aviation English Users

6. Methodology

The researcher opts for the case study research approach as "the catch-all approach" gives more chance for the research to take advantage of different data collection tools and several types of data from a large proportion of respondents. This study focuses on learners, more accurately, novice aviation professionals at Aures Aviation Academy – Algeria. They are all novice pilots (20) en-route to becoming full professional pilots after they finish an eighteen months theoretical and practical training.

Additionally, the researcher seeks the help of five novice air traffic controllers through their responses on a questionnaire same as the novice pilots. On the other hand, eleven subject specialists who are instructors at the academy are asked to give more in-depth information on the target situation through a questionnaire as well. These instructors are able to provide rich responses when it comes to the link between the present and the target situation, as they have been learners, retired professionals, and now as instructors.

A semi-structured interview was designed for the ESP teacher at Aures Aviation Academy to elicit information on the different contents and methods used for teaching English and the frequency of occurrence of formulaic expressions in her course. Also, to have as much information on her perspective concerning formulaicity and its relationship with fluency and communicative competence in aviation. Another semi-structured interview is administered for two aviation professionals, a pilot (captain) and an air traffic controller, to have a clearer idea about the target situation and the use of the

English language by Algerian professionals in addition to the main impediments they face while communicating using the English language.

7. Main Study Recommendations

7.1. Implementing Formulaic Sequences in Teaching General English

The situation analysis revealed that before beginning the ESP programme, the teacher uses the "New Interchange" books one and two in order to teach general English. The beginner and intermediate levels help students' gradual language learning moving to more complex and challenging language aspects and skills. Each programme includes four levels, four units each. So far, it sounds quite satisfactory for the beginning of the educational career of these students as far as the English language is concerned.

However, the researcher encourages and recommends the use of formulaic sequences within the intermediate part of the programme in two ways. First, by introducing formulaicity and its parts to students, as the researcher proposed the first unit within the proposed ESP syllabus. Second, it is best to encourage students to use these formulae while practicing speech activities to develop their communicative competence and acquire prefabricated chunks of language related to general English before acquiring the ones related to their subject specialty.

Finally, and as a step before beginning their careers, formulaicity will help students get higher levels at the compulsory English language proficiency test according to ESP teacher and two nationally certified assessors at Aures Aviation Academy. This is in relation to idiomaticity being a key indicator of language proficiency and adds up points for the candidates "Vocabulary-Level 5" (ICAO Holistic Descriptors in the Linguistic Requirements)

8. Conclusion and Main Results

It is very important for English language instructors and researchers to acknowledge the importance of chunking and teaching formulaic expressions for English language learners as it has been repeatedly proven that a large portion of the English language is prefabricated. In aviation English, it is important to know that the basic language required, which is aviation phraseology, is, itself prefabricated. Thus, it would not be very challenging for novice pilots and air traffic controllers to get used to chunking and learning the language in bulks or chunks as fixed expressions.

Accordingly, the processing and acquisition of formulaic expressions is less complex as a learning process; thus, the retrieval of these chunks at the required time of use would not necessitate much more processing as they are retrieved as a whole for the sake of serving a specific language function. Finally, as we have seen in this paper, it is noticeable that a large population of native speakers are in the aviation business, and their use of language is more spontaneous and consists of a large number of formulaic expressions that may even hold an obscure meaning to what non-native speakers may understand from the words used. As a result, helping learners develop their comprehension of this type of language is very critical to avoid any breakdown of communication that may lead to disasters.

References

Aiguo, W., (2008). Find a Proper Position for Aviation English: A new course of English for specific purposes. *Educational Curricula: Development and Evaluation*, 253.

Basturkmen, H., (2006). *Ideas and Options in ESP*. London: Lawrence Erlbaum Associates, Publishers. Mahwah, New Jersey: London.

Borowska, A., (2016). Do Expert Speakers Need to Practice a Language? *Changing Perspective on Aviation English Training*, (29), p61-72

Campbell-Laird, K., (2004). Aviation English: A review of the language of international civil aviation. In *Professional Communication Conference, 2004. IPCC 2004. Proceedings. International* (253-261). IEEE.

Croft, W. (2001). *Radical Construction Grammar: syntactic theory in typological perspective*. Oxford: Oxford University Press.

Douglas, D. (2000). *Assessing Language for Specific Purposes*. Cambridge, England: Cambridge University Press.

Ellis, N. C., (2012). Formulaic Language and Second Language Acquisition: Zipf and the phrasal teddy bear. *Annual Review of Applied Linguistics*, (32), 17-44.

Ellis, N. C., Simpson-Vlach, R., & Maynard, C., (2008). Formulaic Language in Native and Second Language Speakers: Psycholinguistics, corpus linguistics, and TESOL. *Tesol Quarterly*, 42(3), 375-396.

Goldberg, A. (1995). *Constructions: A Construction Grammar Approach to Argument Structure*. Chicago: University of Chicago Press.

Goldberg, A. (2003). Constructions: A new theoretical approach to language. *Trends in Cognitive Science*, 7(5), 219-224.

Goldberg, A. (2006). *Constructions at Work: the nature of generalization in Language*. Oxford: Oxford University Press.

Gries, S. T., & Wulff, S. (2005). Do Foreign Language Learners Also Have Constructions? Evidence from priming, sorting, and corpora. *Annual Review of Cognitive Linguistics*, 3, 182–200.

Hazrati, A., (2015). Intercultural Communication and Discourse Analysis: The case of Aviation English. *Procedia-Social and Behavioral Sciences*, (192), 244-251.

House, J., (2010). 12. The Pragmatics of English as a Lingua Franca. *Pragmatics across languages and cultures*, 7, 363. Magdalena.

Howard, J. W., (2008). "Tower, Am I Cleared to Land?" Problematic Communication in Aviation Discourse. *Human Communication Research*; 34(3), 370-391.

Howarth, P. (1998). The Phraseology of Learners' Academic Writing. In A. P. Cowie (Ed.), *Phraseology: Theory, analysis, and applications*, 161–188. Oxford: Oxford University Press.

I.C A.O., (2004). Doc, 9835. Manual on the Implementation of ICAO Language Proficiency Requirements. *International Civil Aviation Organization*.

International Civil Aviation Organization (ICAO)., (2004). Manual on the implementation of ICAO language proficiency requirements (Doc. 9835). Montreal, Canada: ICAO.

Li, Y., (2016). *Civil Aviation English for Pilots*: An English Air-ground Communication Course Based on Simulating Videos.

Mackay. R & Mountford. A., (1978). *English for Specific Purposes: A Case Study Approach*. London: Longman Group Ltd.

Mekkaoui, G., (2013). *English for Aviation in the Algerian context: The case of Pilots and Air Traffic Controllers in Zenata-Messalli El Hadj Airport* (Doctoral dissertation). Tlemcen University- Algeria.

Morrow, D., Rodvold, M., & Lee, A., (1994). Non-routine Transactions in Controller-pilot Communication. *Discourse processes*, 17(2), 235-258.

Prinzo O. V., & Hendrix A. M., (2008). *Pilot English language proficiency and the prevalence of communication problems at five U.S. air route traffic control centers* (No. DOT/FAA/AM-08/21). Washington, DC: Federal Aviation Administration.

Shawcross, P., (2011). Flightpath: Aviation English for pilots and ATCOs. Cambridge, United Kingdom: Cambridge University Press.

Stephany, L., (2012). Linguistic Analysis of English phraseology and plain language in air-ground communications.

Stewart, J., (1989). *Avoiding Common Pilot Errors: an air traffic controller's view*. McGraw Hill Professional.

Chapter 2

Linguistic and code-mixing practices in the linguistic landscape of Jordanian cities: The use of English in advertisements on printed product labels

Omar I. S. Alomoush

Tafila Technical University, Jordan

Abstract: This project examines the sociolinguistic position of English on products in Jordan. More specifically, I investigate the role played by discursive representations of economic globalisation and implicit English-centred policies as visible in English language use on diverse products. More than 100 hundred products have been photographed using a digital camera in order to examine monolingual and bi/multilingual practices enacted on different types of products (i.e. water bottles, soft and fizzy drinks, cleaning and washing products, sugar and rice products, and other goods). This allows us to test the theoretical assumption that there are different linguistic and code-mixing practices enacted on these products. On the one hand, the study results indicate that soft drinks, cleaning and washing products, and sugar products often tend to use Arabicised English (AE) in addition to English and Arabic, while the rest of products tend towards the use of Romanised Arabic (RA), English, and Arabic. On the other hand, monolingual English signs are more likely to appear on soft and fizzy drinks and cleaning and washing products than the remainder of goods. To advertise products which have been wholly and purposefully aimed at Jordanian shoppers, companies tend to tailor effective advertising messages to convince the consumer to acquire their own products; one of the most important aspects of the consumer product industry is to correspond neatly with the emblematic and communicative needs of the consumers. Therefore, I conclude that English is seen either as a prestige language associated with luxury or as representing aspirations to global values.

Keywords: Linguistic, ESP, code-mixing

***

Overview

This chapter presents the role of English in the linguistic landscape (LL) of Jordanian cities. It shows how LL can measure and evaluate the impact of English in Jordan. In this regard, the visual display of linguistic and glocal practices is one of the prominent features that marks the visibility of English in the Jordanian LL. More than one hundred products have been photographed in order to examine monolingual and bi/multilingual practices enacted on different types of everyday retail consumer grocery products (e.g. water bottles, soft drinks, cleaning and washing products, sugar and rice products, and yoghurt and similar products). This allows us to test the theoretical assumption that there are varying linguistic and glocal practices enacted on these products. The study results have shown that soft drinks, cleaning and washing products, and sugar products often tend to use Arabicised English (AE) in addition to English and Arabic, while the remaining products tend towards the use of Romanised Arabic (RA), English, and Arabic. Monolingual English signs are more likely to appear on soft and fizzy drinks, cleaning and washing products than the remainder of products. To advertise products wholly and purposefully intended for Jordanian consumers and to correspond neatly with their emblematic and communicative needs, companies tend to tailor their linguistic advertising messages to the perceived socio-demographic profiles of their respective consumers.

I will first introduce the sociolinguistic profile of Jordan and the rationale of the current study. Then, I will provide a brief overview of some empirical and theoretical LL studies conducted in the last two decades. I will profile the survey cities and outline the methodology used for coding the survey data. Finally, I will analyse the quantitative results of the study, in order to draw conclusions concerning the linguistic and concomitant glocal practices enacted in this domain of the Jordanian linguistic landscape.

1. Introduction

Jordan is a predominantly monolingual country with a language shared by other Arabic-speaking countries. According to the 1st and 2nd articles of the Jordanian Constitution (1952, chap. 1), 'the people of Jordan form a part of the

Arab Nation' and 'Islam is the religion of the State and Arabic is its official language'; however, the notion of monolingualism is considered to be gradually declining in favour of bi/multilingualism (cf. Gorter, 2006). The country has needed to adapt to a world that has become increasingly globalised since the collapse of the Soviet Union in 1991, so that English is now the most commonly occurring non-native language in Jordan. In addition to Standard Arabic and Colloquial Jordanian Arabic, English is widely used, especially in higher educational milieus, while the languages of migrant groups (e.g. Circassian, Chechen, Armenian), and French, German, Russian, Italian, and Spanish are occasionally used for a very limited number of functions (e.g. migrant group member identification, and cultural and commercial interests in European countries). Hence the language policy of the state supports bilingual education in Arabic and English, this being mainly reflected in the linguistic repertoires of the Jordanian educated elite and members of the middle and upper classes.

Although a number of studies (cf. Al-Naimat & Alomoush, 2018; Alomoush & Al-Naimat, 2018; Alomoush, 2019) have examined the Jordanian LL, none has so far examined printed labels on products in the country, which illustrate the role of English in both international and local branding, particularly the former. In Jordanian monolingual and bi-/multilingual advertising, English words used on labels on products are designed not to fill lexical gaps, but rather to attract the attention of consumers by means of innovative and creative uses of the language. The primary premise of this article is, therefore, that English significantly contributes to the advertising and promotion of brands and products in the Jordanian context. In order to ascertain the extent of this, 115 products displaying monolingual and bi/multilingual practices on product labels, including branding, sloganising, and similar identifying information, were investigated.

To assist in establishing connections between languages and product types, compared to different and potentially incompatible linguistic policies enacted elsewhere in the commercial written domain (cf. Alomoush, 2019; Spolsky, 2004), and further to understand the use of English for specific purposes in the consumer product industry, the collected data were subdivided into four product groups: water and soft drink brands, washing and cleaning products, rice and sugar products, and yogurt and similar products. On the basis of past research into other, but cognate, linguistic domains, we expect the monolingual and bi-/multilingual practices to vary according to product type.

In this context, the concept of *glocalisation* is utilised as an analytical framework for interpreting the use of English in the Jordanian commercial domain. This is evident in the innovative and creative use of English and Arabic in the Jordanian context, especially in the use of both Romanised Arabic and

Arabacised English. (The former refers to the transliteration of Arabic into Roman letters and Arabic numerals, and the latter to the transliteration of English into Arabic script.) Romanised Arabic is a relatively new phenomenon, and was originally intended to carry out CMC (computer-mediated communication), including but not limited to Facebook, Twitter, and mobile SMSs. Remarkably, it is still used in CMC, despite the fact that the internet and all popular social networking sites have become Arabised in Jordan.

2. Linguistic landscape research: a brief overview

The concept of linguistic landscape is primarily based on Landry and Bourhis' (1997, p. 25) definition: 'The language of public road signs, advertising billboards, street names, place names, commercial shop signs and public signs on government buildings combines to form the linguistic landscape of a given territory, region, or urban agglomeration'. Thus the LL has the potential for including all types of signs presented in public and private spaces. In recent LL studies, the unit of analysis has included a myriad of artefacts in the public space, including but not limited to T-shirts (Coupland, 2010), football banners (Siebetcheu, 2016), tattoos (Peck and Stroud, 2015), and printed shopping bags (Alomoush, 2019).

Studies by Scollon & Scollon (2003) have pointed out the importance of 'place semiotics' in the interpretation of the use of different languages in urban spaces. In other words, the concept of emplacement is the most central aspect of the theory of 'geo-semiotics', the interpretation of signs based on where they are placed in the material world (see Scollon & Scollon, 2003, pp. 142-164). Equally importantly, where the sign is placed in the physical world allows researchers to decide whether the sign has an indexical or symbolic function. The symbolic construction of public spaces is, therefore, examined alongside theoretical and/or methodological frameworks to approach facets of bi/multilingualism in the LL (cf. Alomoush, 2019; Ben-Rafael, 2009). Further advances in the field of linguistic landscape include the incorporation of an ethnographic and discursive approach, and an increasingly wide range of artefacts as mentioned above (cf. Kallen, 2009; Karlander, 2016; Pennycook & Otsuji, 2015).

Meanwhile, LL has recently attracted many sociolinguistic researchers working in the domain of bi/multilingualism (e.g. Alomoush, 2019; Backhaus, 2006; Cenoz & Gorter, 2006; Huebner, 2006). The widespread use of the English language in the LL has received much attention in the last two decades in Europe (e.g. Tufi & Blackwood, 2015), Asia (e.g. Alomoush, 2019), Africa (e.g. Kasanga, 2019), and the Americas (e.g. Weyers, 2016). However, the Arab region has received relatively little empirical and theoretical research attention, a deficit which the current chapter seeks to go some way towards addressing.

3. Methodology

3.1. Research setting

Located in the Arab Middle East, bordering Palestine to the west, Iraq to the east, Syria to the north, and Saudi Arabia to the south, the socio-economic condition of Jordan is characterised by fluidity, hybridity, and constant change. The current population of Jordan is approximately 9 million, 98% of whom are Arabs, while 2% are Circassians, Chechens, Armenians, Kurds, and Turks (see Alomoush & Al-Naimat, 2018; Alomoush, 2015). The many historical places such as Petra, Jerash, and Umm Qais have given rise to a dynamic tourism industry, making it a magnet for international, regional, and local tourists. For the country, 'inbound tourism is the key to the enjoyment of unprecedented prosperity and expansion of business and profitability' (Alomoush & Al-Naimat, 2018, p. 8). Large cities in Jordan (e.g. Amman, Zarqa, and Irbid) are also conceived as the growth engines of the country's economy, even though smaller cities and towns have a key role in the development of the country by virtue of mineral resources and agriculture.

The survey areas include three diverse cities: Amman, Zarqa, and Tafila. Amman is the capital city of Jordan and is situated in north-central Jordan, where more than four million people reside. It is the political, administrative, and economic centre of the state where trade, commerce, and employment are the highest in Jordan, so that patterns of economic and social mobility are in an upward direction. Zarka, bordering the Amman region with a population of more than 635,000, is the second-largest city, and is historically associated with the military, and is heavily industrialised. Tafila, located in southern Jordan with a population of 28,000, although a regional capital, has the characteristics of a market town, and is one of the least privileged cities in Jordan. Therefore, the selected survey areas provide diverse socio-cultural settings for the examination of English in advertisements printed on products, representing large, medium-sized, and small Jordanian cities with predominantly cosmopolitan, industrial, and traditional populations respectively.

3.2. LL signs

The corpus for this chapter was gathered from 115 product labels displaying English, Arabic, Arabizi, and Arabacised English. The data mainly included printed advertisements on local water bottles, rice sacks, washing powder and cleaning materials, and other products. Most signs were photographed using a digital camera in the period April – August 2018. These signs were coded according to language and script and product type (i.e. water bottles, rice and sugar products, washing and cleaning materials, and yoghurt and other products) (see Table 2.1). Out of respect for Jordanian politeness conventions, permission was sought before taking each photograph. All occurrences of the same sign were counted as one sign, and all products displaying visible monolingual and bi/multilingual practices were considered. Since they were irrelevant to the research hypothesis, i.e. they were not examples of advertising displayed on product packaging, a range of non-stationary items displaying similar linguistic practices (such as pamphlets, banknotes, stamps, tickets, handbills, flyers etc.) was excluded from the current study (cf. Sebba, 2010, p. 59).

4. Results

The initial linguistic analysis of proper names reveals the following categories in the written Jordanian product business context (see Figure 2.1):

   a. Duplicated English/Arabic proper names: approximately 80% of all signs recoded include English proper names either duplicated into Arabic script or Arabic ones transliterated into Roman script. The sign in Figure 2.2 shows the brand name *LAMAR* transliterated into Roman script.

   b. Monolingual English/ foreign language proper names: only 15% of the signs recorded are monolingual in English, Arabic, or another foreign language, particularly Turkish.

   c. Unrecognised and/or inventive proper names: 5% of proper names used are not recognised, such as the proper name *Ver nel*, or are inventive, such as the use of newly-coined acronyms such as *MBC* and *KDD* that have particular possible meanings ('Maximum Bacterial Control' and 'KiD Drink' respectively). Coding such proper names is wholly dependent on the original language of commercial sloganising; for example, the brand name *MBC* is followed by *Moisturizing LIQUID HAND WASH*, which indicates a new and inventive use of English in the written Jordanian context. The construction of blends is also one of the manifestations of linguistic creativity and innovation, as in the case of the brand name ارز دايموند / meaning *Diamond Rice*, which constitutes of the Arabic word أرز meaning 'rice' and the English word in Arabic script دايموند.

Linguistic and code-mixing practices 21

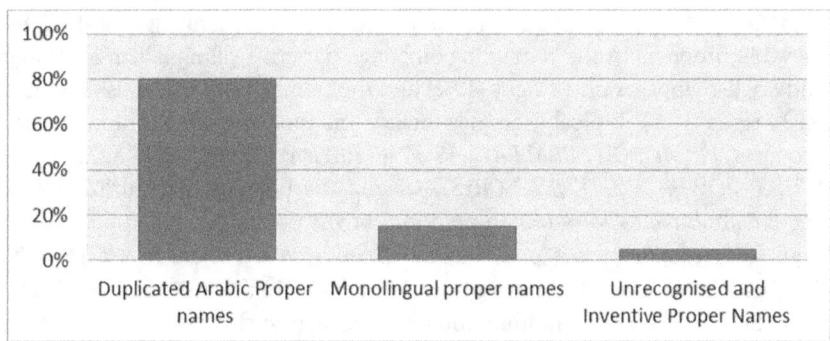

Figure 2.1 Categorization of proper names on labels on products

Table 2.1 Summary of languages used on labels on products

Language	Water and drink brands	Washing and cleaning products	Rice & Sugar Products	Others	Total	%
Arabic	2	-	-	1	3	3
English	2	7	-	5	14	12
Arabic+English	4	5	3	3	15	13
Arabic+English+AE	9	14	13	-	36	31
Arabic+English-RA	12	4	6	15	37	32
English+AE	2	-	-	2	4	4
Other	2	2	-	2	6	5
%	29	28	19	24	115	100

As Table 2.1 shows, within a total of 115 signs, the brand names, linguistic slogans, and identification information displayed on products tend overwhelmingly to be inscribed in English. This provides further evidence that both Arabic and English predominate in the commercial written domain. Unsurprisingly then, the Arabic-English-RA and Arabic-English-AE are the two most commonly used language patterns with a respective total of 37 (32%) and 36 (31%) out of all signs (Table 2.1): examples of the latter include *Lamis Freshness Oud & Saffron* لميس عود و زعفران, *Yaman Water, Bottled Drinking Water* مياه يمان مياه شرب معبأة, and *Abu Nsseir Water* مياه ابو نصير, whilst examples of the former include *Easy Glass Cleaner* ايزي منظف الزجاج, *Rosal, Lemon and Mint Drink* روز الليمون ونعنع, and *LOYAL Concentrated Dishwashing Liquid* لويال سائل جل يمركز

As Table 2.1 shows, English remains the dominant language of Jordan's movable products in the remaining language patterns; bilingualism in Arabic and English appears on 15 signs (13%) and monolingualism in English features on 14 signs (12%). Typical examples include the monolingual washing powder products *Finish POWERBALL, CLASSIC EVERYDAY CLEAN*, and *XTRA PRO-WHITE POWER WHITENING CRYSTALS* and the bilingual fizzy drink *Sprite, 100% Refreshment*انتعاش/ %100. In addition, English alongside AE appears on 4 signs (4%) (e.g. *Tornado*تورنيدو, *Strawberry Drink, Tomato Ketchup*كاتشب, *Hello*هلو, and *New Design* نيوديساين). Other signs (6 signs, approximately 5%) tend to display English in addition to another foreign language such as the monolingual Turkish dishwashing liquid (e.g. *SIR, Bulasik Deterjani*), French and English (e.g. *petit beurre biscuits, Original*), Turkish and English (e.g. *ülker Biscuits*), and the *Lavo* national brand toilet bowl cleaner displaying four different codes: Italian, Arabicised Italian, Arabic, and English. Most strikingly, few monolingual Arabic signs (3 signs, 3%) appear on product labels.

The brand name itself tends to be written in larger font sizes. The lettering in English, AE, and RA is often in larger font sizes than in Arabic, but sometimes it appears in equal font sizes (see Figures 2.1, 2.2, 2.3, and 2.4). It may be true that to some extent the impact of English resembles that of other foreign languages and can be accounted for by reasons of social prestige, as suggested by previous studies (e.g. Barni & Bagna, 2010; Cenoz & Gorter, 2006). However, at least in the Jordanian context, English nowadays is uniquely seen to constitute an essential component of global communication, excellence in commercial activities, and even linguistic innovation and creativity. This omnipresence of English in Jordan today paves the way for further linguistic creativity and innovation, as in the current creative use of code-mixing practices in the LL of the consumer products industry.

4.1. *Water and soft drink brands*

In Jordan, there is an endless list of international and national bottled and cupped water brands which are mainly packaged in plastic cups and bottles. It is very common for these to be heavily distributed to people attending wedding ceremonies, death and mourning rituals, and other social events.

Table 2.2 Percentages of languages used on mobile water bottles and soft drinks

Language	Number	%
Arabic	2	6.15
English	2	6.15

Linguistic and code-mixing practices 23

Arabic+English	4	12
Arabic+English+AE	9	27
Arabic+English-RA	12	36.4
English+AE	2	6.15
Other	2	6.15
Total	33	100

In the analysis of the water and soft drink products obtained from Jordanian social settings, 12 out of 33 signs (approx. 36.4%) are presented in Arabic, English, and RA (see Table 2.2). Most remarkably, the majority of these are merely labels on plastic water bottles and cups (e.g. *Jannat Adan Natural Mineral Water* and *Silsal Ozonated Bottled Drinking Water*, duplicated as جنات عدن مياه معدنية طبيعية and سلسال مياه شرب معباة معقمة بالأوزون. However, some drinks tend to display the trilingual Arabic, English, and RA pattern (see Fig. 2.1). On the other hand, non-alcoholic beverages and soft drinks tend to use English, Arabic, and/or AE; more specifically, approximately one in every four signs (27%) features English alongside Arabic and AE (e.g. *Americana Quality Nectar Orange* امريكانا الجودة نكتار برتقال and *Original Raspberry* اورجنال توت), whilst two signs (6.15%), namely *Sun Top* سنتوب and *7Up Free* سفن اب فري, feature English and AE. 12% of all signs (e.g. a water bottle (معباة مياه العلمين مياه شرب) *Bottled Drinking Water* and a non-alcoholic drink displaying *GOLD* خوخ بدون كحول meaning 'peach, zero alcohol') feature English and Arabic. Other products (6.15%) relates to products displaying a foreign language in addition to Arabic and/or English, such as the *Kean* Greek orange juice brand.

Figure 2.2 Example of the trilingual Arabic, English, and RA pattern on two cartons of apple and orange juice

4.2. Washing and cleaning products

It is worth mentioning that both shopping malls and small shops carry a large number of washing powders and liquids and other cleaning products in a pattern differing from that seen in Western economies: it is normal for Jordanian parents who manage the household to budget for these products when shopping.

Table 2.3 Percentages of languages used on mobile washing and cleaning product packaging

Language	Number	%
English	7	21.9
Arabic+English	5	15.6
Arabic+English+AE	14	44
Arabic+English-RA	4	12.5
Other	2	6
Total	32	100

It is remarkable that Arabic, English, and AE is the most widely used pattern on these products (14 of 32, 44%). Such examples include *GERSY Hair & Body Shampoo* duplicated as جيرسي شامبو للشعر والجسم, and *PASS, Disinfectant & Antiseptic* completely transliterated and translated as باس and مطهر ومعقم respectively. As Table 2.3 shows, English-only signs (7 of 32, 21.9%) are popular in the advertising and promotion of washing and cleaning items, such as *CAMEO Moisturizing LIQUID HAND WASH* and *Ajax Optimal 7*. Also included are signs (5 of 32, approx. 12.5%) that feature both English and Arabic. The product in Figure 2.3 is a prime example of this language combination displaying the brand *Downy* in larger font size than the Arabic wording المركز and إحساس رومانسي duplicated as *concentrate* and *Feel Romantic* respectively. In addition, RA appears alongside Arabic and English on four signs (12.5%) (e.g. سائل جلي العملاق duplicated as *Al Emlaq* Dishwashing Liquid, تركيبة متطورة للمحافظة على نعومة اليدين which has not been translated, and مدار transliterated as *MADAR*, whose slogan القوة المضاعفة is translated as *Superpower*. Again, the brand name itself is normally displayed in larger font size (see Figure 2.3). On these products, unlike English, Arabic is often not a favoured code choice as a brand naming language other than for providing identifying product information.

Figure 2.3 Example of the bilingual Arabic-English combination on cleaning and washing products

4.3. Rice and sugar products

The production of different branded dry food products, here restricted to sugar and rice brands, reflects intense competition among food companies to win the favour of consumers so as to increase sales. Table 2.4 shows the languages used by the most common brands of sugar and rice in Jordan.

Table 2.4 Percentages of languages used on rice and sugar products

Language	Number	%
Arabic+English	3	14
Arabic+English+AE	13	59
Arabic+English-RA	6	27
Total	22	100

Of the signs recorded, 13 of 22 (approx. 59%) feature Arabic, English, and AE, some examples of which include *Tiger* أرز تايجر/ meaning 'Tiger Rice', and *Sunwhite*أرز صنوايت/ meaning 'Sunwhite Rice'. The sign in Fig. 2.4 illustrates the typical linguistic strategy used by dry goods companies to market their products. The brand أرزدايموند/, meaning *Diamond Rice*, appears in larger font size than the rest of the Arabic and English wording, in order to maintain a sense of glocalisation (cf. Alomoush, 2019):

Figure 2.4 Example of the triangular Arabic-English pattern on a rice sack

In the remaining signs, English appears six times alongside Arabic and RA (27%) (e.g. the brand name *Zamzam* followed by *Soft Sugar* translated as سكر ناعم, the brand name الأسرة/ and its identification information سكر ناعم duplicated as *ALOsra* and *Fine sugar* respectively). English also appears alongside Arabic three times: the brand name فلفليم and its identification information أرز كاليفورنيا متوسط الحبة translated as *California Rice Medium Grain*, and *The Swan, Product of Vietnam, Rice Jasmine Fragrance Rice* partly duplicated as أرز فيتنام بنكهة الياسمين.

4.4. Yoghurt and other products

The other surveyed products mainly include yoghurt products, as well as sundry consumables such as tissues, tomato paste, jam, ketchup, etc. It is noticeable that the trilingual Arabic-English-RA pattern is the most commonly used on other products (15 out of 28, approx. 53.6%), examples of which include المختار حلاوة بالمكسرات duplicated as *Al Mukhtar Halawah With Nuts*, البستان مربى المشمش *Bustan Apricot Jam*, and حياة كاتشب طماطم *Hayat Tomato Ketchup*. The tomato paste product in Figure 2.5 illustrates this pattern.

Table 2.5 Percentages of languages used on other products

Language	Number	%
Arabic	1	3.6
English	5	17.8
Arabic+English	3	11
Arabic+English+AE	-	-

Arabic+English-RA	15	53.6
English+AE	2	7
Other	2	7
Total	28	100

As shown in Table 2.5, monolingual English signs are found on five signs (17.8%) (e.g. *MISTER POTATO CriSpS, Pringles Original,* and *Lays' Classic*). As for the remaining signs, one sign features the bilingual Arabic-English pattern and the monolingual Arabic sign طحينة الأسرة meaning 'The Family Tahina'. Three signs (11%) feature Arabic and English. English also appears alongside Arabic twice (7%) (e.g. *Five Cows Brand* totally translated as ماركة الخمس بقرات followed by English-only identifying information *THICK CREAM* in larger font size). Other signs include two examples displaying Turkish and French. Most strikingly, one monolingual Arabic sign features a product (حموده قشطة meaning *Hamoudah Thick Cream*).

Figure 2.5 Example of the trilingual Arabic-English-RA pattern on labels on other products

5. Discussion and Concluding remarks

The study results show that the English language is so popular and ubiquitous that it is widely used as the main language of advertising on a myriad of product types (water bottles, soft and fizzy drinks, cleaning and washing products, rice and sugar products, yoghurt and other products). Building upon the quantitative data gathered from the fieldwork and previous studies conducted in the Jordanian linguistic landscapes (e.g. Al–Naimat & Alomoush, 2018; Alomoush & Al-Naimat, 2018; Alomoush, 2015, 2019), it seems that the originators of these products (i.e. international and national product companies) tend to use English and Arabic in multiple forms to catch the attention of consumers (Chen, 2018). The brand names are typically in Arabic, as a link to the place and the Arab population, in English, as the globe's lingua franca of mobility and accessibility and the language of marketing, and/or in mixed codes (i.e. RA and AE) (cf. Pietikainen & Kelly-Holmes, 2011). This somewhat accords with Pavlenko's (2009, p. 250) claim that multinational companies probably use English to maintain 'an internationally recognised image', whilst the local commercial signs are possibly required to adhere to existing local policies.

Not only has it become normal in Jordan to use English wording in the labelling of products, but it is also common to find new creative and hybrid uses of English. The two processes of Arabicisation of English words and Romanisation of the Arabic letters are further indicative of the glocal practices enacted on product labels. The commodification of products occurs in an environment where English alongside code-mixing practices is conventionalised as a source of successful commercialism, modernity, and elitism. Thus, in using code-mixing practices in visual advertising, it is thought that it contributes significantly to the improvement of the image of the products advertised in the eyes of their customers (cf. Alomoush & Alnaimat, 2018).

In order to have become very distinguished within the discourse of business (cf. Li, 2015; Selvi, 2016), the originators of signs tend to acknowledge the role played by English as most important linguistic feature of the promotional product business, which is in line with the 'good reasons' perspective suggested by Ben Rafael (2009). However, some products tend to use AE, particularly soft drinks and cleaning and washing products, whilst others tend towards the use of RA, as in the case of water bottles and yoghurt products. Meanwhile various new, inventive and creative words and phrases occasionally appear on product labels. Since these are designed exclusively for appeal and attraction, they tend to be visually exciting but overdetermined in meaning. The use of English and code-mixing practices are thus an important tool for maximising the marketing appeal of products in the Jordanian context, and this in turn lends a cosmopolitan flavour to the linguistic landscape throughout the entire country.

References

Al-Naimat, G. K. & Alomoush, O. I. (2018). The Englishisation of materiality in the linguistic landscape of a southern Jordanian city. *Arab World English Journal*, 9(4), 88-107.

Alomoush, O. (2015). *Multilingualism in the linguistic landscape of urban Jordan*. PhD thesis, University of Liverpool.

Alomoush, O. & Al-naimat, G. (2018). English as the lingua franca in visual touristic Jordan: The case of Petra, *International Journal of Applied Linguistics and English Literature*, 7 (4), 1-13.

Alomoush, O. (2019). English in the linguistic landscape of a northern Jordanian city: Visual monolingual and multilingual practices enacted on shopfronts. *English Today*, 35(3), 35-41.

Backhaus, P. (2006). *Linguistic Landscapes: A Comparative Study of Urban Multilingualism in Tokyo*. Clevedon: Multilingual Matters.

Barni, M. & Bagna, C. (2010). 'Linguistic landscape and language vitality'. In E. Shohamy, E. Ben-Rafael and M. Barni (eds.), *Linguistic Landscape in the City*. Clevedon: Multilingual Matters, 3-18.

Ben-Rafael, E. (2009). A sociological approach to the study of linguistic landscapes. In: E. Shohamy & D. Gorter eds., *Linguistic Landscape: Expanding the Scenery*. New York: Routledge, 40-54.

Cenoz, J. & Gorter D. (2006). Linguistic landscape and minority languages. In: D. Gorter (ed.), *Linguistic Landscape: A New Approach to Multilingualism*. Clevedon: Multilingual Matters, 67-81.

Chen, L. N. (2018). Communicating health and wellness: The meaning behind names of handmade soaps. *English Today*, 35(1), 14-19.

Coupland, N. (2010). Welsh linguistic landscapes "from above" and "from below". In: A. Jaworski and C. Thurlow eds., *Semiotic Landscapes: Language, Image, Space*. London: Continuum, 77-101.

Gorter, D. K. (2006) Linguistic landscape: a new approach to multilingualism. Clevedon: Multilingual Matters.

Huebner, T. (2006). 'Bangkok's linguistic landscapes: Environmental print, codemixing and language change'. In: D. Gorter (ed.), *Linguistic Landscape: A New Approach to Multilingualism*. Clevedon: Multilingual Matters, 31-51.

Kallen, J. (2009). 'Tourism and representation in the Irish linguistic landscape'. In: E. Shohamy & D. Gorter eds., *Linguistic Landscape: Expanding the Scenery*. London: Routledge, 270-283.

Karlander, D. (2016). Backjumps: Writing, watching, erasing train graffiti. *Social Semiotics*, 28(1), 41-59.

Kasanga, L. A. (2019). English in advertising in Lubumbashi, Democratic Republic of Congo. *World Englishes*, 38(3), 561-75.

Landry, R. & Bourhis R. Y. (1997). 'Linguistic landscape and ethnolinguistic vitality: An empirical study.' *Journal of Language and Social Psychology*, 16(1), 23-49.

Li, S. (2015). 'English in the linguistic landscape of Suzhou'. *English Today*, 1(31), 27-33.

Pavlenko, A. (2009) Language conflict in post-Soviet linguistic landscapes. Journal of Slavic Linguistics, 17, 1-2, 247-274.

Peck, A. & Stroud C. (2015). Skinscapes. *Linguistic Landscape* 1(2), 133-151.

Pennycook, A. & Otsuji, E. (2015). Making scents of the landscape. *Linguistic Landscape* 1(3), 191-212.

Pietikainen, S. & Kelly-Holmes, H. (2011). 'The local political economy of languages in a Sami tourism destination: Authenticity and mobility in the labelling of souvenirs'. *Journal of Sociolinguistics*, 3(15), 323-346.

Scollon, R. & Scollon, S. W. (2003). *Discourses in Place: Language in the Material World.* London: Routledge.

Sebba, M. (2010). 'Review of linguistic landscapes: A comparative study of urban multilingualism in Tokyo.' *Writing System Research*, 2(1), 73-76.

Selvi, A. F. (2016). 'English as the language of marketspeak'. *English Today*, 32(4), 33-39.

Siebetcheu, R. (2016). 'Semiotic and linguistic analysis of banners in three European countries' football stadia: Italy, France and England'. In R. Blackwood, E. Lanza, and H. Woldemariam (eds.), *Negotiating and Contesting Identities in Linguistic Landscapes.* London: Continuum, 181-94.

Spolsky, B. (2004). *Language Policy.* Cambridge: Cambridge University Press.

The Constitution of the Hashemite Kingdom of Jordan, 1952. Amman: https://www.refworld.org/pdfid/3ae6b53310.pdf (retrieved 12.05.2019).

Tufi, S. & Blackwood, R. (2015). *The Linguistic Landscape of the Mediterranean French and Italian Coastal Cities.* Basingstoke: Palgrave Macmillan.

Weyers, J. R. (2016). English shop names in the retail landscape of Medellin, Colombia. *English Today*, 32 (2), 8-14.

Chapter 3

ESP-Needs Analysis for Khartoum State Vocational Training Centers' English Language Syllabus: An Evaluative Study

Mohamed Abdelsalam Osman Mohamed Ahmed

Dar Al Uloom Private School, UAE

Abstract: This study aims to investigate and evaluate the unified English language syllabus of Khartoum state vocational training centers to see to what extent it meets the trainees' needs. To achieve that the study sets two hypotheses: 1) to some extent the current English language syllabus does not sufficiently meet the trainee's vocational purposes and 2) to some limit the teaching staff at the training centers are not sufficiently satisfied with the current English language syllabus.

The study adopts the descriptive analytical methodology, with a questionnaire for 50 trainees, 9 English language trainers. The findings of the study reveal that the current English language syllabus does not sufficiently meet the trainees' vocational purposes. The trainees will be sufficiently motivated to learn the English language through a course that concentrates more on technical language.

The study recommends that the current English language syllabus should be provided with sufficient amount of technical vocabulary to meet the trainees needs. The trainees' expectations of being taught a sufficient amount of technical vocabulary at the preparatory course should be considered. Further studies are suggested on ESP- needs analysis in a broader way on the opinions and experiences of the trainees and the trainers about the suggested syllabus to examine whether the current study is effective.

Keywords: The current syllabus, The Vocational trainees, Trainers, Coursebook

***

1. Introduction

Before proceeding any further, it is important to give some background information about Khartoum state vocational training centers, where this study was conducted. These are centers built by the government in 2009 with financial and technical support from the European Union, and the United Nations Organization for Industrial Development (UNIDO) respectively. Four centers have been built in different locations in Khartoum State. Each center has different vocations, and now and then a huge number of trainees is admitted with their different interests in different vocations; for instance, Halfaya vocational training center which is located in Bahri has five sections: Welding with three sub-sections, Hotels and tourism, Electronics with two sub-sections, and Electricity installations, Beauty section. The centers' direct aim is to assist the local communities specifically the IDPs (the internally displaced people). The centers provide means of acquiring a quicker skill and the quality of being competent at the same time. CBT system is adopted in the centers (competency-based training system), which means that the trainee stays at/works on the same task until the task is mastered, regardless of how much raw materials are consumed.

Admission eligibility is for those aged between 15 and 25 with the basic school certificate as a minimum admission requirement. After admission, they are called trainees and have to go at first through the preparatory course. This course lasts for thirteen months in which they take six different subjects including English language. The end of the preparatory course is marked by a final assessment that qualifies the successful trainees to the technical level/course. The technical course duration is about sixteen weeks during which trainees take specified vocations upon their choices. Here they remain until they leave certified as skilled workers.

Good communication skills are essential for a successful personal and business relationship and it is hard to gain for learners. The exchange of correct messages serves the reader or speaker's needs, which makes their exact meaning clear and enables them to share information. In the basic model of communication, some basic elements of the communication process are encoding and decoding. Encoding is the process of putting a message into the form in which it is communicated; whereas, decoding is the process by which the receiver interprets the precise meaning. Therefore, the encoder and the decoder have to share the same frame of reference which includes the same code or language, educational background, race, attitudes, some experiences, and much more to successfully communicate (Hamilton & Parker, 1997).

Communication is very important to all organizations. A business person cannot provide a good service if one does not communicate effectively and efficiently. A misinterpreted message can create costly delays; a poorly written report can lead to a wrong decision; confusing instructions can cause injury, the destruction of expensive equipment or the loss of an important customer. Communication errors are often expensive. English has come to be seen as one of the resources that businesses need to manage efficiently if they are to maximize competitive advantage in the market place (Erreygers & Jacobs, 2006).

Brumfit and Roberts (1987) have shed light on the importance of needs analysis and that it is the stage prior to syllabus designing, also it determines the suitable teaching technique. Needs analysis is an initial step in designing a course that motivates the subsequent course activities through its validity and relevancy.

In the investigation of the current English language syllabus or the unified English language syllabus, some questions and hypotheses have been raised to see if the current syllabus is sufficiently appropriate for the trainees' needs. This syllabus is completely (EGP) English for general purposes it has been designed for trainees whose scope and purpose are technical/ vocational.

2. The Objective of the Study

The objectives of the study are as follows:

1. To investigate the unified English language Syllabus of Khartoum State Vocational Training Centers, to see to what extent it fits the trainees' vocational purposes.

2. The study proposes a new syllabus that combines both English for general purposes (EGP) and English for specific purposes (ESP).

3. To encourage curricula designers to pay attention to the vocational trainees' needs regarding English language learning.

4. To promote the awareness of the decision-makers to the importance of the suggested syllabus.

3. Research Methodology

In order to conduct this study, a descriptive analytical method will be followed, and the Statistics package for social science (SPSS) program will be used to analyze the data. A questionnaire for trainees at the technical level in addition to English language trainers at the preparatory level will be used. The questionnaire will be designed according to the main questions and hypotheses of the study. This questionnaire will then be distributed to the selected sample to get their feedback about the current syllabus, and of course, will be checked by some language experts before distribution in order to ensure its validity and reliability.

The population is all centers under the authority of the General Administration of Vocational Training- Khartoum State. The suggested sample is about 60 from 10 trainers (teachers) and 50 trainees.

3.1. The Study Hypotheses

To match the study questions the following hypotheses are formulated:

1. To some extent, the current English language syllabus does not sufficiently meet the trainee's vocational purposes.

2. To some extent, the current English language syllabus does not sufficiently motivate the trainees in language learning.

3. To some extent, the teaching staff at the training centers are not sufficiently satisfied with the current English language syllabus.

4. To some extent, the trainees themselves are not sufficiently satisfied with the current syllabus.

4. Literature review

The emergence of the ESP was mainly affected by three main factors. They are as follows:

4.1. The demands of a Brave New World

The period after the termination of the Second World War in 1945 was an era of expansion in scientific, technical and economic activities. This expansion created a unified world dominated by two factors: technology and commerce. For many parts in that world, there was an urgency to learn English language, not for the pleasure or prestige of knowing the language, rather to benefit from technology and to share world commerce.

4.2. A revolution in linguistics (The shift from grammar to communication)

During the period before 1945, the traditional aims of linguistics had been to describe the rules of English usage, which was grammar. The earliest scholars in linguistics at that time started to think about how language is used in real communication. They were completely convinced that language in different situations varies. For instance; there are big differences between the English of commerce and that of engineering. Making language instruction to meet the needs of learners in a specific context has to be considered. The outcome was that English needed by a particular group of learners could be identified by analyzing the linguistic characteristics of their specialist area of work or study.

4.3. Focus on the learners

The new trends in educational psychology also played a big role regarding the rise of ESP, by making the learners and their attitudes to learning English language the central issue. IF Learners have different needs and interests, then courses have to be designed in accordance with that. This is in short the notion of ESP.

The term ESP goes back to the 1960s. At that time, the textbooks neglected the specific language needed by science students. Ewer and Lattore (1969) pointed out that language forms should be included as a high priority in syllabus design. Strevens (1977, p. 152) notes:

> "...the existence of a major „tide" in the educational thought, in all counties and affecting all subjects. The movement referred to is the global trend towards learner-centred education".

Defined to meet the specific needs of the learners, ESP makes use of methodology and the activities of the discipline it serves by focusing on the language appropriate to these activities. As a specific approach to language teaching, ESP requires that all decisions as to content and method be based on the learner's reason for learning (Hutchinson and Waters, 1987, p. 19).

Many factors led to the growth of ESP. One of them was the failure of traditional language teaching to provide the type of language which meets the new specializations' needs. The second reason was many professions have been created during the 1960s. When the traditional language failed to consider learners needs the call for different approaches (ESP) became a necessity. The beginning of ESP was an attempt to make science textbooks go the same line with students' needs and goals.

4.3.1. ESP versus EGP

ESP is a learner-centered approach compared to teaching English as a foreign/second language (Ahmad, 2012). ESP is a program specifically designed for a specified group of learners, who aim to learn the language for a specific purpose.

Basturkmen maintains that General English Language teaching tends to set out from a definite point to an indeterminate one, whereas ESP aims to speed learners and direct them through to a known destination in order to reach specific objectives. "The emphasis in ESP on going from A to B in the most time- and energy-efficient manner can lead to the view that ESP is an essentially practical endeavor" (Basturkmen, 2006, p. 9)

Day and Krzanowski (2011, p. 5) emphasize 'P' in ESP as a 'professional purpose' and state: "The P in ESP is often a professional purpose — a given skill set that learners presently require in their task or will require in their careers".

ESP courses differ from General English because they broaden one's knowledge about the specific subject matter, by offering intensively specialized vocabulary that in turn prepares learners to use the language in their future professions (Varnosfadrani, 2009). Then Varnosfadrani, in 2009, discusses an extremely valuable point about the ESP course route and direction. A course that puts more emphasis on the learners and how to be equipped with the language which makes them communicatively competent in their future vocations. The researcher agrees with this idea as it supports the study's notion.

4.3.2. Definition of Needs Analysis

The term, "analysis of needs" first appeared in the 1920s in West Bengal, a province of India when Michael West introduced the concept of "needs" to cover what learners will be required to do with the foreign language in the target situation and how learners might best master the language during the period of learning (West, 1994).

According to Iwai et al. (1999), needs analysis is defined as gathering information from a specific group of learners with the intent of developing a curriculum that meets their learning needs. They clarify: In the case of language programs, those needs will be language-related. Once identified, needs can be stated in terms of goals and objectives which, in turn, can serve as the basis for developing tests, materials, teaching activities, and evaluation strategies, as well as for reevaluating the precision and accuracy of the original needs assessment. (p. 6)

5. Results and Discussion

5.1. Descriptive Statistics of Trainees

Table 3.1 Trainees' Age Description

			Statistic	Std. Error
Age	Mean		19.96	.400
	95% Confidence Interval for Mean	Lower Bound	19.16	95% Confidence Interval for Mean
		Upper Bound	20.76	

5% Trimmed Mean	19.88	
Median	20.00	
Variance	7.832	
Std. Deviation	2.799	
Minimum	16	
Maximum	26	
Range	10	
Interquartile Range	5	
Skewness	.394	.340
Kurtosis	-.835-	.668

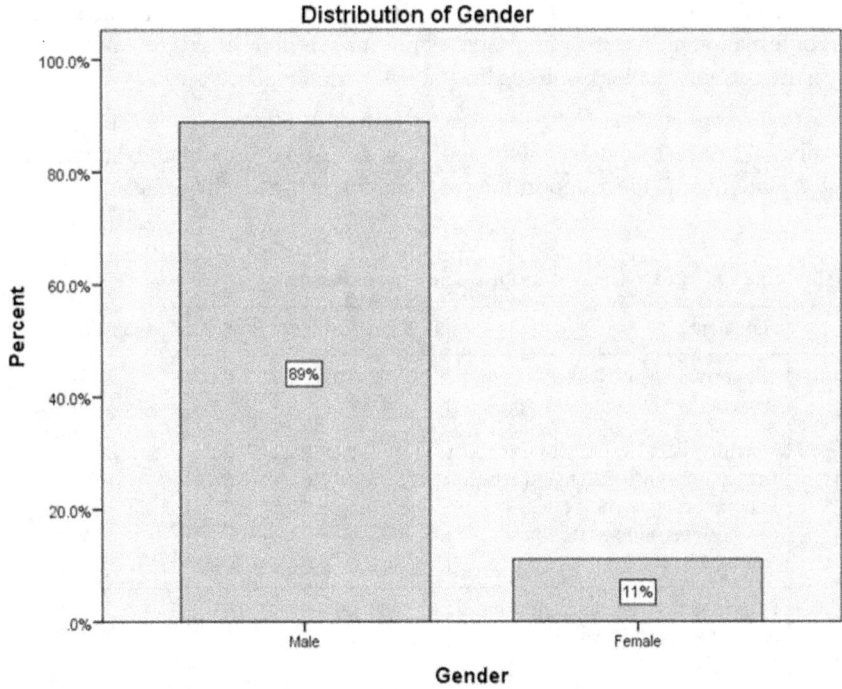

Figure 3.1 Socio-demographic Profile of Trainers (Teachers)

Only one female trainer was taken to the study because the trainer was newly appointed and had not yet taught the new coursebook (The New English File) which is the subject of the study.

5.2. Chi-Square Value, Median and Answers' trend for Trainees' Questionnaire

In order to answer the study questions and to verify the hypotheses, a median will be calculated for each of the statements in the questionnaire. a The answer's trends will be known by calculating the median. A Chi-Square test has been made to know the significance of differences in answers.

5.3. Study Hypotheses Verification

Hypothesis 1

According to Table 3.2 and the Chi-Square test in addition to the trainees' answers 'trend for the first statement (The current English language syllabus does not sufficiently meet my needs as a vocational trainee), it is quite clear that the first hypothesis: - *"To some extent the current English language syllabus does not sufficiently meet the trainee's vocational purposes"*. - Is confirmed. This confirmation reflects the importance of the analysis done, it also reveals the gap in the current syllabus regarding the trainees' vocational needs.

As for trainers questionnaire exactly from the *Statements* measuring the relation between course content and trainees' needs (Statement 2, Statement 6 & Statement 7) they support the confirmation of the first hypothesis.

Table 3.2 Chi-Square Test Results for Trainees' questionnaire

No.	Statement	Chi-square value	P-value	Median	Trend
1	The current English language syllabus does not sufficiently meet my needs as a vocational trainee	67.720	0.00	2	To Strongly Agree
2	I am sufficiently motivated to learn English through a course that concentrates more on technical language	45.600	0.00	2	To Strongly Agree
3	I expected to be taught a sufficient amount of technical vocabulary at the preparatory course	30.200	0.00	1	To Agree

| 4 | The English language syllabus is not designed in the same way as the other courses I studied at the preparatory course | 26.800 | 0.00 | 2 | To Strongly Agree |
| 5 | I might be more satisfied with the current syllabus if provided with the technical language which I might later use at work scope | 12.800 | 0.01 | 2 | To Strongly Agree |

Hypothesis 2

Depending on the findings in Table 3.2 and the response of trainees to the second statements: (I am sufficiently motivated to learn English through a course that concentrates more on technical language) we find that the second hypothesis: - *"To some extent, the current English language syllabus does not sufficiently motivate the trainees in language learning."* - Is confirmed. The results arrived at proclaims the trainees' perception of their needs which could not have been recognized and heard off, unless such a study was conducted. This in turn implies the significance of this study and the consistency and accuracy of its hypotheses. Trainer's interaction to (the second and the fifth statements) in trainers' questionnaire stated in Table 3.3 highlights the same result.

Hypothesis 3

According to trainers' questionnaire analysis as illustrated in the response of trainers to the statements (4, 9) in Table 3.3 the third hypothesis: - *"To some extent, the teaching staff at the training centers are not sufficiently satisfied with the current English language syllabus".* - is confirmed.

Table 3.3 Chi-Square Test Results for Trainers' questionnaire

No.	Statement	Chi square value	P-value	Median	Trend
1	The learner is expected to be sufficiently motivated in language learning when they feel that the course meets their needs	.111	0.739	2	To Strongly Agree
2	The current English language syllabus compared to the other subjects taught at the preparatory course, is not designed according to the vocational purposes	.667	0.717	2	To Strongly Agree

3	The trainees are expected to be more satisfied when the course content meets their vocational needs	2.77	0.96	2	To Strongly Agree
4	Teaching a syllabus meeting the trainees, and vocational purpose satisfy me as a trainer	2.000	0.369	2	To Strongly Agree
5	The trainees are less motivated in learning English, because they see their vocational need are not sufficiently included in the syllabus	0.333	0.550	2	To Strongly Agree
6	The current English language syllabus needs to be provided with technical vocabulary which meets the trainees' vocational purposes	1.556	0.954	2	To Strongly Agree
7	The vocational vocabulary is ignored in the current syllabus	0.111	0.817	4	Disagree
8	The course which sufficiently provides relevant vocational language is expected to satisfy the trainees	1.00	0.739	1	To Agree
9	A course which pays attention to the learners' specific needs is expected to satisfy the trainer	0.667	0.317	2	To Strongly Agree
10	The trainees are expected to be satisfied if their vocational lacks are translated in the syllabus	2.11	0.717	2	To Strongly Agree

Hypothesis 4

As it is clear from the trainers' questionnaire and regarding statements :(4, 9) the fourth hypothesis: - *"To some extent, the trainees themselves are not sufficiently satisfied with the current syllabus"*. – is confirmed according to the trainers' point of view. The confirmation of the fourth hypothesis according to the trainees can be drawn from their response to statements (3, 5) in Table 3.2 as well.

The focus of this study was to investigate the current English language syllabus (New English File- Beginner), or the unified English language syllabus of Khartoum State vocational training centers. This syllabus is completely (EGP) English for general purposes it has been designed for trainees whose scope and purpose are technical/ vocational. Some questions and hypotheses have been raised to see if the current syllabus is sufficiently appropriate for the trainees' needs.

6. Conclusions

From the opinions of the respondents and the findings of this research, the study came out with the following:

- The current English language syllabus does not sufficiently meet the trainees' vocational purposes.

- The trainees will be sufficiently motivated to learn English through a course that concentrates more on technical language.

- The trainees expected to be taught a sufficient amount of technical vocabulary at the preparatory course.

- The current English language syllabus is not designed in the same way as the other courses the trainees studied at the preparatory course.

- The trainees will be more satisfied with the current syllabus if provided with the technical language which they later use at work scope.

- Teaching a syllabus meeting the trainees, and the vocational purpose satisfies the trainer.

- The trainees are less motivated, because their vocational needs are not included in the current syllabus.

- The course which provides relevant vocational language is expected to satisfy the trainees.

- The trainees are expected to be satisfied if their vocational lacks are translated into the syllabus.

- The course which pays attention to the learners' specific needs satisfies the trainer.

6.1. Recommendations

In order to improve the current English language syllabus of Khartoum state vocational training centers, and in light of the study findings the study recommends the followings:

- The current English language syllabus should be provided with a sufficient amount of technical vocabulary to meet the trainees' needs.

- The current English language syllabus should concentrate more on technical language to motivate the trainees in learning the English language.

- Trainees' expectations being taught sufficient amount of technical vocabulary at the preparatory course should be considered.

- The current English language syllabus should be designed the same way the other courses taught at the preparatory course are designed regarding trainee's needs.

- To motivate the trainees in learning English, it is recommended that the course should concentrate on the language they might encounter at work scope.

- To reach the trainers' satisfaction with the course, the course taught should meet the trainees' vocational purposes.

References

Ahmad, D. J., (2012). Theoretical framework & growing demand of ESP in Saudi Arabia. *Arts and Humanities*, 65(5), 114-120.

Basturkmen, H. (2006). Ideas and Options in English for Specific Purposes. London and New jersey: ESL and Applied Linguistic Professional Series: Eli Hinkel, Edition.

Brumfit, C.J. & Roberts, J.T. (1987). An Introduction to language and language learning with comprehensive glossary of terms. London: Batsfords Academic and Education.

Day, J., & Krzanowski, M. (2011). *Teaching English for specific purposes: Anintroduction*. Cambridge; Eng.: Cambridge University Press.

Erreygers, G. & Jacobs, G. (2006). Language, Communication and the Economy. Amsterdam, Philadelphia: John Benjamins.

Ewer, J. R., & Latorre, G. (1969). *A course in basic scientific English*. London: Longman.

Hamilton, C. & Parker, C. (1997). Communicating for results: A guide for business & the professionals. (5th ed.). Belmont, CA: Jossey-Bass.

Hutchinson, T., & Waters, A. (1987). *English for specific purposes: A learning-centred approach*. Cambridge, Eng.: Cambridge University Press.

Iwai, T., Kondo, K., Lim, D., Ray, G., Shimizu, H., & Brown, J. D. (1999). Japanese language needs analysis. Retrieved May 12, 2007 from http://www.nflrc.hawaii.edu/networks/NW13/NW13.pdf

Strevens, P. (1977). New Orientations in the Teaching of English. Oxford: Oxford University Press.

Varnosfadrani, A. D. (2009). Teaching English for specific purposes. *Into thenext decade with (2nd) FL teaching. Rudolf Reinelt ResearchLaboratory EU Matsuyama, Japan,* 181-201.

West, R. (1994). Needs analysis in language teaching. Language Teaching, 27/1, 1-19.

Chapter 4

Where is English Needed at Work? Voices from Iranian Business Sectors

Mohammad Amerian

Allameh Tabataba'i University, Iran

Abstract: EAP courses for various disciplines are designed as a conduit between academic research and practical applications. On the other hand, one of the main missions of the ESP researcher is to prepare learners for the realities of English on the job. This study aimed to provide a profile of target professional English needs of Iranian BA students of business and economics and to explore what real requirements are expected from them at work in the future. To this end, perceptions of two groups of stakeholders, namely, human resource managers (N = 30) and employed graduated students (hereafter called "staff", N = 600) chosen from various established business sectors were asked through triangulation of instruments using questionnaire and interview. The results suggested that while all four main English skills have been considered important in the profession, the employers favored "productive" English skills noticeably more. Moreover, the present professional English level of the staff, as evaluated by their managers, was turned out to have a long distance from the voiced expectations by themselves and the managers. The findings suggested the need for a serious reconsideration of EAP courses in business and economics regarding the teaching methodology, content, and practices in light of future occupational demands of the students and tying different dimensions of such courses to the requirements of the corresponding workplaces. Implications of the study for improving the aforementioned EAP courses are also presented.

Keywords: English for Academic Purposes (EAP), English for Occupational Purposes (EOP), Needs Analysis, Workplace, Iran.

***

1. Introduction

English for Specific Purposes (ESP) is traditionally divided into EAP, the academic dimension, and EOP, the occupational dimension (Dudley-Evans and St John, 1998). While both EAP and EOP are carried out at university, their goals are different in orientation in that the former is purely academic while the latter has an occupational emphasis (Harwood & Petric, 2011). But there are some cases in which EAP flashes forward occupational concerns.

The rate of unemployment in Iran has significantly increased in the recent years (official report of Statistics Center of Iran, 2018) and one of the main reasons has been officially stated as "the lack of required expertise from the part of the university graduate applicants" (Official Reports of Iran Technical and Vocational Training Organization (2017), document VII, p. 25). The necessity of being proficient in English as stressed by Hyland and Hamp-Lyons (2002) concerning all business graduates can be more critical for Iranian undergraduates in business and economics with the extensive waiting business opportunities for them as a result of globalization (Amerian & Marefat, 2019a & 2019b). Consequently, through needs analysis from various job sectors, the study emphasizes the necessity of empowering university undergraduates in business and economics and preparing them for the "real" English needs of the market.

ESP courses are aimed at enabling the learners to function efficiently in a target situation. Hence, the ESP course design process should proceed "by first identifying the target situation and then a careful analysis of the linguistic features of that situation, which is performing Target Situation Analysis or TSA" (Hutchinson & Waters, 1987, p. 12). Certainly, this would be the same for EAP courses and far more critical for those seriously bearing professional demands in mind (Amerian & Marefat, 2019a).

This study follows the same rationale. Falling within the borders of EAP and job market, the present study more specifically aims to address the Professional EAP needs of the students, that is to say, their target professional language needs within EAP. In other words, it aims to analyze the later professional needs of Iranian university students studying in the academic domain generally called "Business and Economics" (including Accounting, Economics, and Management), have a look at the concordance between academic "supplies" and professional "demands", and propose recommendations for the betterment.

Although not extensively followed by the traditional studies and scholars who believed in the rigid separation of EAP and EOP, valuing "the future job" in the academia has an established tradition within EAP. Carter's (1983) English for Academic and Occupational Purposes (EAOP) can be regarded as one of the pioneering attempts in this regard serving academic concerns together with professional and occupational goals such as English for the medical technicians, engineers or business executives. Additionally, Belcher (2004, p. 170) uses terms like "Academic English for Occupational Purposes" or "Academic for Occupational Purposes English" and postulates that "in Academic English for Occupational Purposes, the input should be set for a pedagogy seeking to foster facility with genres in occupational settings". Based on her, this practice facilitates the generation of teaching materials from those actual occupational situations.

The incongruence between what students study in their EAP courses at university and the English skills they need at the workplace has been perceived internationally. Chan (2017) asserts that business English learners should be exposed to authentic workplace discourse and McLaughlin and Parkinson (2018) followed a similar concern in their study of technical vocabulary acquisition through a vocational training course. It is on this basis that Flowerdew (2010) highlighted the mismatches between current EAP courses and EOP demands. Flowerdew and Peacock (2001, p. 12) also suggest that EAP should be subdivided into "EAP designed to help students with their studies and EAP directed towards professional preparation".

According to Flowerdew (2005), it is commonly assumed that most courses taking place in English for Academic Purposes setting at universities are, in the main, concerned with various EAP issues, such as listening to lectures and writing academic reports. Yet, she describes a course while taking place in an academic setting, is designed to equip undergraduates with general skills training in EOP practices to meet the students' future professional needs after graduation. As put forward by Dominguez & Edwards Rokowski (2002), English for Academic Purposes and English for Occupational Purposes share overlapping goals in which the former, undertaken at university, lays the groundwork for the latter in the practical application of acquired language skills.

2. Background: EAP/EOP

According to Paltridge and Starfield (2013), "an increasingly globalized workforce and the overwhelming use of English as a de facto working language have created significant demand for workplace-specific courses" (p. 175). With the same target in mind, a number of studies were conducted in the workplace in which task-based needs analyses carried out through ethnographic on-site observations are often supplemented with more quantitative data. Among the major examples are needs analysis of the German bankers (Edwards, 2000), needs assessment and curriculum preparation for immigrants working in the health care sector (Bosher & Smalkoski, 2002), exploration of the communicative tasks of workers in a factory (Garcia, 2002), investigation of the daily tasks of Waikiki hotel maids through job shadowing (Jasso-Aguilar, 2005), exploring the interpersonal functions of language in English as a Business lingua franca; BELF (Millot, 2017) and using transcripts of the authentic workplace talk in teaching spoken business English (Chan, 2017).

However, especially in recent years, some studies spotted the intersection of "university" and "workplace". The list will majorly include Bhatia and Candlin's (2001) business communication needs analysis in Hong Kong, Dominguez and Edwards Rokowski's (2002) study on the students' and future workers' linguistic and communicative needs, Crosling and Ward's (2002) survey of the oral communication needs in English for business programs (EBP) in the academic and workplace situations of Australia and Belcher's (2006) article on EOP needs for implementation in EAP courses. Also, Kim's (2008) comprehensive exploration of EOP practices in an EFL context, Pattanapichet's (2009) research of discrepancies between university English curriculum and English requirements at workplace and Taillefer's (2007) assessment of the professional language needs of economics graduates in a French context targeted the similar trends. Flowerdew's (2010) needs an analysis on proposal writing for the workplace and Kucherenko's (2013) integrated and balanced syllabus design mediating between EAP and EOP must be also added to the list. These studies all tried to merge EAP and EOP by touching what English skills students are expected to fulfill in their future workplace, defining and characterizing EOP in the academia or what Dovey (2006) discussed under the issue of "new vocationalism": transferability from academic to professional contexts.

Targeting EOP needs for implementation in EAP courses hopefully shapes a growing stream of needs analysis research practice but as reviewing the literature shows, this theme has been still absent from the Iranian research archive on EAP. Thus, following a "common core" agenda for EOP and Deutch's (2003) "global" target needs, this study addresses the following questions:

1. What are the perceptions of graduated students and workplace managers regarding target EOP needs of Iranian undergraduate university students in business and Economics?

2. What are the perceptions of Iranian graduates in business and economics (staff at workplace) and their managers about the staff's present professional English abilities?

3. Having to target the professional English needs of Iranian undergraduate university students in business and economics at focus, what are the problematic areas in their EAP courses as perceived by the corresponding graduates (staff) on the job?

3. Method

The study implemented "exploratory sequential mixed methods" design beginning first with qualitative data which are then analyzed and used for the quantitative phase (Creswell, 2014).

Table 4.1 The Profile of Business Sectors

Professional Sector	Banking	Insurance	Stock Exchange	Industry	Commerce	Tourism
Corporation	1. Bank Melli Iran 2. Bank Mellat 3. Bank Sepah 4. Bank Tejarat 5. Bank Maskan	1. Asia Insurance 2. Alborz Insurance 3. Novin Insurance 4. Parsian Insurance 5. Dey Insurance	1. Mofid Securities 2. Hafez Securities 3. Agah Securities 4. Aban Securities 5. Khwarazmi Securities	1. Iran-Khordo Co. (IKCO; Automobile Industry) 2. Iranian National Oil Company (NIOC; Oil & Gas Industry) 3. National Iranian Steel Co. (NISCO; Steel Industry) 4. National Iranian Copper Industry Co. (NICICO; Steel Industry) 5. Electronic Industries of Iran Co. (Telecommunications Industry)	1. Paksan Co. (Detergents) 2. Refah Chain Stores (Retailing) 3. Golrang Co. (Retailing) 4. Irancell (Telecommunications) 5. Daroo-Pakhsh (Medication)	1. Ghogh-noos 2. Deltaban 3. Alibaba 4. Sahel-Gasht 5. Diba

3.1. Participants

To enjoy reliable data, after consultation with 20 university professors in business and economics disciplines, six standard professional workplaces (i.e., business sectors) for graduates in business and economics officially announced in the most recent update of International Standard Classification of Occupations in 2012 (ISCO-08) were considered as the yardstick. The classification is issued by International Labor Organization (ILO) and includes (1) Banking, (2) Stock Exchange, (3) Insurance, (4) Industry, (5) Commerce and (6) Tourism. The participants were, then, selected through stratified sampling. Also, to choose the Iranian companies from each sector, Iran's standard ranking of Top 100 Iranian Companies (*IMI-100*, 2018) conducted by the country's Industrial Management Organization (IMO) and officially announced annually, was referred to. Based on that, the five topmost corporations from each sector (in total, 30 corporations) were chosen, as shown in Table 4.1.

3.1.1. Managers

Concerning the managers, five human resources (HR) managers from each of the six work domains were kindly requested to participate, comprising 30 altogether. The reason the researcher mainly zoomed at HR managers, putting their corresponding university degrees aside, was that due to the nature of their positions, they were well aware of the different knowledge, skill and competency requirements of their staff (including their English proficiency levels) and hence, were practically the best informants. Table 4.2 summarizes their demography.

Table 4.2 Demographic Profile of The Managers (MGT: management, Eco.: economics, B: bank, Ins.: insurance, SE: stock exchange, Ind.: industry, Com.: commerce, T: tourism)

Business Managers	Total Number	Gender		Degree			Major		Business Sector					
		M	F	BA	MA	PhD	MGT	Eco.	B	Ins.	SE	Ind.	Com.	T
	30	24	6	1	11	18	24	6	5	5	5	5	5	5

3.1.2. Graduate Students in Business and Economics ("Staff")

Graduate students from the addressed majors now working in different business sectors comprised another group of the participants in this study.

From each professional sector, 100 personnel were asked to take part so that the researcher could know more about their different English needs at work and also delve more into their impressions of the EAP courses they had experienced before at university (all had at least B.A.) and their suggestions for making EAP classes more efficient and profession-tailored. Together, they included 600 individuals whose demography is detailed below (Table 4.3).

Table 4.3 Demographic Profile of The Staff (MGT: management, Eco.: economics, Acc.: accounting, B: bank, Ins.: insurance, SE: stock exchange, Ind.: industry, Com.: commerce, T: tourism)

	Total Number	Gender		Degree			Major			Business Sector					
		M	F	BA	MA	PhD	MGT	Eco.	Acc.	B	Ins.	SE	Ind.	Com.	T
Staff	600	368	232	338	240	22	542	18	40	100	100	100	100	100	100

As it was aimed to ask the participant staff about their current English requirements on the job and their perceptions of the university English courses they had just experienced before entering the workplace, only the recent graduates whose work experience was less than 7 years were considered. Concerning the managers, this changed to at least 15 years to make sure about the richness of their expertise and familiarity with their staff.

3.2. Instrumentation

The study is mixed-method research and opted for the triangulation of instruments. Henceforth, following Long's (2005) suggestion for mixing "inductive" and "deductive" procedures (p. 31) to fit the context, both quantitative instruments and qualitative measures (i.e., questionnaire and interview) were utilized as their "carefully sequenced use" would produce "better quality information" (p. 33). The questionnaire also included "self-assessment" and "peer-assessment" items. Apart from the enrichment of the final data interpretation, the rationale behind implementing them is mainly rooted in the nature of Human Resources Assessment (HRA) in which 360-degree assessment of the staff (being assessed by all the stake-holders including themselves) is applied for developmental purposes to enjoy a wide variety of viewpoints on the individuals' performance (including survival of their English-related tasks on the job).

3.2.1. Questionnaire

In order to determine the perceptions of the two groups of participants on the job (managers and staff) about the professional target language needs of the university students in business and economics, a questionnaire was designed and validated on basis of the theoretical and empirical literature on needs analysis and preliminary exploratory interviews with ESP and subject-matter experts and the graduates. The needs were carefully asked for, transcribed, coded and classified with a skill-based lens and in the shape of professional tasks. Following a handful of similar studies (e.g., Taillefer, 2007), the required and the present English proficiency levels of the staff at work based on the Common European Framework of Reference (CEFR) were also added to the questions using CEFR's standard assessment grid. Moreover, as recommended by the aforementioned ESP experts, a separate section was added to check the suitability of the current EAP classes for the future profession of students and ask for suggestions for incorporating professional considerations into EAP classes.

All the items were designed based on a five-point Likert scale and two open-ended questions were attached to the end of the questionnaires in order to assess the "problematic areas" of incorporating professional English tasks into EAP classes and "solutions" to them. The questionnaire for the staff didn't have the first eleven questions (which needed the expert opinion of the managers). The questionnaires were administered to the participants in Persian to avoid any sort of ambiguity or misunderstanding. To make sure not to have any lost idea during translating the questionnaire from Persian to English, back-translation was conducted with the help of an EAP expert. Then, the inter-translator reliability coefficient among 10 English translators was calculated ($r = 0.83$) (to see the full English version of the questionnaire, see Appendix A).

Regarding the psychometrics of the questionnaire, the content validity was estimated through a panel discussion of EAP experts. The questionnaire was piloted and the results were implemented to estimate the reliability of different parts of questionnaires via Cronbach's alpha reliability measure. The reliability of the first section (*abilities of staff*) came out as 0.77 and the indices for later sections proved to be 0.79 (for *problems in English*), 0.81 (for the *importance of English at work*), 0.93 (for *professional English tasks*), 0.95 (for *abilities in professional English tasks*), 0.87 (for *needed/present level for a future job according to CEFR* which together shaped eight binary items), and 0.72 (for *suitability of current EAP classes*), respectively. To assess the construct validity of the questionnaire, exploratory factor analysis (EFA) was run and the results were used for confirmatory factor analysis (CFA). At this part, 17 factors were extracted as below (Table 4.4):

Table 4.4 Results of EFA for the Questionnaire

Part (number of items)	Factor	Item no. (Loading)
1 (11 items)	present sufficiency of EAP classes for students	Items 2 (0.85), 3 (0.86) and 4 (0.76)
	the general importance of English at work	Items 5 (0.89), 6 (0.94), 7 (0.77), 8 (0.88) and 9 (0.65)
	importance of English skills at work	Items 1 (0.59), 10 (0.65) and 11 (0.82)
2 (12 items)	abilities/problems in English	Items 12 (0.82), 13 (0.73), 14 (0.85), 15 (0.81), 16 (0.78), 17 (0.75), 18 (0.80) and 19 (0.78)
	importance of English at workplace	Items 20 (0.90), 21 (0.63), 22 (0.90) and 23 (0.87)
3 (20 items)	importance of speaking on the job (according to CEFR)	Items 24 (0.77), 25 (0.78), 26 (0.83), 27 (0.88) and 28 (0.88)
	importance of listening on the job (according to CEFR)	Items 29 (0.84), 30 (0.85), 31 (0.88), 32 (0.74) and 33 (0.79)
	importance of reading on the job (according to CEFR)	Items 34 (0.82), 35 (0.81), 36 (0.90), 37 (0.82) and 38 (0.78)
	importance of writing on the job (according to CEFR)	Items 39 (0.83), 40 (0.87), 41 (0.44), 42 (0.81) and 43 (0.89)
	present abilities in job-related speaking activities (according to CEFR)	Items 44 (0.86), 45 (0.93), 46 (0.90), 47 (0.94) and 48 (0.90)
	present abilities in job-related listening activities (according to CEFR)	Items 49 (0.87), 50 (0.88), 51 (0.86), 52 (0.74) and 53 (0.79)
	present abilities in job-related reading activities (according to CEFR)	Items 54 (0.87), 55 (0.91), 56 (0.91), 57 (0.92) and 58 (0.79)
	present abilities in job-related writing activities (according to CEFR)	Items 59 (0.87), 60 (0.89), 61 (0.87), 62 (0.87) and 63 (0.83)
4	needed level in four English skills for future job according to CEFR	Items 64 (0.72), 66 (0.87), 68 (0.91) and 70 (0.90)
	present level in four English skills for future job according to CEFR	Items 65 (0.89), 67 (0.91), 69 (0.89) and 71 (0.90)
5	suitability of current EAP classes for future profession of students	Item 72 (0.87)
	'suggestions for incorporating profession-oriented considerations into EAP classes	Items 73 (0.73), 74 (0.81), 75 (0.78), 76 (0.74) and 77 (0.53)

3.2.2. Interview

An interview protocol was developed for the managers enjoying ideas from the most recent relevant resources (e.g., Atai & Hejazi, 2019; Atai & Shoja, 2011; Lehtonen & Karjlainen, 2008; and Spence & Liu, 2013). The semi-structured interviews were arranged and conducted by the researcher at different offices. The questions focused on priorities of managers among different English skills/sub-skills concerning job requirements, the relationship between general English (GE) and EAP, the importance of different English skills to fulfill various occupational requirements, managers' rough evaluation of the EAP courses in fulfilling professional requirements, and suggestion for tailoring EAP classes to occupational needs. To make sure of the clarity of the questions, avoid any possible misunderstanding and elicit credible and relevant answers, the interviews were conducted in Persian (applying the same back-translation procedure and inter-translator reliability calculations as done for the questionnaire; $r = 0.87$) and on average, each interview lasted for 15 minutes (the full version of the interview questions is available in Appendix B).

3.3. Procedure and Data Analysis

Data collection for the study was completed during the one-year time span of June 2017-June 2018. The questionnaire was administered to the addressed respondents during office meetings to maximize the return rates. The qualitative data gathered from the interviews were analyzed using data codification and reduction. Also, by content analysis of the answers given to the two open-ended questions at the end of the questionnaire, major problematic areas of EAP classes in relation to the future profession of the students in business and economics were investigated and checked.

4. Results

4.1. Target EOP needs

The ability of staff to "read" was indicated as the most important skill they should satisfy as was chosen by 28 of 30 managers (93.3%). Next, 27 managers (a noticeable majority equal to 90% of the participants) suggested that "listening" and "speaking" are either "much" or "very much" important in the job the staff is doing and "writing" comes last with being favored by 80% of the participants as an important skill on the job. In a nutshell, all English skills were judged by at least 80% of the managers as highly important for their staff. The ability of staff to "read" was indicated as the most important skill they should satisfy being chosen by 28 of 30 managers (93.3%). Next, 27 managers

(90%) suggested that listening and speaking are "very important" in the job the staff is doing and writing comes last being favored by 80% of the participants. Among the items considered for speaking, "talking with foreigners" was indicated as the most important English-based professional tasks. Considering listening, understanding professional audio-visual materials (55%) and "understanding technical speech" (52.3%), regarding reading, reading on-line technical materials (63%) and reading technical books (62%) and in writing, writing resume and job applications and cover letters were embraced the most.

4.2. Present professional English abilities

The managers indicated that graduates from university (i.e., their staff) are not highly proficient in English and are weak in oral skills. In detail, 20 managers out of 30 rated their staff's listening proficiency as weak and nearly the same number (19 managers, 63.3%) believed the same concerning speaking. On the other hand, the participant staff admitted their weakness in language skills and this is noticeably bolder for the oral skills. Beginning with listening, over 65% of the participants (nearly 400 individuals) indicated that their ability is "little" or stands on the average and the rate rises to 67% (402 persons) concerning speaking.

To managers, none of their staff stands in C2 in any of the skills and based on almost all, the staff is not C1, as well. Together, it simply suggests that staff were evaluated by their managers as being in, at most, "B" levels. Another important suggestion of the results is that the staff were assessed to be at either A2 (elementary basic user) or B1 (intermediate independent user) in receptive skills (reading and listening) by the majority of the managers (63.3%) which is, even, replaced by "A" levels (A1 and A2) for productive skills (63.3% and 53.4% for writing and speaking, accordingly).

4.3. "Professional English" problems

Based on the managers, the chief problematic skills for their staff in fulfilling their job demands are listening (23 managers, 76.7%) and speaking (20 managers, 66.7%). Writing followed the oral skills by being opted by 16 managers (53.4%) and reading was portrayed as the least challenging skill for the staff by 10 managers (26.3%).

When required to give feedback on their "problems" in different language skills, the majority of the staff indicated that they feel their problems lie on "little" or "average" in 3 out of 4 skills namely reading (64.7%), listening (62%) and writing (61.7%) with 388, 372 and 370 individuals, respectively. Regarding speaking, the trend changed to "average" and "much" with 62% (372 ones).

The last part of both managers' and staff's questionnaires asked them two open-ended questions about the "problematic areas in EAP courses" concerning the students' future profession and their "suggestions to solve them". Using qualitative data reduction methods, the expressed responses of 30 managers and 600 staff members to this part were content analyzed (thematic analysis) and then summarized in the form of 10 most frequent (above 15 times of occurrence) statement *themes* extracted from "telling" words and expressions. These are listed in Table 4.5.

Table 4.5 Emerged Themes in Response to Open-ended Questions of the Questionnaire

	Problems
1	Lack of knowledgeable, proficient and motivated teachers
2	Low general English proficiency (GEP) of students when entering university
3	Few EAP class hours (credits)
4	Not taking EAP courses seriously by all stakeholders
5	Ignoring English in other academic courses
6	Lack of motivated students
7	Lack of attention to professional English needs (the delivered content is mostly "general")
8	No connection between workplace (needs) and university (courses)
9	Irrelevance of the university degree and future working position
10	Diversity of the students' future professions and hence, their needs

As for the "solutions", using knowledgeable, professional and highly-motivated teachers, conducting placement tests and leveling the EAP classes, increasing EAP class time, making high performance in EAP courses compulsory for promotion/graduation, running all university courses in English, motivating the students via considering bonuses, using informed teachers who connect university instruction with professional needs on the job, making EAP classes practical, and designing "umbrella" vision of the EAP courses to suit the extension of the needs and tasting the stream of "general" occupational demands in EAP classes were the top and most frequent themes extracted.

4.3. Managers' Interviews

To yield an in-depth coverage of the present and target needs and exploration of the participants' dynamic notions (Long, 2005), the 30 participant managers in this study were also asked for an interview. The contents of all the interviews (totally comprising more than 7 hours of recording) were transcribed and then carefully analyzed, codified and categorized by three EAP experts based on the themes supposed in the interview protocol. The results are summarized in the form of eight items below in Table 4.6.

Table 4.6 Summary of the Managers' Interview

Item	Frequency
1. The managers' priorities among English (sub)skills	(a) Vocabulary and Reading (N = 24), (b) Oral Skills (N = 21)
2. Practicality of the staff's EAP courses in satisfying English-related duties	Impractical (N = 27)
3. Suggestions for improving the efficiency of EAP courses	(a) Task-based EAP courses in shape of practical and participatory classes and workshops (N = 18), (b) contextual syllabi (N = 17) and (c) continuous EAP courses to immerse the students (N = 10)
4. Concentration of EAP classes' topics and resources on professional needs students will encounter in their future vocation	Agree (N = 27)
5. Practicing simulated professional tasks in EAP classes	Agree (N = 29)
6. Participation of the staff in in-service English courses due to serious shortages in EAP classes in attending real job-related demands	Agree (N = 28)
7. "Professional English" should be a priority in universities' EAP courses	Agree (N = 30)
8. "Professional" EAP courses should have more than 4 educational credits (hours per week)	Agree (N = 29)

Overall, the results from the interview section were in-line with those gathered from the questionnaires. All four main English skills were, again, judged by the managers to be important in job-related tasks while the supremacy of oral skills in the personnel's occupational success gained prominence. The big gap between the "targeted" and "actual" proficiency levels was, also, approved once more in the interviews.

5. Discussion, Conclusion and implications

As Belcher (2006) puts, ESP assumes that there are problems or lacks, that they are unique to specific audiences in specific contexts and that they should be instruction-tailored. The job sector is no exception. Merging EAP and EOP and characterizing workplace in the academia, except for a few studies (e.g., Dominguez & Edwards Rokowski, 2002; Kucherenko, 2013), has been quite an absent theme from the EAP research practice. This study was after marrying academia and workplace within the realm of the Iranian EAP for business and economics. The study was chiefly concerned with general shared profession-based English needs of those who are in the occupational positions from one side and optimizing the according EAP courses from the other, to provide a job-tailored "common core" of English skills to be practically portrayed in the targeted Iranian students' syllabi.

The results derived from the questionnaire and interview underlined such areas as optimizing teachers (content knowledge) and classes (placement, hours, method, resources, facilities), empowering students' pre-university general English proficiency, taking EAP much more serious in the higher-order procedures, motivating class members, tying academia and workplace (needs analysis, workshops, simulated tasks, inviting professional practitioners) and increasing the business interaction of Iran with the world.

Despite all the time and budget spent on proliferating the content of the Iranian EAP courses, the suggestions made by this study, as informed by the "real" stakeholders outside the academia, may imply the urgent necessity of setting framing changes to make EAP domain act more efficiently in response to its innate missions concerning post-academic life of the graduates on the job. As verified by the verbalized gaps in the study, the findings seem to provide vital implications for renewing the EAP programs in the realm of business and economics and enhancing the accountability of EAP instruction in the very field, which covers individual, pedagogic and organizational levels.

The results of this study recommend policymakers of the EAP courses in business and economics to make the courses more goal-oriented towards the future professional tasks to be experienced by the students. The findings also encourage using knowledgeable and professional teachers with high interest in the relevant subject matter and extending the weekly class hours to expand the chances students obtain to practice real-work business English conditions. EAP course designers can, also, use the findings to tailor university instruction with professional English needs on the job using update, practical and effective teaching methodologies and coherent career-related syllabi lending themselves as much as possible to the authentic vocational environments incorporating the productive skills.

It is hoped that these findings will encourage ELT policymakers to invest more in "professional" aspects of EAP and provide guidance for propositions and revisions with respect to EAP materials and classroom practices. It is also hoped that the findings are both rewarding and practical for the current pedagogy and research on ESP/EAP in the international domain, as well, since the worrying unemployment rate of the degree-holders all over the world as a result of English proficiency deficit has been repeatedly alarmed by the global figures, especially in the recent decade. Certainly, much more research is required to probe various professional English needs at miscellaneous workplaces and varying levels and, as Flowerdew (2013) recommends, certainly seeking help from more qualitative, ethnographic and critical-oriented methods and tools can more comprehensively suit the crucial need.

Acknowledgments

The researcher is thankful to all who contributed to this study, especially the managers and the staff in various business sectors who kindly accepted to take part as participants.

References

Amerian, M. & Marefat, F. (2019a). A Triangulated Study of Professional English Needs of University Graduates in Business and economics in Today's Iranian Business Sectors. *Applied Research on English Language*, 8(2), 227-260.

Amerian, M. & Marefat, F. (2019b). Perceptions on EAP for Business: Fresh Findings from Academia and Workplace. *Journal of Teaching Language Skills*, 37

Atai, M.R. & Hejazi, S. Y. (2019). Assessment of academic English language needs of Iranian post-graduate students of psychology. *Ibérica*.

Atai, M. R. & Shoja, L. (2011). A triangulated study of academic language needs of Iranian students of computer engineering: Are the courses on track? *RELC Journal*, 42, (3) 305-323.

Belcher, D. (2004). Trends in ESP. *Annual Review of Applied Linguistics*, 24, 165-186.

Belcher, D. (2006). English for specific purposes: Teaching to perceived needs and imagined futures in worlds of work, study, and everyday life. *TESOL Quarterly*, 40, 133-56.

Bhatia, V., & Candlin, C. (2001). *Teaching English to meet the needs of business education in Hong Kong*. Hong Kong: Center for English language education and communication research.

Bosher, S., & Smalkoski, K. (2002). From needs analysis to curriculum development: Designing a course in health-care communication for immigrant students in the USA. *English for Specific Purposes*, 21(1), 59-79.

Carter, D. (1983). Some propositions about ESP. *English for Specific Purposes*, 2, 131-137.

Chan, C. (2017). Investigating a research-informed teaching idea: The use of transcripts of authentic workplace talk in the teaching of spoken business English. *English for Specific Purposes. 46*, 72-89.

Creswell, J. W. (2014). Research Design: Quantitative, Qualitative and Mixed Methods Approaches. NY: Sage.

Crosling, G., & Ward, I. (2002). Oral communication: the workplace needs and uses of business undergraduate employees. *English for Specific Purposes* 21(1), 41-57.

Deutch, Y. (2003). Needs analysis for academic legal English courses in Israel: a model of setting priorities. Journal of English for Academic Purposes, 2, 125–146

Dominguez, G., & Edwards Rokowski, P. (2002). Bridging the gap between English for Academic and Occupational Purposes. *Journal of ESP World*, 2(1), Retrieved from: http://www.esp-world.info/ESP_list.htm

Dovey, T. (2006). What purposes, specifically? Re-thinking purposes and specificity in the context of the "new vocationalism." *English for Specific Purposes*, 25, 387-402.

Dudley-Evans, T., & St John, M. J. (1998). *Developments in English for specific purposes: A multi-disciplinary approach*. Cambridge: Cambridge University Press.

Edwards, N. (2000). Language for business: Effective needs assessment, syllabus design and materials preparation in a practical ESP case study. *English for Specific Purposes*, 19(3), 291-296.

Flowerdew, L., & Peacock, M. (2001). *Research perspectives on English for academic purposes*. Cambridge: CUP.

Flowerdew, L. (2005). Integrating traditional and critical approaches to syllabus design: The what, the how, and the why? *English for Academic Purposes*, 4, 135-147.

Flowerdew, L. (2010). Devising and implementing a business proposal module: Constraints and compromises. *English for Specific Purposes*, 29, 108-120.

Flowerdew, L. (2013). Needs analysis and curriculum development in ESP. In B. Paltridge & S. Starfield (Eds.), The handbook of English for specific purposes. Boston: Wiley-Blackwell.

Garcia, P. (2002). An ESP program for entry-level manufacturing workers. In T. Orr (Ed.), *English for specific purposes* (pp. 161-174). Alexandria, VA: TESOL.

Harwood, N., & Petric, B. (2011). In Simpson, J. (Eds.) *The Routledge handbook of applied linguistics*, New York: Rutledge.

Hutchinson, T., & Waters, A. (1987). *English for specific purposes*. London: Oxford University Press.

Hyland, K., & Hamp-Lyons, L. (2002). EAP: Issues and directions. *English for Academic Purposes*. 1, 1-12

Jasso-Aguilar, R. (2005). 'Sources, methods and triangulation in needs analysis: A critical perspective in a case study of Waikiki hotel maids'. In Long, M. (Ed.), *Second language needs analysis* (pp.127-158). Cambridge: Cambridge University.

Kim, D. (2008). *English for occupational purposes*. London: Continuum.

Kucherenko, S. N. (2013). An Integrated View of EOP and EAP. *The Journal of Teaching English for Specific and Academic Purposes*, 1, 3-9.

Lehtonen, T., & Karjalainen, S. (2008). University graduates' workplace language needs as perceived by employers. *System*, 36(3), 492-503.

Long, M. H. (2005). Methodological issues in learner needs analysis. In M. H. Long, (Ed.), *Second Language Needs Analysis* (pp.19-75). Cambridge: Cambridge University.

Millot, P. (2017). Inclusivity and exclusivity in English as a Business Lingua Franca: The expression of a professional voice in email communication. *English for Specific Purposes*. 46, 59-71.

McLaughlin, E., & Parkinson, J. (2018). 'We learn as we go': How acquisition of a technical vocabulary is supported during vocational training. *English for Specific Purposes. 50,* 14-27.

Official Reports of Iran Technical and *Vocational Training Organization (2017),* Retrieved from: http://irantvto.ir/uploads/1_259_27.pdf

Pattanapichet, F. (2009). Development of a Competency-based English Oral Communication Course for Undergraduate Public Relations Students. ESP World, 4 (25): 1-46. Retrieved from: http://www.esp-world.info/Articles_25/the_competency-based_English_oral_communication_course_for_PR_students.doc

Paltridge, B. and S. Starfield (eds.). (2013). *The handbook of English for Specific* Purposes. Boston: Wiley-Blackwell

Spence, P., & Liu, G. Z. (2013). Engineering English and the high-tech industry: A case study of an English needs analysis of process integration engineers at a semiconductor manufacturing company in Taiwan. *English for Specific Purposes.* 32 *(2),* 97-109.

Summary results of Workforce Statistics plan for 2018, Statistics Center of Iran. Retrieved from: https://www.amar.org.ir/Portals/0/Files/abstract/1396/ch_ntank_96-2.pdf

Taillefer, G. F. (2007). The professional language needs of economic graduates: assessment and perspectives in the French context. *English for Specific Purposes 26,* 135-155

Top 100 companies in Iran (IMI-100) in 2018, Industrial Management Institute of Iran. Retrieved from: http://imi100.imi.ir/Pages/RankingFirst100.aspx

Section II:
ESP through technology and culture

Chapter 5

Transnational Digital Literacy Practices of Two Karen Refugee Female Adolescents: Multimodality and Spaces

Sonia Sharmin

East West University, Bangladesh

Abstract: This chapter focuses on two Karen refugee female student participants who are doubly minoritized by virtue of their racial and ethnic differences. This qualitative study investigates the in and out-of-school literacies of two Karen refugee adolescents living in the Southeastern United States. The scholarship is particularly lacking in the literacy development of refugee women like these and their use of writing as a medium of social communication. This study finds that their digital lives out-of-school abound with rich literacy practices that can be incorporated in enhancing their literacy practices in school. While not all digital practices help them grow as learners, practices that connect them with their community, family and friends to fulfil their emotional and mental spaces immensely help them become better learners. Although these resettled refugees are originally from media-impoverished backgrounds, they have become proficient users and learners of technology with time. If teachers are informed about the transnational digital literacy practices of refugee learners, they can integrate those practices when designing instruction.

Keywords: Transnational, Digital Literacy, Refugee, Spaces, Multimodality

***

1. Introduction

Karen female adolescents have been chosen for literacy practices as Karens are one ethnic refugee group from Burma. In this study, Karen female students are followed to see their literacy practices in everyday life both in and out of school. I focused on digital literacy practices, with the theoretical assumptions that space is not limited to formal space but emotional, mental and other multimodal spaces (Kress, 2000) that need to be considered by the teachers of these learners. Multimodal spaces cover "all modes of communication that are co-present in the text" (Kress, 2000, p. 337). Often multimodal spaces that are connected to multiple literacies go unnoticed in monocultural and monolingual schools (Stewart, 2014). In order to learn from "dynamics and emergent conditions of lived experiences by moving away from stereotypical notions of culture," (González et al., 2005, p. 25) I wanted to explore female refugees' digital literacy practices. Prior research (Gilhooly & Lee, 2014; Omerbašic, 2015) has focused on how digital practices connect refugee communities to the world. Specifically, Omerbašic (2015) focused on how digital spaces were an opportunity for girls to negotiate the concept of citizenship; Gilhooly and Lee (2014) specifically studied the Karen digital practices; and Stewart (2015) proposed how we can learn from refugee digital narratives. My research adds to this work by showing two Karen female adolescents' transnational digital literacy practices, and how those practices might be incorporated into school curricula.

2. Participants

Two girls, Ming (pseudonym) and Saw (pseudonym), who attend a high school in Georgia. They were born in Burma, and they spent some years in a refugee camp in Thailand when they were children before coming to the United States. Like many Karen, Ming and Saw's out of school activities are influenced by their Baptist faith. Saw goes to the Karen church every Saturday and Sunday; Ming visits the church less frequently and stays home to take care of the family. Both Ming and Saw use their L1, Karen, to communicate with people in the church, but they cannot write in Karen.

Ming's family in the U.S. consists of her mother, two sisters and one brother. Her father is still in Thailand and is married to a different woman. Her grandmother lives nearby. She came to the United States with her mother when she was nine years old. She wasn't even eighteen when the research was conducted. Saw has two sisters and one brother, and she is the oldest child in the family. She lives with both parents.

Ming and Saw are now digital natives with daily immersion in the digital world. Like many teens, Ming spends hours outside of school on social network sites, posts pictures, and sends texts to maintain her social life. Unlike Saw, Ming does not have access to a computer at home because her family cannot afford one. Instead, she uses an iPod. Saw, on the other hand, has a smartphone. All of her three siblings have iPods. When Saw was asked what she did with her phone, she answered that she used it both for fun and family matters. In all, then, technology is an integral part of their daily lives. Moreover, being responsible members of their families, they help their siblings and parents with social media. Observations and interviews showed that their digital literacy practices online in order to grasp how they engage themselves culturally.

My research focuses on refugees who are on the margins of society and learning to use their second language to reclaim their multiple identities through their digital practices. They are engaged in different spaces in their daily lives both in school and out-of-school.

3. Theoretical Framework

A New Literacies (Gee, 2000; Street, 1993; Lankshear & Knobel, 2011) framework is commonly invoked among scholars who are working in online contexts. New Literacy "refers to a particular sociocultural approach to understanding and researching literacy (Lankshear & Knobel, 2011, p. 27). This is a study of literacy that does not measure students' skills but rather examines the social practices they engage in daily life. This theoretical lens is used in this study to explore how digital media scaffold the literacy practices of these two girls. For students to fully demonstrate their communicative capabilities, traditional practices such as testing are not enough. In addition, digital media are an integral part of the literacy and meaning-making practices used by adolescent multilingual writers in their daily life (Black, 2005). Using a sociocultural approach to literacy, this study set out to demonstrate why and how these Karen female adolescents use technology to create different meanings to forge connections between their family and friends in their daily lives.

Informed by a New Literacies perspective, this study analyzed multimodal digital literacy practices of these adolescents. I asked what reading and writing practices can benefit them and what implications might be of their multimodal transnational digital literacy practices. Transnational "refers to the fact that individuals who have migrated from one country to another may continue to incorporate daily routines, activities, and institutional affiliations that connect them to their country of origin, even as they are actively engaged in their everyday lives in their destination country" (Lam, 2009, p. 379). Transnational digital literacy practices include diverse cultural practices that refugee learners are engaged in and how they bring them into their online writing. In that connection, they have spaces that many of their local American peers do not have. By developing a diverse and broad range of resources in classrooms, learners can better comprehend the world. These transnational digital spaces are significantly related to the lives of two female resettled refugees.

The purpose of this study was to uncover "the codes and practices that work to silence or disempower them as readers, viewers, and learners in general" (Alvermann & Hagwood, 2000, p. 194). Since multimodality is a significant part of their digital lives as immigrants, their multimodal literacy practices cover a range of areas including the mental, emotional, and social. For them, meanings are negotiated in different cultural contexts and situations in multiple spaces from their American peers. This multimodal analysis of their digital practices is an exploration of the texts that they produced online. As a researcher, my goal was to make sense of all these transnational multimodal digital practices and document how these practices fill different spaces of their life. The research questions for this study are: 1. What knowledge is produced and distributed as these two girls connect their lives with digital literacy? 2. Why is it important to incorporate transnational digital literacy into the school curriculum? 3. What pedagogical implications might we draw from the study as educators?

4. Data Collection

As a transnational researcher not affiliated with the girls' school district, first I needed to be familiar with the school system and students' life-style. I started volunteering at the participants' school in 2015. In 2016, I began a systematic analysis of these youths' school and out-of-school literacy practices. I conducted several semi-structured interviews, observed participants for 42 hours, and analyzed documents in school as well as out of school focusing on their writing on Facebook, postings on Instagram and Snapchat. In order to gain full access to their Facebook writings, I decided to make both of them my Facebook friends while not involving my subjectivity as I kept observing them on Facebook.

4.1. Data Analysis

I analyzed my data drawing utilizing social constructionist approach to grounded theory (Charmaz, 2008). "Grounded theorists adopt a few strategies to focus their data gathering and analyzing, but what they do, how they do it, and why they do it emerge through interacting in the research setting, with their data, colleagues, and themselves" (Charmaz, 2008, pp. 397-398). As I coded the data, I selected codes based on their digital literacy practices, how they use technology and for what purposes. Some of the early codes included Facebook, Korean soap operas, and responsible family member. I also performed a multimodal analysis to find out how these students are putting their multimodal practices (e.g. texts, videos, photos, sounds, Facebook posts, etc.) together.

4.2. Ming and Saw's Digital Experiences in the United States

I explored Ming and Saw's digital life both in school and at home. Their multiple identities are expressed through various practices that they are engaged in everyday life. Both of their digital literacy practices are portrayed in Table 5.1 and Table 5.2.

Table 5.1 Ming's Digital Literacy Practices

Applications	Literacy Practices	Purpose
Facebook	Reading and writing	Networking and connecting with relatives
Google Doc	Reading and Writing for class	Writing
YouTube	Listening to songs watching videos	Entertainment
iMessages and FaceTime	Reading and writing	Communication
Instagram	Posting photos	Entertainment
Snapchat	Posting photos and life events	Entertainment
Korean Soap operas	Drama and language	Entertainment
Thai Movie	Drama	Entertainment

Table 5.2 Saw's Literacy Practices

Applications	Literacy Practices	Purpose
Facebook	Reading and writing	Networking and connecting with relatives
Google Doc	Writing for class	Writing
YouTube	Biblical Gospel both in English and Karen	Preparing for music on Sunday
iMessages and FaceTime	Reading and writing	Communication
Korean Soap Operas	Watch them when she is bored	Entertainment
Snapchat	Posting photos	Entertainment
Instagram	Posting photos and life events	Entertainment

4.3. Ming and Saw's Use of Technology in Daily Life

When I asked Ming what she does with an iPod, she answered that she uses it in numerous ways. For instance, "At home [she] will be watching YouTube on [her] iPod." She listens to songs in different languages that she enjoys immensely. Her answers reflect how much she misses Karen songs and how the iPod is a good source for her to keep in touch with that culture as she does not want to forget her first language (L1) that they use at home. Her iPod is an all-purpose source of entertainment when she is bored at home. Comparing her situation before she had access to an iPod, she related how her American classmates used to laugh at her. As a refugee, she appreciates any technology more than U.S. born peers because her phone is the only source of entertainment as she does not have a car to go to places.

Engagement. When I asked Ming what she does as a digital native, she did not understand the meaning of the phrase. Once I explained the term, she answered that she uses Facebook, iMessage, games and other apps that engage her throughout the day when she is at home.

Even though she says that she is not a big fan of games, Ming still plays some games on her cell phone at home. She added, "at the school bus and at certain times when I am bored at home." She then added a story about how engrossed she gets while playing games. "One day I was supposed to do my French homework. I was playing all day and then I forget about doing the homework. I was just like, 'next day I will do my homework and submit the next day.'" She was engaged while playing games for the whole day with her little sisters and brothers. I burst into laughter when I heard this story from her. At the same time, I was thinking of how we can utilize this practice in literacy instruction.

Commenting on *Facebook* is also a way for Ming to build her own community as a forum where she can share her ideas. Comment boxes are her favorite. For example, she said that she has a friend who is a tomboy, and she posts comments under her friend's photos such as "Wear a dress" or "Put your hair down." She went on, "One day I told her to wear a dress and post on Facebook and she did that." She enjoys this kind of online activity. She is engaged in digital writing while she is on Facebook. Not only that, coming from a Karen cultural background, she also approves of the stereotypes and the gender performance of how a girl should look like. To me, her Facebook comments display that background. The engaging of cultural practices to participate in hegemonic narratives through digital spaces seems like a very important point in how their digital literacy practices mediate their Karen identities.

Talking with her, I learned that she has various groups of friends, and she differentiates among them in how she communicates with them online by maintaining different modes of spaces and languages for communicating with different people. For Ming, online spaces are a "set of places where ... [she] can affiliate with others [that] is based primarily on shared activities, interests, and goals" (Gee, 2004, p. 73). With friends from a "white church," she communicates in a friendlier register via iMessage about church activities. With her friends from the Karen church, she uses iMessage, but she has a different approach to connect to different groups. She tends to make more informal group conversations. Writing on Facebook allows her to write for entertainment. In her interview with me, she pointed that out, but when I checked her Facebook wall, it was not shared with me. This tells me that she differentiates and keeps separate communication among her various affinity groups. Davis (2011) likewise did a study of an American adolescent's use of digital tools that found different dynamics with different people.

For Ming, online communication is a primary means of social communication because she does not have an extensive face-to-face social network to interact with. She has online friends who talk about their boyfriends on Facebook groups. Ming said, "We talk about our secret dates." She also shared that in that group, her friends share secret information. In that digital space, one of her friends wrote, "I love you" and her boyfriend replied, "I love you too." All these conversations took me deep inside her digital life. Significantly, however, she does not share this information with her parents or teachers, and much of her digital social life may be invisible to them. Adolescents will share this secret, but what I see as a woman of color is that because of the culture she is coming from, girls will not be open to their parents about their boyfriends like many American children are. Also, my observation in school demonstrates that Ming is not very extroverted to her teachers about her needs, especially when she is with her American peers who are loud and direct to their teachers.

Ming finds school work hard; hence, for her, it is difficult to find a meaningful connection between in-school and out-of-school literacy. Like Davis (2011), my data emphasizes that youth use digital tools every day and have different dynamics with different people. Moreover, my data indicate that multilingualism adds more complexity and symbolic linguistic tools to the mix. For example, when Ming chats with other Burmese and Karen students, she types in Burmese, even though she struggles with that since she was never taught how to type in Burmese or Karen. So clearly the semiotic value of communicating in Karen with this group outweighs its inconvenience for her. I found that she is also a technology peer-teacher to her American-born brother how to use various apps. Her constant negotiation with her literacy practices as an adolescent impressed me.

When I asked Ming whether she prefers reading online, she said "Yes." She uses an app at home called Manga Rack to read comic books. It helps her read faster, and there are many books in the app for her to read. Whatever she knows about new technology, she shares with her friend circle, and whatever her friends know, they share that with her. The implication is that writing is not necessarily a solitary activity. Regarding Manga Rack, she said, "It does help me. I can choose stories." Inspired by those graphic stories from the app, she randomly draws pictures that stem from her online literacy practices. Like Cary (2004), my results show the positive outcome of comics. Along with engaging second language learners more in reading, comics can also remove the fatigue of being a second language learner. As refugees, their education levels could be stunted in learning a second language and using that as a tool in other areas.

Saw does not enjoy Facebook as much as Ming. She has an iPhone, and whenever she needs to look up vocabulary, she uses her phone. I emphasize vocabulary because that is what she told me she struggles with the most when she reads a book in English. However, as I follow her on Facebook, I get to see how much she likes to post. Being a practicing Christian, her posts are mainly related to the church, God, and her belief. Through my observational notes, I got to know that she does not have any motivation for technologies that do not engage her in school. She seemed rather silent and aloof. However, she creates her own world, where she enjoys her own life on the Internet. Like Ming, Saw uses technology to keep up with music. She usually listens to Karen music when she does her school work in school. When I asked her how she uses the Internet at home, she noted that after her parents leave for work, she does not have anything to do. Also, she does not have a car. Therefore, being online is often the only source of recreational activities for her and her siblings. Digital media provide powerful affordances as for social interaction through writing for students who are otherwise socially isolated by their status as refugees.

While talking to her, I got to know that she feels lonely and engages her time in finding relief by immersing in her own Karen world where she can think of her belief, listens to her Karen songs, and be herself. When she is in school, she keeps on listening to Karen music.

4.4. Academic Uses of Technology in School

In Saw's English class, she was assigned an essay on current topics to be composed using ideas from newspapers and online sources. When she was given an open prompt, Saw chose to explore questions of refugee politics even if the actual writing was not about Karen people. That says something large about her identity. For her English writing assignment on Google Docs, she looked for different sources to support her opinion as a refugee. Below is an excerpt of the final product:

> According to the survey from NBC, most Americans oppose accepting Syrians. I say we should accept Syrians because I personally once was a refugee. Living the life of a refugee is a life that no one wants to live. ... Just like that many of Syrians childrens [sic] are going the same situation, and some are worst than what I went through. These refugee peoples need our help. They want to live in a better place where they don't need to be worry about where should they run for the next target.

To me, the frustration Saw has portrayed in her essay shows how she thinks what Americans' conception of who refugees are. Also, the fear of being a refugee and the history is portrayed in her writing shows how frustrated she is with her life as a refugee. Uncertainty about life and her family's history and coming to the United States make her feel like a fish out of water. The family history she portrays in her essay is compelling and expresses how much she wants to talk about the struggle as a refugee. She justifies her point as to why Syrians refugees should be in the United States by comparing her situation as a refugee. This assignment was an effective way to ask someone like her about her opinion about a topic where she can bring her background and give strong supports as a writer.

Saw repeatedly told me that she does not enjoy reading and writing. However, for the essay that she wrote, she consulted multiple online sources to create her own piece. Since it resonated with her refugee background, she could relate it to her experience. Emotional resilience and productivity can be increased if teachers can address their emotional needs as refugee learners.

4.5. Korean Soap Operas in Digital Media and Identity Negotiation

Korean soap operas address an important niche in both Ming and Saw's out of school lives. This seems to be a gendered activity as my larger data shows that while Karen boys tend to gravitate towards soccer in their leisure hours, girls often pass their time watching Korean soap operas. Since her family cannot afford to subscribe to Netflix to watch Hollywood movies, one of the reasons she watches Korean soap operas is because those soap operas are available free online. In fact, Ming said that she had binge-watched these dramas whole nights without sleeping. For example, one series, *Gogh, the Starry Night*, influenced Ming so much that she chose to write an essay for her English class. After watching this drama several times, she creates her own fantasies. Perhaps, with all of her challenges, as a child from a struggling refugee family, she likes to create escapist fantasies. *Gogh, the Starry Night* reflects her life. This soap opera is a woman's journey of fear and uncertainty of life with two men. While she is struggling with her career, she is also torn between two men who seem not to be good for her. I think that this soap opera resonates with her life since it's a woman's struggle. Being an adolescent in a resettled refugee family and her uncertain relationship with her boyfriend influence her to write this imaginative piece. This is an excerpt from what Ming has written on Google doc for her class:

> *This story is back in the old time like around 2012, It was Me, my sister and our prince from our dream...Yes reader, we doing everything to us save and others mermaid because we can't let our mermaid die and we wanted save otherwise if they die we have no choice but eat it. Now reader you know why we don't want our mermaid dead because we don't want to eat it because it hurt us but that a law that the old man made. He a scary man who knows everything so we as the mermaid we have to be really careful.*

This piece sounds like "the Little Mermaid," too, and what she did in this essay is that she tried to narrate the struggle of a girl with men. This is a powerful connection between her life and her family life with the fantasy world. The imageries are explicit and it is a powerful expression. Similarly, Saw believes that through the subtitle of these dramas, she learns better English.

While Saw learns from the soap operas, she told me in an interview that those soap operas are reflections of life. These motivate her to watch these movies more. Teachers need to know more about students' multicultural and multilingual media consumption out of school.

5. Connecting Family to the Community

While Ming and Saw are having fun with the community at their school, they are also connecting to the broader world through technology. When I asked Ming about her parents' role in her digital life, she expressed that she does not feel any pressure from her mother to curtail her uses of technology. Whenever she is at home, she can use technology. She said, "At home I am free. I can get on anytime I want." Her mother also plays the same games that Ming plays, and her mother learns new technological uses from her. She informed me that the only time that her mother controls her technology use is when she gets a phone call from the school from her teachers. Otherwise, her mother is an inspiration for her to continue her digital journey. To me as a researcher, this is huge support from her mother.

For Saw, technology is a source of connection with family members who are in Burma and Thailand. For example, in an interview with Saw, she related:

> *S: I mean... I use Facebook because I have relatives in Burma you know and so sometimes, we need to contact each other.*

Sonia: You don't call them to Burma?

S: No. It's easier to talk on Facebook.

In an especially dramatic example of how technology is bringing her family closer, Saw found her lost uncle on Facebook after ten years. She and her family started communicating with him henceforth. Her mom communicates using Saw's Facebook account about farming in Burma. Because Saw came to the United States with her parents in 2012, she and her family in the U.S. are curious about her aunt's position and cousins' position in Burma, as well as how they are in Thailand. Since they cannot help them in bringing those family members to the U.S., they need to communicate with them. That digital space is much needed for her to be in touch with close and distant family members.

6. What These Two Women Taught Me

At the moment, nothing of their experiences seems different than other digital natives in this country. These two women have taught me immensely regarding how media influence them. A transnational digital literacy perspective shows that the audience actively produces meaning and that way, they become part of history. Also, future cultural texts can be produced this way. Students' work that I have represented are products of their historical and social life. To build emotional resilience, persistence, and personal productivity, bringing their digital literacy practices into classrooms are imperative. When I observed them in classrooms, I found both are silent while their American peers are not. In that situation, where teachers are busy controlling unruly students, these refugee students' needs remain unnoticed and invisible. Addressing their silence in classrooms through an appropriate manner might help them. Their transnational digital literacy practices together offer culturally rich resources that can be used in classrooms. Their classroom silence masks their very active multicultural, multilingual digital media proficiency out of school. Also, classrooms are not organized to draw this out.

7. Conclusion

Addressing the transnational literacy practices of these students through digital practices can motivate them as readers and writers. It showed that the pedagogical learning perspectives can bring huge differences in addressing these students' silence. The portraits of Ming and Saw as digital citizens reveal that technology is an important and integral part of their lives. Their in- and out-of-school practices show that they use technology to connect with people and the world around them while they assimilate American culture. At the same time, they are not content with all technologies that they are exposed to in school as the use of those technologies does not always make lessons fun. Most importantly, some digital practices in class do not engage them as learners because of the lack of connection between their everyday life and those digital practices. The integration of transnational digital literacies at school could be facilitated if we asked students about those practices at home and incorporated those practices in teaching.

Since Ming likes playing games, one of the implications is that more games can be incorporated in classrooms to make lessons more interesting. Students are willing to work hard at writing if they are engaged with meaningful digital communication. School-based literacy practices need to be more student-centered and student-determined to get student investment. Regarding affinity space, Gee (2007) wrote: "The common endeavor is organized around a whole process (involving multiple but integrated functions), not single, discreet, or discontextualized task" (Gee, 2007, p. 206). Since games can create affinity spaces that engage learners in multiple ways, incorporating various games will be more productive.

Students might participate better in writing if they are given more chances in creating escapist fantasies. Teachers can use digital tools content, while addressing the topics that students are interested in because that way these students can relate more to their regular life. Bringing funds of knowledge (González et al., 2005) to their classroom setting will make the process of learning easier. Educators need to be well prepared to nurture students who bring transnational and complex multilingual identities in classrooms. Incorporating refugee narratives will fulfill the need to some extent.

During my participant observation in classrooms, I observed that students did not find digital technologies in themselves inherently engaging. Rather, they enjoyed digital technologies such as videos that were connected to their lives. Asking each student about their literacy practices at home and incorporating those ideas in teaching would help them. For example, ideas from Korean soap operas and using more graphic novels would help these youths become better learners. Since schools must use state-mandated curricula, using texts are important. However, using adaptations of graphic novels that have more illustrations and less traditional texts will be more helpful.

Perry & Hart (2012) found that teachers did not know much about their refugee students and in their study, they mentioned that many teachers expressed the fact that they were unprepared to face the challenge of teaching refugee students. Literacy varies within cultural groups and technological advancement makes the process even more complex, especially for students with transnational identities. Like Stewart's (2014) study, this study demonstrates the value of out-of-school literacy practices and how teachers can continue creative practices that motivate them to be better learners.

Incorporating ideas from the narratives of these girls with an effort to address their emotional, mental and social spaces will help these learners more. School and teachers might know better what they can do in teaching reading and writing through my research since my field notes suggest that their transnational digital literacy practices are invisible to the teachers. The purpose of this small project is to inform public institutions about the steps the institutions and teachers can take dealing with refugee second language learners in classrooms so that teachers do not feel unprepared because of cultural differences (Stewart, 2015). It will enable others to develop more equitable and inclusive curricula and teaching methodologies for these global citizens.

8. Suggestions

- Interesting reading will engage learners and using relevant apps can help these learners. Choosing reading materials from different online apps (e.g. graphic novels) can help students to improve their comprehension skills.

- Another idea to promote learning would be using videos, something related to their culture such as Korean soap operas.

- Creating online space for students to share their ideas will open possibilities to share their interests. Students will be able to write in their affinity space about the topics they are interested in.

References

Alvermann, D., & Hagood, M. (2000). Critical Media Literacy: Research, Theory, and Practice in "New Times". *The Journal of Educational Research, 93*(3), 193-205.

Black, R. W. (2005). Access and Affiliation: The Literacy and Composition Practices of English-Language Learners in an Online Fanfiction Community. Journal of Adolescent & Adult Literacy, 49(2), 118-128.

Cary, S. (2004). Going graphic: Comics at work in the multilingual classroom. Portsmouth: Heineman.

Charmaz, K. (2008). Constructionism and the Grounded Theory. In J.A. Holstein and J. F. Gubrium (Eds.), Handbook of Constructionist Research (pp. 397- 412). New York: The Guilford Press.

Davis, K. (2011). A life in bits and bytes: A portrait of a college student and her life with digital media. Teachers College Record, 113(9), 1960-1982.

Gee, J. P. (2000). Teenagers in New Times: A New Literacy Studies Perspective. Journal of Adolescent and Adult Literacy, 43(5), 412-420.

Gee, J. P. (2004). *Situated language and learning: A critique of traditional schooling*. New York: Routledge.

Gee, J. P. (2007). What video games have to teach us about literacy and learning. New York: Palgrave Macmillan.

Gilhooly, D. & Lee, E. (2014). The Role of Digital Literacy Practices on Refugee Resettlement: The Case of Three Karen Brothers. The Journal of Adolescent and Adult Literacy. (57) 5. pp 387-396

González, N., Moll, L. C., & Amanti, C. (2005). Funds of knowledge: theorizing practices in households, communities, and classrooms. Mahwah, N.J.: L. Erlbaum Associates, 2005.

Kress, G. (2000). Multimodality: Challenges to thinking about language. *TESOL Quarterly*, 34, 337–340.

Lam, W. S. E. (2009). Multiliteracies on Instant Messaging in Negotiating Local, Translocal, and Transnational Affiliations: A Case of an Adolescent Immigrant. Reading Research Quarterly, (4), 377.

Lankshear, C., & Knobel, M. (2011). New Literacies. Berkshire, England: McGraw-Hill Education.

Omerbašić, D. (2015). Literacy as a Translocal Practice: Digital Multimodal Literacy Practices Among Girls Resettled as Refugees. Journal of Adolescent & Adult Literacy, 58(6), 472.

Perry, K.H., & Hart, S.J. (2012). "I'm just kind of winging it": Preparing and supporting educators of adult refugee learners. Journal of Adolescent & Adult Literacy, 56(2), 110–122. doi:10.1002/JAAL.00112

Stewart, M. (2015). "My Journey of Hope and Peace": Learning From Adolescent Refugees' Lived Experiences. Journal of Adolescent & Adult Literacy, 59(2), 149-159.

Stewart, M. (2014). Social Networking, Workplace, and Entertainment Literacies: The Out-of-School Literate Lives of Newcomer Latina/o Adolescents. Reading Research Quarterly,49(4), 365-369.

Street, B. V. (1993). Introduction: the new literacy studies. In (Ed.), Cross-cultural approaches to literacy (pp. 1–22). Cambridge, UK: Cambridge University Press.

More to Explore List

1. Explore MangaRack to find out interesting graphic novels for Karen students
2. Know about Burma's Civil War: https://www.vice.com/en_us/article/bu rma-is-complicated-so-i-made-a-book
3. Read Karen literature and history to incorporate in class: http://www.karen.org.au/docs/Karen_people_booklet.pdf
4. http://wowlit.org/blog/2017/03/20/2017-outstanding-international-books-3/ To explore the life of refugees from around the world

Chapter 6

ESP and the Beatles:
Songs are not only for fun

Ian Michael Robinson

Univeristy of Calabria, Italy

Abstract: Songs can be a useful tool in general English lessons but are often excluded from the more 'serious' work of ESP. This chapter reports on a project that involved giving songs by the Beatles a decisive role in a university-level ESP course for students of Social Work and Social Policy. In this 42-hour language course, almost every lesson involved a Beatles' song. The songs were used for different activities and functions: for example, vocabulary building, grammar practice, listening, reading, topic introduction, and study skills. Questionnaires were used to elicit information from the fifty students involved as to whether they felt that this approach to ESP was appropriate, valid and effective. Overall, it would appear that students appreciate the use of songs by the Beatles in their ESP lessons and that this approach may be considered effective in this context.

Keywords: Beatles, songs, ESP, listening skills, Social Policy

***

1. Introduction

Songs have a consolidated place in the teaching of general English, however very often they are seen as a filler activity, one that is just for fun. This chapter investigates the use of songs in the teaching of English for Specific Purposes university-level language lessons. In the project reported here these songs were used in a variety of ways for different activities and functions: for example, vocabulary building, grammar practice, listening, reading, topic introduction, and study skills. The songs employed in this endeavour are all Beatles' songs. Having used the songs and related activities, the students involved were administered a questionnaire to gather their perceptions of the utility and validity of using songs in an ESP class. This is something which until now has not been studied and so two objectives of this chapter are to add to the literature on this subject and add another tool to the ESP teachers toolbox.

2. Literature review

English for Specific Purposes (ESP) has changed over time, starting in the 1960s (Dudley-Evans & St John, 1998) it came out of the communicative language approach (Richards and Rogers 2014) and at first, was seen as something distinct from general English (Strevens, 1977), but Dudley-Evans and St John, with their absolute and variable characteristics of ESP, state that ESP "may" be different from general English in its methodology. It can also be different in the range of skills involved, Woodrow (2018, p. 6) writes that one characteristic of ESP can be the "limited range of skills taught". Another contrast with general English courses is the level of motivation that specialising is hoped to achieve, Woodrow (ibid, p. 6) adds that in ESP "learners have high external motivation", which he sees as being in contrast to general English in "a school setting where English is mandatory and students may lack motivation" (ibid, p. 6-7). This seems to be in contrast with Jordan (1997, p. 71) who reveals, however, that in an English for Academic Purposes (EAP) course it can be difficult to sustain "interest and motivation".

A recent definition of ESP defines it as

> *"an approach to language teaching that targets the current and/or future academic or occupational needs of learners, focuses on the necessary language, genres, and skills to address these needs, and assists learners in meeting these needs through the use of general and/or discipline-specific teaching materials and methods."* (Anthony 2018, pp. 10-11)

This changing from an absolute difference from English for general purposes to a possible difference to a point where aspects of general English are included in ESP shows how more nuanced ESP has become, as does the fact that the skills do not have to be "limited". What makes ESP different from general English according to Anthony (2018) is that it is based on what he refers to as the "four pillars" of ESP: Needs Analysis, Learning Objectives, Evaluation, and Materials and Methods. He also goes on to try to give an as inclusive as possible list of what sub-categories there might be under this umbrella term: for example, English for Academic Purposes (EAP); English for Vocational Purposes (EVP); onto specialised subjects such as English for Solid-State Physics. He also notes the thin line that exists between teaching a subject in English (EMI, English Mediated Instruction), bilingual teaching and

ESP. ESP must be primarily concerned with the language and the skills needed, rather than the learning of the content of the subject matter. All of these have to be thought about when designing a new ESP course.

ESP developed from a narrow focus on English for Science and Technology (Hyon, 2018; Woodrow, 2018), and Hyon (2018) traces how, with an understanding of different genres, it has become a much more complex field. It has become important to identify the specifics of the certain area of ESP under consideration as they are not all the same. To help do this, Hyon refers to Swales' communicative events and discourse community as being essential in describing ESP.

Woodrow (2018) applies Tomlinson's principles of SLA material development to ESP, stating the material must "have an impact", "promote positive affect", "be perceived as useful by the learners", "facilitate learner self-investment", "expose learners to authentic use", "draw attention to linguistic features", "provide learners opportunity to use target language" and "account for learner styles". All of this must come after a careful needs analysis for the course. Indeed, Woodrow (2018, p. 5) notes that "The single most defining feature of ESP courses is that they are based on the analysis of learner needs". In his book, Brown (2016, p. 16) notes that "needs can at best be described to be sets of judgements and compromises justified by observation, surveys, test-scores, language learning theory, linguistics, or otherwise". A very detailed needs analysis such as that devised by Munby (1978) is very long and complex and so Brown advocates a simpler version and defines it as being the "Current Best Shot at a defensible curriculum". The result of the Needs Analysis will be dependent on the scope and scale of it, which are in turn dependent on resources available. Brown (2016, p. 27) notes it is also necessary to take into account "how specific ESP should be".

One aspect of the specificity of the ESP course is the type of English it should promote. Ideas of English as a Lingua Franca and those of World Englishes are feeding into ESP and are shifting the focus away from native-like proficiency towards levels of proficiency which are seen as being appropriate to the needs of the students. Woodrow (2018, p. 13) writes that "the level of specificity of ESP and the use of appropriate models of English are determined by the contexts in which communication will occur". The context for this project is described in the next section.

2.1. What is not mentioned in any of the ESP literature is the use of songs in ESP

Songs are often used in EFL lessons; Jolly (1975) was advocating for the use of songs in teaching foreign languages back in the 1970s and Leith in the same decade (1979, p. 540) stated, "There is probably not a better nor quicker way to teach phonetics than with songs". Harmer (2007, p. 320) notes that "One of the most useful kinds of texts for students to work with is song lyrics" and that teachers can "choose songs ... which are appropriate in terms of topic and subject matter". Tegge (2018) writes about the positive effects reported for using songs ("superior retention of songs compared to written texts", the "multimodality of stimuli – music, rhythm, linguistic sound patterns, mental imagery, kinaesthetic experiences").

Simpson (2015) says that music is a "great teaching tool" because of its "universal appeal, connecting all cultures and languages" and that because of this it is "one of the best and most motivating resources in the classroom, regardless of the age or background of the learner". However, there are authors who point to some problems involved; Lorenzutti (2014, p. 14) warns that "Despite the rich potential of songs as authentic and stimulating texts, when it comes to designing a listening activity for a song, teachers tend to rely upon the Gap Fill as the sole activity". Various authors (Budden, 2008; Domoney & Harris 1993; Eken, 1996; Griffee, 1992; Gugliemino, 1986; Lo & Li, 1998; Lorenzutti, 2014; Monreal, 1982; Murphey, 1992; Shen, 2009) suggest various tasks that can take the teacher beyond this limitation and give reasons for doing so.

In a recent article Tegge (2018) found that most teachers involved in his research thought of songs as "a useful tool in the language classroom to foster second language acquisition" (ibid, p. 277) and used them with "clear meaning – and language-focused goals in mind and in the context of a directed and diverse teaching unit which included complementary activities" instead of just five-minute fillers. Tegge also identified various activities used by teachers with songs: Cloze/gap-fill; discussion; sing-along; focus on comprehension questions; ordering activity; writing activity; true/false statements; dictation. He also (ibid, p. 279) found the following goals being set in the use of songs: "to create a positive and motivating learning situation"; "to accommodate individual learners' needs"; "to provide authentic language and culture"; "to teach clearly defined language skills and linguistic knowledge". These were all for general English. He sees (ibid, p. 283) that one problem of using songs is "the time and effort spent on preparing and conducting the lesson".

3. The study

This study involved post-graduate students enrolled on a Social Policy and Social Work Master's degree and those on the Social Research and Sociology Master's course in a southern Italian university (here the Master's course is a two-year course that follows on from the three-year undergraduate course as part of the three-plus-two system introduced in the Bologna Process). The English course is an obligatory course for the students and involves forty-two hours of lessons with the main teacher as well as ten hours with language instructors in smaller groups. The majority of these students had already done English lessons as part of their undergraduate degree and had passed a B1 level final exam. However, the group demonstrated a heterogeneous language level varying from A2 to C1. Fifty-four students were enrolled on the course, but not all students were always at all of the lessons. It is an ESP/EAP course aimed at meeting the specific language skills needed by these students.

The students in these postgraduate degree courses need academic skills of reading articles, listening to seminars, reading books and the language necessary to do field research. Some students are interested in studying abroad on the Erasmus Plus programme. They need occupational English to work abroad, deal with EU directives and articles of interest and the language necessary to deal with immigrants (this last part is important for students of the two interested degree courses as Calabria, in the south of Italy, is an important landing area for refugees fleeing from North Africa). They also need to overcome resistance to learning English as an L2 as many reports having had problematic language learning experiences at school.

This particular field of study deals with social sciences and therefore a need to understand texts concerning society and everyday problems and communicate about these issues. This gives a vast array of possibilities as to what can be taught within the course. Students also need a good level of general communication skills as these are needed in social research or in dealing with people, especially immigrants, who maybe do not have a good command of the students L1, which in most cases here is Italian, but who might be better at English. This all leads to specific teaching objectives; students need to be able to discuss the context they are in – the university and the geographical region; they need to be able to function linguistically in their academic field of interest; they need to be able to function linguistically in their possible future jobs. The language needed is not native-speaker like proficiency but rather a practical proficiency for dealing with a variety of Englishes. The general language policy of the university as explicated by the Language Centre is that postgraduate students should leave the university with at least a B1 upper level in at least one L2.

As well as more traditional style ESP material, this course involved the use of eighteen songs by the Beatles. The decision to use the Beatles was mainly a subjective one based on personal preference, but also given their large canon of songs this offered variety but also a limit; this limit was seen as an incentive to creativity in the preparation of tasks following Pope's (2005, p. 122) suggestion that "through game-like constraints … playful creativity is stimulated to emerge". It was hoped that by being constricted to only use works from one group then more creative use of these songs might come about.

There follows a brief guide to the songs that were used, the task that involved the song and the follow-up exercise. Here the songs are presented in alphabetical order.

3.1. Songs

"**A Day in the Life**": past tense verbs were removed and the students were asked to put the verbs in the brackets into the correct form in the past. The song uses newspaper headlines in its lyrics. The song task was followed by a table of eight headlines from the BBC online news service and, mixed up, the eight corresponding first sentences of the articles. Students had to match headlines to titles. All the articles were connected to social problems. In pairs, students then had to write a newspaper headline and first paragraph for a contemporary social problem in the local area.

"**A Hard Day's Night**": students are asked to listen and underline the idiomatic expressions in the song. In a table of idiomatic expressions and their meanings, students had to match the idiom with its meaning. As a further exercise in identifying and using some of the most commonly used idiomatic expressions, students had to put words in the correct order to make idiomatic expressions and then decide what they mean. Students then wrote dialogues which used idiomatic expressions and then acted out the dialogues.

"**Don't Bother Me**": words at the end of each line were removed and mixed up. Students had to listen and complete the lines with the correct words. Very often, people do not want to be "bothered" by social problems, preferring to ignore them. In small groups, the students designed ways to bring social problems to the attention of the general public or of local politicians/Public Administrators.

"**Eleanor Rigby**": words were removed and scrambled. Students had to use the letters in the brackets to make the correct word for the space. This song talks about a lonely person and so leads on to a text entitled "The Dangers of Loneliness". Students had to read the text about loneliness and answer some comprehension questions. This was followed by a discussion on the topic.

"**Hello, Goodbye**": students were asked "What vocabulary learning techniques can you deduce from this song?". It was noticed that this song uses opposites (hello – goodbye) and that this is a good way to learn vocabulary. There followed an exercise concerning opposites (antonyms) of words. The song also uses a lot of repetition and students were encouraged to discuss ways to repeat vocabulary to help them learn new words and phrases in the L2.

"**Help!**": words were removed from the lyrics and cryptic clues were given to help them reconstruct the lyric, e.g. When I was __1_____ so much __1_____ than today

The clue was 1) Not older, and the answer is, obviously, "younger".

This led on to a series of short discussions about *help*, for example:

Discuss with your friends how studying this degree course can help you in your future career.

Discuss with partners how you can help society?

Discuss how knowing English can help you?

Each discussion was timed so that they lasted only three minutes before the students moved on to the next discussion.

"**I'm A Loser**": words were removed from the text and the letters mixed up, students had to use the mixed-up letters in brackets to create the correct word. They then listened to the song to check their answers. The song discusses love and the loss of love. Students were then asked to discuss what different types of love there are. This was followed by a reading task with an article that gives descriptions of seven types of love taken from ancient Greece, for each one there is an example which had been cut out of the text and written below. The students had to match the description of the type of love to the example (1. Eros: Love of the body: 2. Philia: Love of the mind: 3. Ludus: Playful love: 4. Pragma: Longstanding love: 5. Agape: Love of the soul: 6. Philautia: Love of the self: 7. Storge: Love of the child). They then discussed in groups how this type of distinction helps us understand society and the problems in it.

"**Lady Madonna**": the song was divided into two halves, A and B, and the lines in the song were mixed up. The students had to listen and put the lines in the correct order. The song refers to the day-to-day economic problems of a woman with a child, the exercise that followed was a table of the sources of financial problems, the reasons for such problems and their solutions, all mixed up. Students had to connect the relevant problem to the source and the solution. This led to a discussion of how to help people with economic problems.

"**Lucy In The Sky With Diamonds**": students had to read the song and find any references they thought they could find to drugs (it should be noted that John Lennon, the writer of the song, always denied that this song refers to drugs in any way). This led on to a series of discussion questions concerning drugs, e.g.

Discuss in small groups why it could be a good idea to legalise (some) drugs.

Why do people take illegal drugs?

How can we help people who abuse drugs?

Who is worse, the pusher or the drug addict?

Is drinking alcohol the same as taking drugs?

"**Run For Your Life**": in this song, a word (or phrase) was removed from each line, students had to put it back where it belongs using cohesion strategies, then listen to the song to check their answers. The song, rather surprisingly for a Beatles' song, refers to the threat of violence towards a reluctant lover and leads on to a text entitled "Domestic Violence Threats". This article describes types of domestic violence and then gives a real-life example of each. The examples were removed and put at the end of the text. Students had to replace the examples in the text.

"**She Said, She Said**": at the end of each line there is a choice of two words, students must listen and decide which one is correct. The song is a dialogue; students then had to write a dialogue with a partner about a discussion of a social problem. The dialogue had to be at least sixty words long.

"**She's Leaving Home**": words were removed from the lyrics and students were asked to identify the type of word (adjective, noun, etc.) that had been removed and then try to insert the correct word. They then listened and checked, and where necessary, corrected.

The song concerns somebody leaving home. This was followed up with a text about why children run away. In this text, some words were removed, they are the last three words of a sentence and the first three words of the next. Students must put the phrases back into the text in the correct places.

After this, students were asked to form small groups and discuss what advice to give to young people who are thinking of running away, thus using the language of advice-giving. This was connected to another text about giving advice to people and students were asked to read this part of the article and identify which ideas they mentioned (if any) in their groups.

"**Taxman**": words were removed from the song as a gap fill. Students listen and complete the song.

The follow up is a text concerning how taxes are spent. For the main categories of expenditure, the letters in the words were mixed up, the students had to unscramble the words. Tax money is needed for social service; in small groups, the students had to write an argument as to why the government should spend more money on social services here in Calabria.

"**The Fool On The Hill**": verbs were removed from the lyrics, students had to complete the lyrics with the correct verbs, then listen and check their answers.

The following text was entitled "When a mental health condition becomes a disability". At the end of the text, there were ten "answers". Students had to write the corresponding questions.

"**When I'm Sixty-Four**": twelve expressions in the song were highlighted and had to be connected to the correct corresponding picture, e.g. "When I get older losing my hair" connects to a picture of a man suffering hair loss. The follow-up exercise refers to a paragraph and a graph. Students must read the paragraph and look at the graph and then decide whether the ten statements below are True (T), False (F) or they do not know because the information is Not in the Text (NT). This particular task is later found at the end of the course exam.

"**Within You, Without You**": some lines in the song were tampered with, students had to listen to the song and decide whether the lines in the lyrics are correct or not. If there is a word that is not correct, they had to replace it with the correct word. The next task used mistakes that past students had committed in their writing tasks in previous exams. The students in the class had to correct the mistakes. An example of such a mistake is "Italy important place in history of European nation".

"**Yesterday**": personal pronouns were removed from the lyrics and students had to replace them. They then listened to the song to check their answers. After this, the students had a text of an interview with a social worker about his time, in the past, working with adults. The verbs were removed and the infinitive put in brackets next to the gap with an indication as to whether the verb was in the past or present tense and whether it was in the continuous or simple form. Students had to complete the text with the verbs in the correct form.

"**You've Got To Hide Your Love Away**": some of the words from the song were muddled up, the students had to put them back in the right order. They listened to get feedback.

In his book explaining the Beatles' lyrics, Davies (2014) says that some people have suggested that this song by John Lennon is a message to the Beatles' producer, Brian Epstein, who was homosexual in a time when being gay was illegal. This could be John Lennon telling his friend to be careful. This song then led on to a text about a British Government LGBT Action Plan and a multiple-choice closed task on grammar.

This variety of use of songs and the connected tasks and exercises attempts to cover many of the language needs of the students. The songs are used for their themes, vocabulary or phrases, as well as for their grammatical content. The material described here accounts for about half of the material that was specifically produced for the ESP language course.

It was not explained to the students why these songs were being used.

At the end of the course, the students were asked to complete a questionnaire concerning the songs (see appendix).

4. Results and comments

Fifteen of the songs were chosen as being the favourite of the songs used, with the most popular one being 'Yesterday' which was nominated by 6 students and then "She's leaving Home", "Taxman" and "Within you, without you" each being cited 4 times. This result encourages the use of a variety of songs as, obviously, different people relate to different songs in different ways.

Twenty-two different types of exercise were enjoyed the most, with 4 people choosing the gap-fill exercise and 5 choosing the short discussions connected to the idea of "help". This suggests the work involved in devising all these various activities was appreciated as the members of the class who liked the activities in different ways and so this variety probably helped the lessons become more enjoyable and so, hopefully, more motivating. The ESP lessons for these students were part of the compulsory lessons that they have to attend as part of their degree course. This means that the high motivation that Woodrow expects of ESP classes is not necessarily present as these lessons could easily reflect the mandatory English lessons of school with the potential for lack of motivation.

Twenty-eight students said that by using these song tasks, their English has improved, four said no and one was undecided. Sixteen said that this improvement was in learning new words, fourteen said that this improvement was in pronunciation. Other reasons included improving general listening comprehension skills. Two people said that they had not improved because they did not understand the words in the songs. The mixed-ability of the class was cause for concern for the adequate completion of the tasks at times.

Twenty-four students felt that in the limited time available to learn English that this was an effective way to teach English, noticing that this method was "interactive", gave "structure" to the lessons and was "interesting". Six said it wasn't, one of these asking for more exercises directly connected to the final exam, and one student was undecided. This positive result suggests that songs should be employed in ESP lessons, but that maybe, because university students can tend to be very exam-oriented, a little more effort is needed to explain how the songs and the connected tasks relate to this objective.

The students noted that the songs were used for specific reasons: twelve saw this as a way to practice pronunciation; fourteen as a way to learn new words; eleven as grammar practice; five as a way to practice understanding the message in a listening text; one student saw it as a "simple and fun way to learn". It is satisfying that the students realised that they had learnt specific aspects of language, however, maybe a more direct objective could be explained during the lesson.

Answering the question "Do you think it was a good idea to use songs?" thirty-three replies were in the positive, one was negative and one person replied "sometimes". The reasons, where they were given, included this is a "good way to learn without weighing down the lesson". The dissenting voice called for "exercises for the exam".

When asked whether they would have preferred not to have used songs, twenty-seven replied that they would not have preferred this, one would have preferred not to and one was undecided. The songs were seen as an "enjoyable", "interesting", "simple method to study English" that helps students with their pronunciation and to learn new words. This corroborates the findings from the previous question and gives validation to the use of songs in ESP lessons.

The lessons included only songs by the Beatles and when asked whether they would have preferred a wider range of artists twenty-four said they would and nine said they were happy with this choice of a Beatles only policy. Three people replied that with different music students might pay more attention, one wrote that "if students don't like Beatles, he/she doesn't want to listen. Maybe disturb", two students said they did not like the Beatles, whereas four students expressed their appreciation of the group, two preferred more modern music; other artists were also suggested (Queen, Bob Marley, Pink Floyd). One student wrote that he/she was happy to see only Beatles' songs because "Beatles have helped spread the English language in the world", another wrote that "Beatles wrote songs well" and one stated that "Beatles use a clear pronunciation, easy to understand, happy rhythm". This preference could lead to a change in the future courses, while still using many of these songs, but here the use of only Beatles' songs was also a provocative one which tried to get a reaction from the students. The choice of songs with corresponding singers or groups is always going to be subjective and be received subjectively by the students. The students soon came to recognise that all the songs would be by the Beatles and accepted this, and as some students noticed, there can be good cultural arguments for this choice.

When asked directly if these songs had helped them learn English, twenty-three said yes, two said "quite"; "no", "not too much" and "more or less" each had one person replying in such a way. Six people again focused on new words as the area where this improvement had taken place, four on pronunciation. Two people noticed that "The music rests in your mind when the lesson finishes", one noted that "Songs are important to understand the language" and it was seen as "fun". One student replied that notwithstanding all these songs and the input "I still have difficulty in English". Songs cannot, therefore, be seen as a way of certainly obtaining language learning, but there are good reasons to support the idea that they can be effective for the majority of the students.

The questionnaire also involved twelve statements for the students to agree or disagree with, these can be found in Table 6.1 along with the average reply of the students.

Table 6.1 Statements to agree or disagree with

On a scale of 1 to 5 (where 1 = **Not at all** and 5 = **completely**) do you agree with these statements?	Average result
Songs should not be used in English lessons.	1.4
Songs should only be used in general English lessons.	3.3
It was useful to use these songs in the lessons.	4.3
The songs made the lessons more fun.	4.4
I wanted more songs in the lessons.	3.2
The songs are not in the exam and so are not important.	2.6
Traditional grammar style exercises are more useful than these songs.	3.4
Students should be allowed to choose which songs to use in the classroom.	2.9
The songs made the lessons more boring.	1.3
The songs used are relevant to my degree course.	2.8
There were too many songs used in this language course.	2.7
I enjoyed the course with this mix of songs and other tasks.	4.2

On a Likert style scale, the answers with average values in the 2 range (2.0 to 2.9) produce equivocal replies which do not indicate acceptance of or dissent with the statement. In general, these replies in Table 1 show that students strongly agree that songs should be used in their lessons and perceived these songs as useful although, contradictorily as this was an ESP class, they also felt that songs were more applicable to general English lessons and were not certain that these songs were relevant to the degree course that they were following. However, the songs were overwhelmingly seen as making the lessons more fun, less boring and that this mix helped the students' enjoyment. Students still feel, although marginally (3.4.) that traditional grammar exercises are more important. Although noted above, some students wanted exercises and practice that they felt were more directly connected to their final exam, the general point of view of the students did not feel this to be the case as they did not express a strong opinion one way or another that songs were not important as they are not in the exam. They did suggest from their answers that they wanted more songs in the course. There was only a very slight tendency to suggest that students should be allowed to choose the songs used.

Eighteen students recommended continuing with songs in the ESP class, four said not to and one was undecided. This suggests that the students were engaged with the use of songs and that, as seen above, found them useful for their studies in English. This is important for others involved in ESP. The students were aware of the fact that theirs was an ESP course and that the objectives for the course of lessons were directly related to their specific needs in English. These students felt overwhelmingly that this project of using the Beatles songs to help them learn English had been useful and had helped them become more motivated, because of the enjoyment factor, to study.

Students were asked whether future courses should continue to use songs or not. The reasons to continue included the following: "they can help students", "songs are interesting", "I liked listening to these songs", "the best way to learn", and "because those songs touch some issues that we study in our degree course, for example, violence or drugs". Some people wanted different artists and two stated "It will be more important for them to do more exercises for the exam".

There were very few final extra written comments from the students, but these included "Keep it up and English lessons will always be done with pleasure", "Course is interactive", and "The course was very effective". This seems to validate the project and the use of songs.

5. Conclusion

The project used songs in a variety of ways within the confines of a tertiary level ESP class in an Italian university. All of the songs came from the Beatles vast canon. The activities were designed to avoid just using the songs as gap-fill exercises and not just as a five-minute fun filler exercise. By using songs in almost every lesson with the students, it was necessary to become creatively engaged so as to avoid repetition, as well as respond to the needs of the students. This use of songs and the variety of exercises connected to them was seen by some students as giving structure to the lessons. These ESP lessons are obligatory for all students on the Social Work and Social Policy degree course and the Social Research and Sociology degree course. This means that the students have not chosen to study ESP for these specific fields but must do and so the high level of motivation that Woodrow (2018) expected of ESP students might be lacking. It is therefore essential to find a way to motivate these students and songs can be an ideal way to do this, as suggested by Simpson (2015). Tegge (2018), above, wrote that it takes time and effort to find suitable songs and to create the activities to go with them, this certainly holds true for the activities involved in this project. However, the positive results and feedback from the questionnaire indicate that this is a worthwhile investment. The fact that this investment was appreciated by university students doing an obligatory ESP course as part of their degree course, strongly suggests that this is an approach that can be replicated elsewhere. It should, of course, be remembered that the nature of the degree courses under consideration here might have meant that the courses leant themselves particularly well to the use of songs. It could be that a more scientific degree course might prove more problematic. It was easy to find songs that were in some way pertinent to the field of study of these students, even if not all the students recognised this particular effort. These students involved in this project found this use of Beatles songs a valid and effective way to conduct ESP lessons.

If we return to Anthony's (2018) four pillars of ESP (Needs Analysis, Learning Objectives, Evaluation, and Materials and Methods) then this approach has allowed us to meet some of the needs of the students, remembering that the course also involved other tasks that were not connected to these songs, it helped meet the learning objectives, and the materials were deemed to be consistent with Tomlinson's principals that Woodrow applied to ESP in that they "have an impact", "promote positive affect", were "perceived as useful by the learners", "expose learners to authentic use", "draw attention to linguistic features", "provide learners opportunity to use target language" and "account for learner styles". Some of the learners even went so far as to say that they wanted more songs in the ESP lessons.

References

Anthony, L. (2018). *Introducing English for Specific Purposes*. Abingdon: Routledge.

Budden, J. (2008). Using music and songs. https://www.teachingenglish.org.uk/article/using-music-songs (last accessed 27/02/2019)

Brown, J. D. (2016). *Introducing Needs Analysis and English for Specific Purposes*. Abingdon: Routledge.

Davies, H. (2014). The Beatles Lyrics: *The Unseen Story Behind Their Music*. London: Weidenfeld & Nicolson.

Domoney, L., & Harris, S. (1993). Justified and ancient: Pop music in EFL classrooms. *ELT Journal*, 47, 234-241.

Dudley-Evans, T. & St John, M. J. (1998). *Developments in English for Specific Purposes: A multi-disciplinary Approach*. Cambridge: Cambridge University Press.

Eken, D. K. (1996). Ideas for using pop songs in the English language classroom. *English Teaching Forum*, 34, 46-47.

Griffee, D. T. (1992). *Songs in action*. Prentice Hall.

Gugliemino, L. M. (1986). The affective edge: Using songs and music in ESL instruction. *Adult Literacy and Basic Education*, 10, 19-26.

Harmer, J. (2007). *The Practice of English Language Teaching (4th Edition)*. Harlow: Pearson Education Limited.

Hyon, S. (2018). *Introducing Genre and English for Specific Purposes*. Abingdon: Routledge.

Jolly, Y. S. (1975). The use of songs in teaching foreign languages. *The Modern Language Journal*, 59(1/2), 11-14. http://dx.doi.org/10.2307/325440

Jordan, R. R. (1997). *English for Academic Purposes*. Cambridge: Cambridge University Press.

Leith, W. D. (1979). Advanced French conversation through popular music. The French Review, 52, 537-551.

Lo, R., & Li, H. C. (1998). Songs enhance learner involvement. *English Teaching Forum*, 8-11, 21, 36.

Lorenzutti, N. (2014). Beyond the Gap Fill: Dynamic Activities for Song in the EFL Classroom. *English Teaching Forum*, 1, 14-21.

Monreal, M. E. (1982). How I use songs. *English Teaching Forum*, 20, 44-45.

Munby, J. (1978). *Communicative Syllabus Design*. Cambridge: Cambridge University Press.

Murphey, T. (1992). *Music and song*. Oxford University Press.

Pope, R. (2005). *Creativity: Theory, History, Practice*. Abingdon. Routledge.

Richards, J. C. & Rodgers, T. S. (2014). *Approaches and Methods in Language Teaching (3rd Edition)*. Cambridge: Cambridge University Press.

Shen, C. (2009) Using English Songs: an Enjoyable and Effective Approach to ELT. *Language Teaching*, 2(1), 88-94. Retrieved from www.ccsenet.org/journal.html.

Simpson, A. J. (2015). How to use songs in the English language classroom. https://www.britishcouncil.org/voices-magazine/how-use-songs-english-language-classroom

Strevens, P. (1977). *New Orientations in the Teaching of English*. Oxford: Oxford University Press.

Tegge, F. (2018). Pop Songs in the Classroom: time-filler or teaching tool? *ELT Journal*. 72/3. Oxford: Oxford University Press. 274-284.

Woodrow, L. (2018). *Introducing Course Design in English for Specific Purposes*. Abingdon: Routledge.

Appendix

BEATLES QUESTIONNAIRE

In this course we have used a lot of Beatles songs. Please answer the following questions about this.

The information is collected anonymously, so feel free to express your true opinion. This data will only be used for research purposes and will not have any effect on your academic career. By handing in this completed survey, you are agreeing to the use of this data.

Which song did you like the most? _____

Which exercise did you think was the best? _____

Was there an exercise related to the songs that you did not like?

If yes, which one? _____

Do you think that by using these songs your English has improved?

If yes, how? If not, why not? _____

_____

In the limited time we had to learn English, do you think this was an effective way to teach English?

If yes, why? If not, why not? _____

_____

What were the songs used for? _____

_____

_____

_____

Do you think it was a good idea to use these songs in the lessons? _____

_____

_____

Would you have preferred not to use songs in the lessons?

If yes, why? If not, why not? _____

_____

Would you have preferred a wider range of artists to have been used? Yes / No

If yes, why? If not, why not? _____

_____

Have these songs helped you learn English?

If yes, how? If not, why not? _____

_____

*On a scale of 1 to 5 (where 1 = **Not at all** and 5 = **completely**) do you agree with these statements*

a) Songs should not be used in the English lessons.	a)	_____
b) Songs should only be used in general English lessons.	b)	_____
c) It was useful to use these songs in the lessons.	c)	_____
d) The songs made the lessons more fun.	d)	_____

e) I wanted more songs in the lessons. e) _____

f) The songs are not in the exam and so are not important. f) _____

g) Traditional grammar style exercises are more
useful than these songs. g) _____

h) Students should be allowed to choose which songs
to use in the classroom. h) _____

i) The songs made the lessons more boring. i) _____

j) The songs used are relevant to my degree course. j) _____

k) There were too many songs used in this language course. k) _____

l) I enjoyed the course with this mix of songs and other tasks. l) _____

Would you recommend that the teacher use the same songs and exercises next year with other students?

If yes, why? If not, why not? _____

_____

_____

_____

Any other comments about this course and / or the songs used in it.

_____

_____

_____

_____

Chapter 7

Challenges of E-Learning in Teaching ESP: Prospects and Drawbacks

Svetlana Rubtsova, Tatiana Dobrova

Saint Petersburg State University, Russia

Abstract: The 2030 Agenda for Sustainable Development, adopted by all United Nations Member States in 2015, provides 17 Sustainable Development Goals (SDGs). Goal number 4 stands for ensuring inclusive and equitable quality education and promoting lifelong learning opportunities for all, specifying in 4A the necessity "to build and upgrade education facilities that are child, disability and gender sensitive and provide safe, non-violent, inclusive and effective learning environments for all". Modern digital technologies have been increasingly changing our world, and have undoubtedly been having a serious impact on the system of education and its main tools. Digital technologies cannot but help bring SDGs into effect, especially Goal 4. Institutions of higher education started developing a wide range of distance learning programmes that are not surprisingly in great demand. This case study presents the experience in the field of distant ESP teaching and online ESP teaching gained by the Faculty of Modern Languages of Saint Petersburg State University.

Keywords: e-learning, teaching ESP, drawbacks

***

1. Introduction

This chapter is devoted to new approaches in teaching ESP in higher education in the era of digitalisation. The authors focus on the experience of the Faculty of Modern Languages of Saint Petersburg State University (SPbU).

Nowadays, we are concerned about the future from a global perspective. This concern was made public for the first time in October 1987 when the report "Our Common Future" (the Brundtland Report) was released. This document coined and defined the term "Sustainable Development" (Report of the World Commission on Environment and Development, 1987). It is the development that meets the needs of the present generation without endangering future generations. Sustainable development is defined in terms of environment, economy and society. The 2030 Agenda for Sustainable Development fosters inter-cultural understanding, tolerance, and mutual respect. It provides 17 Sustainable Development Goals (SDGs). Goal number 4 stands for ensuring inclusive and equitable quality education and promoting lifelong learning opportunities for all. It specifies in 4A the necessity "to build and upgrade education facilities that are child, disability and gender sensitive and provide safe, non-violent, inclusive and effective learning environments for all" (2030 Agenda for Sustainable Development, 2015). Modern digital technology has been increasingly changing our world. We cannot avoid mentioning digital technology as far as SDGs are concerned, especially Goal 4. Here higher education has come to the fore with a wide range of distance learning options in demand. We focus on possible ways of achieving sustainable development goals in higher education through ESP. An individual approach plays a pivotal role in reaching sustainable development goals that provide equal chances for getting a degree for those who live in remote places, not to mention students with disabilities. Due to globalisation and new technologies, an individual has to adapt to the constantly changing world and to "recycle" a huge amount of information. It is lifelong learning that is aimed at solving this problem. SDGs have posed new challenges to all levels of education including higher education.

It is obvious that the traditional model of education, aimed only at obtaining knowledge, is hopelessly outdated. The goal is to transform the educational paradigm itself and revise existing approaches and learning models. These are aimed at developing general digital literacy skills, and social and intercultural skills to meet the demands of the new digital world. They are set out in the Federal State Educational Standards of the Russian Federation (FSES) (Federal State Educational Standards of the Russian Federation (FSES) n.d.). This is a set of requirements that are compulsory for the implementation of educational programmes of all levels by educational institutions that have state accreditation. In the field of higher education in all areas, the FSES include full-time, part-time and individual training plan education. The FSES stipulate that future specialists are supposed to have a good command of self-organisation and self-education, i.e. be disposed to lifelong learning. As far as modern IT technologies are concerned, the FSES provides wide use of e-learning and distance learning technologies. When training physically challenged students, e-learning and distance learning technologies should ensure the possibility of receiving and transmitting information in accessible forms. Graduates can solve standard tasks of professional activity with the use of information and communication technologies. They can also collect and process research material using traditional methods and modern information technology, and upload the results of their research in information networks. In terms of foreign languages, according to the FSES, graduates are supposed to have the ability to: carry out oral and written communication in foreign languages; solve problems of interpersonal and multicultural interaction; and work in a team, tolerantly perceiving social, ethnic, confessional and cultural differences (Federal State Educational Standards of the Russian Federation (FSES) n.d.). SPbU closely follows the FSES, with the Faculty of Modern Languages providing foreign language teaching for more than twenty areas of education. The educational standard is established by SPbU. It ensures the unity of the educational space of the Russian Federation and the continuity of the main educational programmes at various levels (Educational Standards of SPbU n.d.). Here we present the experience in the field of distant ESP teaching and on-line ESP teaching accumulated by the Faculty of Modern Languages. The authors cover the issues of e-learning with an individual approach in teaching ESP using the example of the undergraduate and postgraduate programmes of Saint Petersburg State University.

2. Digital Technology in Education

The role of digital technology in people's lives has significantly increased recently. Modern society has become involved in a general historical process of digitalisation. This process includes the possibility for any citizen to get access to many information sources, and the penetration of digital technology in scientific, industrial, and public spheres. The processes occurring in connection with the digitalisation of society contribute to the acceleration of scientific and technological progress, and the intellectualisation of all types of human activity. They also contribute to the creation of a qualitatively new information environment, ensuring the development of human creativity. One of the priorities of the digitalisation process of modern society is the digitalisation of education. This is a system of methods, processes and software and hardware integrated to collect, process, store, distribute and use information in the interests of both students and educators. Education technologies are aimed at facilitating learning and improving educational outcomes by using relevant processes and resources (Robinson et al., 2008).

Nowadays, we are entering the stage of smart society. It is characterised, first of all, by the presence of communication technologies of collective activity. They transform significantly business, education and other activities in human society, and human society itself. Education, through the use of electronic and collective technologies, is becoming more widespread and effective. At the same time, in smart education, the use of electronic technologies is combined with individual training in critical thinking and creativity. This is impossible without human participation.

In the economy, a new quality of services is being formed: they are generated by users themselves, citizens of the smart society, interacting with public authorities and private businesses through horizontal links rather than vertical ones. Citizens get the opportunity to participate in working out plans and roadmaps and their implementation to develop their cities and regions and to influence state decisions. The availability and openness of any information resource ensure full transparency with citizens' control of public authorities. It is assumed that in the smart society, there is a transition from the traditional model of learning to e-learning, and then – to smart education. At the same time, the role of educational institutions is changing. They are not designed any more to "deliver knowledge", but to create the best conditions for students to acquire their own experience and skills. In this regard, the main function of the teacher is high-quality navigation of ICT and world information resources rather than conveying "ready-made truths". Smart education allows students to generate new knowledge, and forms the personality of a smart person who is proficient in ICT to search, analyse information and create innovations (CNews Club, 2013.). Therefore, the smart state is supposed through constant training, reducing routine work to form a smart citizen with the help of smart management. Smart citizens are highly educated people who use modern technology for life, act collectively and participate in governance. That is why it is necessary to transform the educational paradigm itself and revise existing approaches and learning models to develop skills for the student to be successful in the new digital world.

In the 20th century, to be an educated person meant, first of all, to be literate. Nowadays, the essence of the term has evolved, and literacy goes far beyond being able to read and write. One needs distant literacy in the first place. What is digital literacy? Modern society, the market of goods, services and labour are characterised by rapid changes, which are largely caused by the intensive development of digital technology. The role of the personal computer in the life of an average person is rapidly increasing. With the help of computer systems, documentation is maintained, as well as e-mail and communication with databases are provided. The Internet connects both people who are on neighbouring premises, and those who live and work on different continents. Today, the Internet is a place where people work, meet each other, have fun, study, pay for services, and buy food and clothes. So, the task of educators is to make students ready to live in this new digital world, to be digitally literate.

As early as 1997, Glister used the term digital literacy in his book with the same title. According to Glister, digital literacy means the ability to evaluate sources of information found in newsgroups, bulletin boards, and other online sources using certain search strategies. Jones-Kavalier and Flannigan (2006) define digital literacy as the ability to perform tasks effectively in a digital environment, i.e. the ability to read and interpret media, to reproduce data and images through digital manipulation, and to evaluate and apply new knowledge gained from digital environments. Jenkins (2009) claims that digital literacy refers to "an individual's ability to find, evaluate, and compose clear information through writing and other media on various digital platforms". Digital literacy is evaluated by skills and the ability to produce writings, images, audio and designs using technology. Nowadays, the term is widely used in higher education especially in international and national standards (Knobel and Lanskear, 2008).

To sum up, digital literacy is a set of knowledge and skills that are necessary for the safe and effective use of digital technology and Internet resources. It is based on digital competencies, i.e. the ability to solve a variety of problems in the use of information and communication technologies and to master different LMSs. The European Commission prepared its definition of digital competence within the framework of the action plan for the development of digital education (DEAP). It emphasises the importance of conscious and responsible use of digital technology in education, at work, and in public life. Digital competence is supposed to include the ability to digitally collaborate, provide security, and solve problems (The European Commission's science and knowledge service, n.d.). This chapter deals with digital competence in ESP teaching and learning.

3. ESP Through E-Learning in SPbU

The first time the term e-learning was used was in October 1999 in Los Angeles in a professional environment at the seminar CBT Systems. UNESCO defined e-learning as an approach to facilitate and enhance learning by means of personal computers, CD-ROMs, and the Internet (Chatelier and Voicu, 2018). UNESCO does not recommend translating the term and the concept of e-learning into national languages. They have very specific contents, which are not always adequately conveyed by the translation. With the rapid development of digital technology, the term e-learning has evolved. It emerged to describe the application of information and communication technologies to enhance distance education, implement open learning policies, make learning activities more flexible, and enable those learning activities to be distributed among many learning venues (A Virtual University for the Small States of the Commonwealth, 2003). Nowadays, e-learning is understood as an umbrella term that refers to the use of any digital device for teaching and learning, especially for delivery of or accessing the content. Thus e-learning can take place without any reference to a network or connectivity. The digital device used by the learner to access materials needs no connection to a digital network, either a local area network or to the Internet or even to a cell phone network if a tablet is used as a terminal or access device (Moorea et al., 2010). In the last two decades, hundreds of scientific articles, books, and conference proceedings have been published to explore the possibilities of using e-learning technology in educational programmes from kindergarten to university, from the public sector to business corporations.

Online education is a powerful trend among modern pedagogical technologies and educational innovations. It accounts for 1.1% (20.7 billion roubles) of the total education market in Russia (Research of the Russian market, 2016). Online education is in demand in society, it is actively promoted by educational organisations. Moreover, it is an object of interest of the state, which is confirmed by the launching of the project for 2016–2021 "Modern digital educational environment in the Russian Federation". The main goal of the project is to increase the availability of education and the implementation of the concept of continuous education "through the development of the Russian digital educational space" (Паспорт приоритетного проекта). One type of online education is massive open online courses (MOOCs). They enable the solution of the problems of building an individual educational trajectory and the additional professional training of the student; and the formation of their ability for self-organisation and self-development, which is a key competence necessary for the implementation of the concept of continuous education. Meanwhile, it is necessary to mention both the advantages and disadvantages of MOOCs. Advantages include full flexibility, including studying while travelling, no tuition fee, and globally distributed teachers with access to authentic training material and constant updating (The Advantages and Disadvantages of E-learning, 2013). However, the disadvantages can be very significant. They include the lack of any fixed schedule and routine, which may lead to procrastination and therefore, a waste of time, as well as the lack of immediate feedback. The latter along with the lack of face-to-face communication with teachers and classmates may cause some serious problems. The issues of teacher-student communication effectiveness and students' psychological safety are among the important issues in pedagogical psychology. Creative educational relationships contribute to the effectiveness of education and training. Not all students can cope with the challenges of mastering MOOCs. Left by themselves, students may experience confusion in self-development, and communication problems in general (Zhang and Fan, 2017). Having become aware of the importance of the problem, MOOCs developers try to overcome these disadvantages by encouraging discussions in course forums or stimulating community meetups or hangouts (Bowden, 2017). SPbU widely uses these tools to ensure the psychological safety of the students.

It is worth mentioning that in modern scientific and pedagogical discourse, the terms "distant learning" and "e-learning" are sometimes used as synonyms in the definition and description of online courses. This is incorrect. "Distant" means produced or operated at a distance, and "electronic" means existing in digital form (e-book) or carried out using network technologies (e-mail or electronic business). The difference between e-learning and distant education technologies is stipulated in Article 16 of the Federal law on education (Education in the RF, 2017). However, nowadays, in the era of digital technology, distance education is impossible without digital technology, this fact explains the terminological synonymy in the modern methodology discourse.

Blended learning is an effective way to overcome the drawbacks of MOOCs and other types of e-learning. It is a combination of traditional forms of classroom learning with elements of e-learning, which uses special information technology, such as computer graphics, audio and video, interactive elements, etc. Thus, the learning process is a sequence of phases of traditional and e-learning, which alternate over time. Progress in information technology has contributed to the development of blended learning, primarily through the ability to share information via the Internet. Questions for exams, samples of project tasks, and training materials can be simply uploaded on the SPbU educational platform or e-mailed to students. Continuous assessment in blended learning can be automatically performed by testing systems.

Stanford University researchers analysed more than a thousand empirical studies comparing traditional, online, and blended learning (Means et al., 2010). The results of the analysis enabled the authors to argue that, between 1996 and 2008, online learning did not have a significant advantage over traditional forms of learning. However, blended learning proved to be significantly more effective than learning that occurred entirely online. This study significantly strengthened the position of blended learning and gave even more momentum to its development.

We would like to focus on the lingua franca issue in fostering professional language competence. Today we live in a globalised world. Globalisation is a complex of multidimensional processes in all spheres of society when territoriality as an organising principle of social and cultural life disappears. Globalisation processes cover all aspects of human life – economy, finance, labour, information, intellectual resources, education, science and art. Today there are about 1.5 billion people in the world who speak English. Being the most taught language, English does not replace other languages but complements them.

The processes of globalisation have linguistic aspects that should not be reduced to only quantitative indicators of the spread of a certain language in the modern world. Today we can witness a different process in the world when a huge number of people from different countries effectively and in a short time master the English language for everyday and professional communication. Language learning has become more functional: unprecedented demand has demanded unprecedented supply. Unexpectedly, foreign language teachers found themselves at the centre of public attention: legions of impatient specialists in various fields of science, culture, business, technology and all other areas of human activity demanded immediate training in foreign languages as a tool of production (Foreign language as a means of professional communication, 2019). In fact, in 90 countries, English is either widely studied or is a second language (Streltsova, 2017). The world community has entered the era of national-English bilingualism.

The Russian Federation follows the trend, with SPbU being no exception. All SPbU students learn English as the first foreign language. The aim of the English language curriculum is to create a stable system of fostering a professionally-oriented foreign language communicative competence. It provides students with a competitive advantage in the implementation of educational mobility or continuing education, as well as in the labour market. The level of a student's English is determined by the results of online placement testing, conducted with the help of the Blackboard educational platform. According to the results of the placement test, the educational trajectories specified by the curriculum are defined. As a result of mastering the curriculum, all students are supposed to reach level B2 of English language communicative competence. Nowadays, foreign language communication has become an essential part of the future professional activity of a graduate of SPbU. Therefore, a professionally-oriented approach to teaching a foreign language is relevant, i.e. there is a need to ensure the complex of English: EAP (English for Academic Purposes), ESP (English for special purposes) and general English. The Faculty of Modern Languages staff provide English classes for more than 20 different professional spheres for all first- and second-year students of SPbU. All types of e-learning are effectively used in teaching professional foreign languages, first of all, ESP and EAP in SPbU.

The Blackboard platform is not a new technology. Since its inception in 1997, the system has steadily developed becoming one of the market leaders. It is an effective interactive element between the teacher and students, complementing and modernising the educational process. Blackboard enriches the traditional learning process with additional features. The system allows teachers to create courses and online tests, upload educational materials, check works for plagiarism, introduce video components into the course programme, i.e. to use all the advantages of distance e-learning. Students have remote round-the-clock access to the course materials, can take study papers online, communicate with each other in chat rooms, ask questions to teachers, and get up-to-date information. Through the Blackboard system, teachers assess students' progress promptly respecting the anonymity and security of personal data. In addition, all users can quickly send alerts and announcements about changes in the schedule and other necessary information. SPbU has been using it for about ten years. The introduction of the Blackboard platform did not affect the assessment system, but students have the opportunity to better prepare for the tasks of the current assessment and understand their grades. Thus, the functionality of Blackboard allows you to create tests for self-examination, i.e. students can check their level of readiness on a particular topic and, if necessary, refresh their memory on some of the material. The teacher can upload all grades received during the semester and provide them with personal comments. Besides, it has facilitated the process of accepting written works, namely essays. In the Blackboard system work is created and the load time is determined. You can set the parameters so that if the work is not loaded on time, they are not accepted at all. It is very disciplining for students. Besides, the teacher receives a report of the built-in plagiarism check system. Understandable value is created when students see how the Blackboard system helps them to get better prepared for the class, discuss pressing questions in the chat, or ask them directly to the teacher using the same platform. Moreover, whether we like it or not, this digital form of communication is close to today's students, and the supply of information through electronic systems is often more familiar and understandable for students born in the 21st century. The Blackboard system requires an additional effort of the teachers, as, at the beginning of the semester, they have to upload course materials. This one-time effort optimises the entire further process, therefore there is no need to print materials or send individual assignments by e-mail as everything can be placed in the Blackboard system, which will do everything automatically. The Blackboard system is used for all courses of the University. ESP/EAP teachers started to use Blackboard for students to do the placement test and to register students' attendance. These two functions are still the most vital ones. Besides, at present, the Blackboard system is used as a storage of ESP/EAP materials. Unfortunately, students do not use many of the opportunities provided by the system as it is difficult to work on the platform using mobile phones.

The learning management system Moodle is friendlier from the perspective of the students. Moodle is an abbreviation of the Modular Object-Oriented Dynamic Learning Environment. It is a free learning management system focused primarily on the organisation of interaction between teachers and students. To use the Moodle system only a web browser is needed, which makes the use of this learning environment convenient for both the teacher and the trainees. According to the results of the students' performance, the teacher can put grades and give comments. In 2018, we decided to use the Moodle system for ESP/EAP teaching and learning in SPbU. The teachers of the Faculty of Modern Languages have uploaded more than 30,000 exercises in 22 professional fields, which enable the students to practice ESP/EAP or check their knowledge at any time from anywhere using their mobile phones. The structure of the exercises that are set follows the structure of the relevant ESP/EAP course. In May 2019, we first used the Moodle system to conduct a continuous assessment. To receive feedback a small survey was conducted. The developed questionnaire was filled out by students immediately after the continuous assessment test. The purpose of the questionnaire was to reveal the functions of the Blackboard and Moodle systems that students use regularly and consider useful to improve the effectiveness of e-learning. 224 students of 18 bachelor's programmes in different professional fields took part in the survey. The questionnaire included questions concerning both compulsory activities in the systems (tests), and ones about the things they do using not only the systems but other sources. The results are presented in Table 7.1.

Table 7.1 SPbU e-learning environment in teaching ESP/EAP

	Do you find useful the following opportunities	Yes	No	fifty-fifty	Why?
1	placement test on Blackboard	24%	34%	42%	too long not always adequate
2	do my ESP homework on Blackboard	11%	63%	26%	cannot use my mobile phone to do it
3	check my rating on Blackboard	48%	13%	39%	
4	use ESP and General Language textbooks on Blackboard	3%	86%	11%	cannot read PDF files on my phone
5	do weekly tests on Moodle	79%	5%	16%	too often
6	do final term test on Blackboard	77%	5%	18%	inconvenient time to do the test

The analysis of the survey results shows that students prefer to use different educational systems for different goals. Although less than a third of the respondents consider that Blackboard completely meets the needs of the placement test, the majority (approximately two-thirds of the respondents) claim that the Blackboard system can be used to provide the placement test. This result is predictable since, during the first two weeks of the term, a student can change their trajectory with the consent of the two teachers of the respective groups on these trajectories. Therefore, some inaccuracy of the test is corrected taking into consideration the personality of the student, which allows us to ensure an individual approach to each student. The survey results show that the only thing students do themselves in the Blackboard system, and not because it is compulsory, is checking their ranking in the group. Only 13% of the respondents consider it needless. According to the respondents, Moodle is more useful for their weekly routine activities. They prefer doing weekly tests in Moodle rather than consulting the grammar and vocabulary materials in the Blackboard system. It is not surprising, especially taking into consideration the fact that in the Blackboard system materials are usually stored in PDF files. The main advantage of Moodle is the ability to log in using a mobile phone, which means from anywhere at any time. The vast majority of the respondents are satisfied with both systems as the tool to do the final tests. Only a few of them say that the fixed time of the test is inconvenient. At present, the university cannot ensure honesty, openness and verification of the student's identity if the test is performed remotely. Anyone can log in using the username and password of the student and perform the test for him. Therefore, the final test is conducted only at SPbU premises at a fixed time, which is considered inconvenient by a few respondents. Thus, the survey shows that the students use the Moodle system regularly to perform weekly tasks and repeat poorly learned material. Whereas the Blackboard system can be successfully used to provide placement and final tests.

The ideas of blended learning are implemented at SPbU in the framework of close cooperation with the Centre of E-learning Development. It is the newest division of SPbU intended to provide access to knowledge for everyone. There is a combination of the long-term academic traditions of SPbU with e-learning and distance learning modern educational technologies. It provides an opportunity to receive a quality education within a convenient period of time and anywhere in the world. The main goal of the centre is online resource integration in the modern information educational space. MOOCs created in SPbU are the basis for the development of innovative areas of education where the ideas of life-long learning are implemented. Since 2018, applicants to the master's and postgraduate courses who have a certificate of online courses of SPbU have received five additional points when participating in the competition.

In 2017–2018 the Faculty of Modern Languages together with the centre created a number of MOOCs. We started with the MOOC "English: Post-Graduate Qualified Exam". To become a PhD having completed a postgraduate course, the student must pass three main qualifying exams: English (or another modern foreign language); philosophy; and a professional exam in the field of research. The MOOC meets modern requirements providing the opportunity for distant learning, which is especially vital for working graduate students and applicants, as well as residents of remote regions and people with disabilities. Therefore, we try to meet the objectives of sustainable development of humanity in the framework of higher education by providing equal opportunities for all. The MOOC introduces students to the requirements for passing the postgraduate qualified English exam. Postgraduate students and those who sit the test without attending classes are supposed to demonstrate knowledge of grammatical phenomena and lexis of academic English. They must have the skills for working with authentic scientific texts, and knowledge of the basics of communication for academic purposes. Students also get acquainted with the content and structure of the postgraduate qualified English exam. The exam consists of the following three parts including Portfolio. First part: at least 3–5 completed tasks in accordance with the Work programme of the discipline, with a compulsory task of written translation of the scientific article or monograph (12,000 printed characters). Second part: reviewing an authentic scientific article in English on the subject of the main areas of research, including a list of keywords of the article (4–7 words). Third part: structured oral communication in academic English with the examining board on one's scientific research within 15 minutes. Each of the three parts of the exam is compulsory. The marks are portfolio – 40 points; reviewing the article – 30 points; communication in academic English – 30 points. The MOOC is designed for 72 academic hours within 8 weeks: one module per week, with five units per module. Each module contains two videos with PowerPoint presentations and two blocks of exercises. Feedback is provided through the forum. Each week topics relevant to the subjects of the modules are created, and users can produce their own topics to discuss issues that interest them. It enables teachers and students to communicate, ask questions and get answers, express their opinion, and participate in the discussion. In autumn 2018, the MOOC took part in the 4th International Competition of MOOCs "EdCrunch Award OOC 2018". It is a competition that allows everybody to get acquainted with the best practices of e-learning and distance learning technologies. The MOOC was highly appreciated and awarded with the Diploma of the III Degree in the nomination "The Best MOOC According to Consumers". The MOOC certificate is counted as part of the exam and gives 40 points for the portfolio. In May 2019, we produced a survey for postgraduate law students to reveal whether the MOOC was in demand and if so to what degree. 24 postgraduate law students who planned to take the postgraduate qualified English exam in late May 2019 participated in the survey. The results are shown in Figure 7.1.

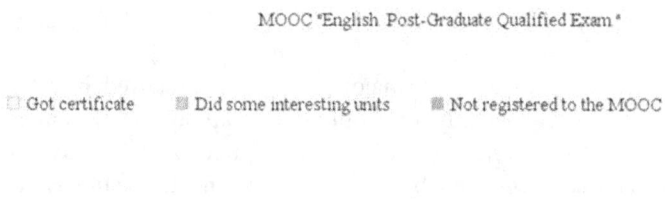

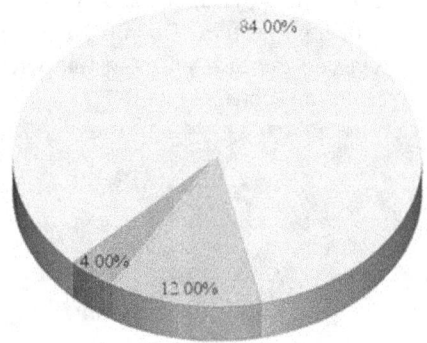

Figure 7.1 MOOC "English: postgraduate qualified exam"

The survey confirmed the interest of law students in the MOOC. The vast majority completed the MOOC and received the certificate. Thus, 84% of the postgraduate students got 40 points for their portfolio as a part of the exam, having produced the MOOC certificate. It should be noted that three of the postgraduate students lived in remote areas and did not have an opportunity to attend classes. 17 postgraduate students who attended classes every week also preferred to master the MOOC and get certificates.

In 2018, the Faculty of Modern Languages together with the Centre of E-learning Development created a distant version of the additional educational programme "Translation and Interpreting in the Sphere of Professional Communication". In its off-line version, the programme has been implemented for more than 25 years with continued success. The programme is designed for two academic years, with graduates receiving their degree a certificate of translator and interpreter in the relevant professional sphere. Every year more than 100 university undergraduates take the programme. Therefore, we can state with confidence that the programme is quite successful. However, we repeatedly get questions concerning any opportunity to take the programme online, or partially online. In 2018, SPbU decided to provide such an opportunity in the framework of implementing SDGs. The online version includes seven theoretical MOOCs and English classes face-to-face with a teacher via the Internet using the Blackboard system. ESP is an integral part of the MOOC "Cross Cultural Communication in Interpreting and Translation." Our offline students had the opportunity to master disciplines online. Nevertheless, the majority of them preferred blended learning. We developed a questionnaire to offer to our offline students aimed at finding out their preferences, namely whether they prefer online or face-to-face theoretical classes. Understandably, 98% of all respondents said they are happy to have an opportunity to master theoretical courses online. Unexpectedly, the following question "Do you need face-to-face lectures on these disciplines?" revealed the differences in the perception of students of different ages. The results are shown in Figure 7.2.

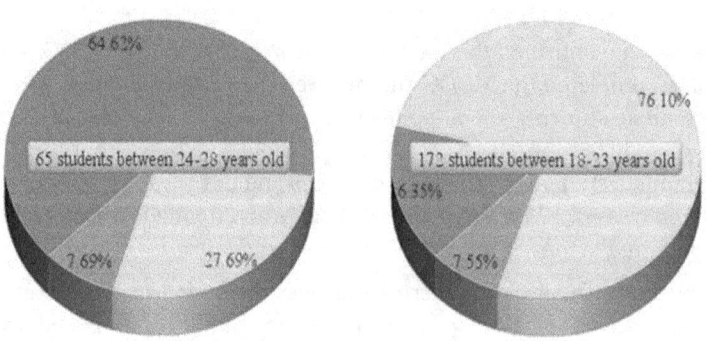

Figure 7.2 Online Additional Educational Programme "Translation and Interpreting in the Sphere of Professional Communication"

The survey showed a great difference in the opinions of respondents of different ages. We have divided 237 respondents into two age groups. The majority constitutes the students between 18–23 years old (172 persons). The second group includes 65 students between 24–28 years old. About 76% of younger respondents did not express a desire to listen to lectures in the classroom; they were quite happy with the opportunity to master theoretical courses at any time from anywhere. However, those respondents who were between 24–28 years old answered that at least sometimes they needed face-to-face contact with the lecturer to master the discipline more effectively. Some of them added that mastering the course together with their classmates is important for them. Thus, not only face-to-face communication with the lecturer but also the opportunity to discuss some vital issues with the classmates can contribute. Otherwise, they can feel isolated and depressed, which may even lead to leaving the programme. Thus, we received confirmation that blended learning is more effective than just online learning.

4. Conclusions

To sum up, we can state with confidence that e-learning, especially blended learning, is an integral part of education at Saint Petersburg State University. The Faculty of Modern Languages widely uses the Blackboard and Moodle systems, as well as MOOCs providing ESP/EAP teaching and learning for students of 22 professional spheres. The conducted research revealed the most effective ways of using these tools. Thus, the Blackboard system is quite effective in conducting placement and final tests, as they can only be done personally at the premises of the University. While, according to students, to master certain ESP/EAP issues, the Moodle system is more convenient. It enables students to do exercises and perform other tasks from their mobile phone, which means at any time and anywhere. This is quite important for students born in the 20th century. The teachers of the Faculty of Modern Languages have developed and uploaded in the Moodle system 30,000 ESP/EAP exercises in 22 professional spheres. This provides students with the opportunity to work independently to master the issues they need most of all. Our students with the help of this educational environment can decide themselves what and how intensively they need to practice at a certain moment. The experience of creating MOOCs has shown that they are quite popular with the students as they provide equal opportunities for all, including physically challenged students and those who live in remote areas. However, students over 23 years old feel the necessity to attend classes to communicate not only with the teacher, but also with their classmates to master the material more effectively. Therefore, blended learning is preferable wherever this is possible.

References

A Virtual University for Small States of the Commonwealth, 2003, viewed 10 October 2018, from http://www.colfinder.net/resources.htm.

Bowden, P. (2017). *Advantages and Disadvantages of Online and Classroom Learning*, viewed 16 October 2018, from https://onlinelearningsuccess.org/advantages-and-disadvantages-of-online-and-classroom-learning.

Chatelier, G. & Voicu, I. (2018). *E-Learning within the Framework of UNESCO*, viewed 10 October 2018, from http://www.ijcim.th.org/SpecialEditions/v26nSP1/26n1page6.pdf.

CNews Клуб. (2013). *Смарт-общество: нескромное обаяние smart-технологий* [CNews Club (2013), *Smart society: the immodest charm of smart technology*], viewed 25 September 2018, from https://club.cnews.ru/blogs/entry/smartobshchestvo_neskromnoe_obayanie_smarttehnologij.

Об образовании в Российской Федерации: Федеральный закон от 29.12.2012 No 2730ФЗ n.d. [Education in the Russian Federation: Federal law], viewed 16 October 2018, from http://base.garant.ru/7029 1362/#friends#ixzz3qq5FE2Mj (дата обращения: 01.04.2018)

Eu Science Hub n.d., *The European Commission's science and knowledge service*, viewed 10 October 2018, from https://ec.europa.eu/jrc/en/digcomp/digital-competence-framework.

Иностранный язык как средство профессиональной коммуникации, (2019). [Foreign language as a means of professional communication], Пермь.

Glister, P. (1997). *Digital Literacy*. Wiley and Computer Publishing, New York.

Jenkins, H. (2009). *Confronting the Challenges of Participatory Culture: Media Education for the 21st Century*, The MIT Press, Cambridge, MA.

Jones-Kavalier, B. R. & Flannigan, S.L. (2006). *Connecting the Digital Dots: Literacy of the 21st Century*, viewed 28 September 2018, from http://connect.educause.edu/Library/EDUCAUSE+Quarterly/ConnectingtheDigitalDotsL/39969.

Knobel, M & Lanskear, C. (2008). *Digital Literacies: Concepts, Policies, and Practices*, Peter Lang Inc., New York.

Means, B., Toyama, Y., Murphy, R., Bakia, M., & Jones, K. (2010). *Evaluation of Evidence-Based Practices in Online Learning: A Meta-Analysis and Review of Online Learning Studies*, viewed 16 October 2018, from https://www2.ed.gov/rschstat/eval/tech/evidence-based-practices/finalreport.pdf.

Министерство науки и высшего образования РФ n.d., *Федеральные государственные образовательные стандарты* [Ministry of science and higher education of the Russian Federation n.d., *Federal State Educational Standards of the Russian Federation*], viewed 15 September 2018, from https://fgos.ru.

Moorea J. L., Dickson-Deaneb, C. & Galyenb, K. (2010). «*E-learning, online learning, and distance learning environments: Are they the same?*», viewed 10 October 2018, from https://www.sciencedirect.com/science/article/abs/pii/S1096751610000886.

Паспорт проекта «Современная цифровая образовательная среда в Российской Федерации» [Passport of the project "Modern digital educational environment in the Russian Federation".]. (2017). viewed 16 October 2018, from http://www.consultant.ru/document/cons_doc_ LAW_216432/

Robinson R.S., Molenda M. & Landra R. (2008). *Facilitating learning. In Educational technology: A definition with discussion*, ed. A. Janusciewski and M. Molenda, Erlbaum, New York.

Исследование российского рынка онлайн-образования и образовательных технологий n.d. [Research of the Russian market of online education and educational technologies]. (2016). viewed 16 October 2018, from http://edumarket.digital (дата обращения 01.04.2018).

Санкт-Петербургский государственный университет (СПбГУ) n.d., *Образовательные стандарты СПбГУ* [Saint Petersburg State University (SPbU), Educational standards of SPbU], viewed 15 September 2018, from https://spbu.ru/openuniversity/documents/obrazovatelnye-standarty

Санкт-Петербургский государственный университет (СПбГУ) n.d., *Использование системы Blackboard в учебном процессе* [Saint Petersburg State University (SPbU), *The Blackboard system in the educational process*], viewed 22 October 2018, from https://gsom.spbu.ru/all_news/event2017_05_24_1/.

Streltsova A.D. (2017). *"English as the language of international communication // Young scientis"*, viewed 22 October 2018, from https://moluch.ru/archive/183/46933.

The Advantages and Disadvantages of E-learning. (2013) viewed 16 October 2018, from https://www.optimuslearningservices.com/practical-ld/advantages-disadvantages-elearning/

United Nations. (1987). *Report of the World Commission on Environment and Development: Our Common Future*, viewed 15 September 2018, from http://www.un-documents.net/our-common-future.

United Nations. (2015). *Transforming our world: the 2030 Agenda for Sustainable Development* viewed 15 September 2018, from https://sustainabledevelopment.un.org/post2015/transformingourworld.

Zhang, Y., Fan, H. (2017). *The Influence Factors Analysis of Graduate Students' Psychological Safety*, viewed 16 October 2018, from https://www.researchgate.net/publication/315923054_The_Influence_Factors_Analysis_of_Graduate_Students'_Psychological_Safety.

Chapter 8

Common Perceptions and Misperceptions about ESP: an overview

Amina Gaye

Fatima College of Health Sciences, UAE

Abstract: Dudley-Evans and St. John (1998) defined ESP as an approach to course design that starts with the question: *Why do these learners need to learn English?* The learners' needs should be at the center of any teaching activity. A review of the literature shows that ESP is now known as a learner-centered approach to teaching ESL/EFL. It is not a matter of teaching specialized varieties of English. Using a language for a specific purpose does not imply that it is a special form of the language, different in kind to other forms; a view that echoes that of the genre analysis movement's advocates (Swales, 1990; Bhatia, 1993). However, many EFL instructors tend to limit ESP to the teaching of vocabulary and therefore exclude other aspects of language proficiency. This study discusses such misconceptions about ESP in an attempt to provide simple responses that can help improve the teaching-learning of English in specialized contexts.

Keywords: ESP, conceptions, misconceptions, myths, realities

***

1. Introduction

Since the 1960s, ESP has become a vital and innovative discipline within the teaching of English as a Foreign Language (EFL) or English as a Second Language (ESL) and has played an important and influential role in English Language Teaching (ELT). Specialization in the content of English teaching curricula is currently increasing, and every author agrees that English is not to be studied simply for its own sake, but rather for the communicative uses to which it can be put. The need for ESP teachers is rapidly growing, and many studies have been conducted to discover good ways to meet learners' expectations in ESP. However, although the demand for courses in Language for Specific Purposes (LSP) has been growing very fast, ESP theory and applications have been very controversial as there are many perceptions and misperceptions about ESP as a field of ELT. This study addresses common statements about what ESP is and how it should be taught in order to provide simple responses that can help improve the teaching-learning of English in specialized contexts.

2. Method

A literature search was conducted to find articles that deal with the most controversial issues in ESP. The following keywords were used: ESP, conceptions, misconceptions, myths and realities. Some articles were found relevant and selected. This study highlights the main findings of those articles, questions and interprets them in order to provide simple responses to some common conceptions and misconceptions about ESP.

3. Findings and Analysis

3.1. All researchers agree on the definition of ESP

The concept of ESP is so broad that there has been controversy about the interpretation of its meaning. At the first Japan Conference on English for Specific Purposes, held at Aizu University in Fukushima in November 1997, many definitions were given for ESP. Some simply defined it as the study of English for a specific purpose, the term "specific" in ESP highlighting very well the specificity of the purpose for learning English, whereas others described it as the teaching of English for vocational or professional purposes, for example, teaching English to those who want to use it in specific fields such as business or tourism (Orr, 1997).

In their attempt to clarify the meaning of ESP, Dudley-Evans and St. John (1998) gave an extended definition of ESP in terms of *absolute* and *variable* characteristics. According to them, meeting the specific needs of the learners, using the underlying methodology and activities of the discipline served, and being centered on the language (grammar, lexis, and register) skills, discourse, and genres appropriate to those activities are absolute or fundamental characteristics of ESP. As to the variable ones, they refer to the fact that ESP may be related to or designed for specific disciplines, may use, in specific teaching situations, a different methodology from that of general English; is likely to be designed for adult learners, either at a tertiary-level institution or in a professional work situation (it could, however, be for learners at the secondary school level); is generally designed for intermediate or advanced students, and assumes some basic knowledge of the language system, but can be used with beginners.

Hutchinson and Waters (1987) were more precise, describing it as an "approach to language teaching in which all decisions as to content and method are based on the learner's reason for learning" (p. 19). This focus on the learner's reason for learning has led Belcher (2009) to argue that there are as many types of ESP as there are specific learner needs and target communities.

If we start our definition by referring to Dudley-Evans and St. John's (1998) tree diagram in Figure 8.1 below, ESP is divided into two main branches, namely English for Academic Purposes (EAP) and English for Occupational (also vocational or professional) Purposes, although whether EAP could be considered part of ESP in general or not is a debate within the field.

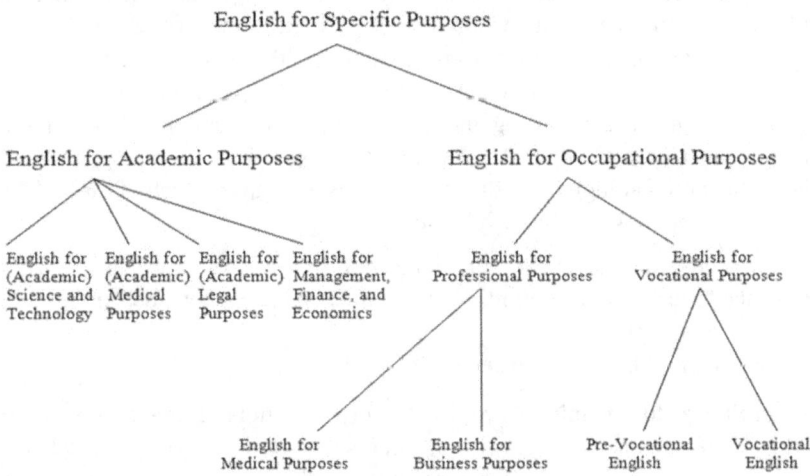

Figure 8.1 ESP classification by professional area (Dudley-Evans & St. John, 1998, p. 6)

3.2. To conduct a Needs Analysis is to simply ask the learners what they need

Almost all theorists agree on the fact that needs analysis is of primary importance in ESP and plays a crucial role. It is considered to be the starting point of any ESP activity. According to Howatt and Widdowson (2004), the idea of analysis of students' needs is said to have begun with Richterich and Chancerel (1980) pioneering work for the Council of Europe, through the phrase *analysis of needs*. However, with the change in views on language and communicative competence, approaches to needs analysis also changed. So, what is Needs Analysis?

Munby's (1978) language-centered approach defines needs as the ability to comprehend and/or produce the linguistic features of the target situation. Needs are also understood in terms of *learning needs* and *target situation needs*. The learning needs represent what the learner needs to do in order to learn the language, whereas the target needs are what the learner needs to do in the target situation.

Hutchinson and Waters (1987) look at those *target needs* in terms of necessities (what learners have to know to function effectively in the target situation), deficiencies (the necessities learners lack), and wants (the learners' view of what their needs are).

Needs Analysis is the process of establishing *the what and the how* of a course and is a major feature that distinguishes ESP from general English. Richards (1997), as cited by Jordan (1997) in his book titled *English for Academic Purposes*, describes needs analysis as "the process of determining the needs for which a learner or group of learners require a language and arranging the needs according to priorities" (p. 1). For example, while General English instructors emphasize all four language skills (speaking, writing, listening, and reading), in ESP, the teacher has to analyze which of these skills students need most for their work (Fiorito, 2005, p. 1).

Can Needs Analysis be therefore reduced to simply asking the learners what they need? Based on the definition above, the response is obviously no.

3.3. ESP cannot be taught to beginners

According to the definition proposed above by Dudley-Evans and St. John (1998), ESP can also be used with beginners who have no general knowledge of English. Although ESP and general English differ on many points such as vocabulary and content, ESP learner still needs to have some basic knowledge in general English, and that issue has created many debates. Fiorito (2005) explains that ESP students are usually adults who already have some acquaintance with English and are learning the language in order to communicate a set of professional skills and to perform particular job-related functions. Therefore, ESP is being considered to be taught in vocational schools or colleges where learners are aware of their target needs. However, with some changes in the education system, many vocational high schools currently aim to prepare their students for the professional world and might choose to teach ESP rather than general English at the secondary level.

3.4. Researchers agree on one way to serve the ESP learners' needs

According to the register analysis theory advocates, language use is predetermined by the situation speakers are in or by the subject matter they are talking about. In other words, there is a special language or register that matches different types of subjects or situations. Therefore, a good way to serve ESP learners' needs would be, as Strevens (1977) suggested, to provide them with the key grammatical features and lexis of their specialist area by creating corpora of texts taken from specific disciplines and analyzing them. It is said that such a theory rested on the assumption that a scientific text, for example, would be made up of certain features unique to itself that could then be identified and used as the basis for teaching materials. However, researchers rapidly found out the disadvantages of such an approach. Coffey (1984) argues that register analysis not only operated only at the sentence level and says nothing about the broader features of texts that operate at the inter-sentential level but also had results showing that there was very little actual difference in *scientific* language as compared to general English. In short, "register cannot be used because there is no significant way in which the language of science differs from any other kind of language" (pp. 4–5). Nevertheless, it is good to specify that although register analysis in its purest sense was abandoned in ESP after the 1960s, its influence has reached out through the 1980s and to the present day.

Discourse or rhetorical analysis developed as a movement in ESP that came to fix the problems created by register analysis. Unlike register analysis, this approach tried to look beyond the sentence. Discourse analysis does, in fact, study language use *beyond the sentence boundary*, but also analyzes *naturally occurring* language use. It has had a strong influence in ESP research, and out of it has developed the *genre analysis approach* by Swales (1991), an approach that has evolved as an important system of analysis in ESP over the last two decades. Swales' enthusiasm for genre analysis is also shared by Dudley-Evans (1987), who argued that "we need a system of analysis that shows how each type of text differs from other types" (p. 73).

Hyon (1996) explains that the genre analysis approach launched the second important stage of the development of ESP, with *genre* being primarily seen as a tool for analyzing and teaching the spoken and written language required of non-native speakers in academic and professional settings. According to him, genre research in ESP can be broadly divided into two phases:

> *firstly, earlier work based on analyzing the moves and steps involved in discourse—'structural move analysis'—and, secondly, later work which has broadened the definition of genre analysis to look at how extra-*

linguistic features and more recently intercultural aspects, have affected both the form and sequencing of language. (p. 695)

This has led to the rise of needs analysis in ESP with *needs* being an important term to look at before starting any ESP activity.

3.5. ESP is an approach to English Language Teaching

According to Hutchinson and Waters (1987), ESP is not "a product but an approach to language teaching which is directed by specific and apparent reasons for learning" (p. 16). What lies at the heart of successful language teaching is subject matter matched to the learners' experience and interests. Indeed, as Dudley-Evans and St. John (1998) defined it, ESP is an approach to course design that starts with the question: *Why do these learners need to learn English?* According to them, the main concerns of ESP have always been, and remain, with needs analysis and preparing learners to communicate effectively in the tasks prescribed by their study or work situation.

In the 1980s, the *skills approach*, another broad movement of ESP that started in the register analysis period, matured and developed to cover specific skills, including speaking and listening. That approach aimed to concentrate on the particular language skills determined by the results of a needs analysis, instead of trying to deal with all of them at the same time. This led to the development of the *learning-centred approach* in ESP thanks to Hutchinson and Waters.

ESP is now known as a learner-centered approach to teaching ESL or EFL, and as the latter stated, "ESP is not a matter of teaching 'specialised varieties' of English. According to Hutchinson and Waters (1987), the fact that language is used for a specific purpose does not imply that it is a special form of the language, different in kind to other forms; a view that echoes that of the genre analysis movement's advocates explained earlier. Genre analysis focuses on how language is used within a particular setting (Swales, 1990) and is concerned with the form of language use in relation to meaning (Bhatia, 1993). Bhatia's definition of genre is highly inspired by Swales' (1990), which is characterized by the "communicative purpose(s) it is intended to fulfill" (Bhatia, 1993, p. 13).

3.6. To teach ESP is to teach subject knowledge and content

Another subject that has created a lot of controversy among scholars in current research is the debate about the role of content and lack of expertise in ESP classrooms. Content significantly plays an important role in the teaching of ESP. In ESP, learners should be able to apply what they learn in English classes to their field of study or job. In fact, whether the general English teacher or a specialist in the field should teach ESP courses is a matter of controversy among theorists. Many studies have been conducted to asses this. ESP is defined as a combination of subject matter and English language teaching, and many theorists assume that the ESL teacher, although having a good command of the language, does not possess enough knowledge of the subject matter and lacks the necessary expertise needed in the ESP classroom.

Although ESP practitioners without any scientific and technical knowledge may encounter difficulties in the classroom, they face ESP students who know the content rather than English. As mentioned earlier, EAP is a part of ESP, according to Dudley-Evans & St. John's (1998) classification of ESP. Many researchers agree that the purpose of EAP is to meet the needs of learners studying different subjects at university through the medium of English. Those needs revolve around the four language skills (listening, speaking, reading, and writing) and study skills including critical thinking. The focus of ESP is not on the knowledge, or even specific language of any particular subject (Business or Biology) but on core skills and generic language that can cover any discipline. Teaching subject knowledge alongside language is actually Content and Language Integrated Learning (CLIL) but not ESP.

Many theorists have suggested that ESP practitioners may not need as much specialist (or target situation) knowledge as has been assumed. According to Ferguson (1997), what ESP practitioners need is knowledge about an area, that is, its values and preferred genres, rather than in-depth knowledge of the area. Dudley-Evans and St. John (1998) similarly remark, "Business people do not expect a Business English teacher to know how to run a business; they expect knowledge of how language is used in business" (p. 188).

Such views echo those of Maleki (2008) who conducted research in Iran. For Maleki, what needs to be addressed are the intended learning outcomes. The goal of ESP is not primarily to teach a subject in EFL but to teach English with specific content that is normally mixed with general topics, and EFL teachers are the ones who are solely qualified for the job. Maleki goes further in his paper titled "ESP Teaching: A Matter of Controversy" to confirm in this case study that "many of students' problems in understanding what they read are not caused by the specialist vocabulary of their subject of study; rather, their main problem in reading is with general English words" (p. 8). Therefore, he sees no reason for sending specialists in the field to ESP classes.

3.7. Vocabulary in ESP means a focus on the specialist vocabulary

The aim of ESP is not to teach special terminology or jargon in a specific field of study (Maleki, 2008) but rather to look beyond the sentence and deal with genre analysis when designing courses and teaching materials.

ESP teachers leave the teaching and learning of subject-specific terms and concepts to the subject-specific experts. According to Chazal (2012), EAP materials should include core and academic language which is generic to any discipline – e.g. *analysis, significant, is based on, seems to suggest that.* ESP practitioners are discourse analysts and should teach the types of discourse and texts that students have to read and write in their discipline. This knowledge requires the teacher to know the repertoire of genres used in a profession and the occasions when they are used. However, the knowledge of the code is not enough. Bhatia and many other theorists such as Flowerdew (2002) suggest researchers might additionally take a *text-first* or *context-first* approach to the analysis of a particular genre whether the researcher is primarily interested in looking at linguistic and discourse features of the texts (text-first), or understanding more about the context in which the text is produced (context-first). The latter is particularly important as the results of studies conducted show that EFL instructors working in content-specific areas mainly deal with reading comprehension activities and consequently use many texts in their teaching. Adopting a context-first approach to their teaching of professional genres in ESP would help them become more aware of the importance of the context in which the language is used, thus preventing them from teaching a special jargon outside of the context in which it will be used—that is, at jobs.

4. Conclusion

In conclusion, there are many thoughts on English for Specific Purposes as a field of ELT. Some are myths and some are realities. Researchers actually do not always agree on what ESP is, who should be taught ESP and how it should be taught. This overview of the most common controversial conceptions of ESP addresses the issue and was done in an attempt to reflect on the existing research. It also aimed to bring new theoretical lenses that could help improve the teaching of English for Specific Purposes.

In that attempt to bring responses to arguments about what ESP is and is not, we can draw the following conclusions:

- ESP is not necessarily concerned with a specific discipline.

- ESP is not only taught to a specific age group or professionals but can also be taught to Beginners.

- ESP is not about teaching subject knowledge and content.

- ESP is not about teaching specialist vocabulary (i.e. subject-specific words).

- ESP is rather "an approach to language teaching in which all decisions as to content and method are based on the learner's reason for learning" (Hutchinson & Waters, 1987, p. 19).

- ESP includes core academic language related to any discipline and focuses on discourse and genres used in any profession rather than scientific terms.

References

Belcher, D. (2009). What ESP is and can be: An introduction. In D. Belcher (Ed.), *English for specific purposes in theory and practice*. Ann Arbor, MI: University of Michigan Press.

Bhatia, V. K. (1993). *Analysing genre—Language use in professional settings*. London, England: Longman, Applied Linguistics and Language Study Series.

Chazal, E. (2012). English for Academic Purposes 7 Myths and Realities. Oxford: Oxford University Press ELT.

Coffey, B. (1984). ESP—English for specific purposes. *Language Teaching, 17*(1), 2–16.

Dudley-Evans, T., & St. John, M. J. (1998). *Developments in English for specific purposes: A multidisciplinary approach*. Cambridge, England: Cambridge University Press.

Ferguson, G. (1997). Teacher education and LSP: The role of specialized knowledge. In R. Howard & J. Brown (Eds.), *Teacher education for LSP* (pp. 80–89). Clevedon, England: Multilingual Matters.

Fiorito, L. (2005). Teaching English for specific purposes. Retrieved from http://www.usingenglish.com/articles/teaching-english-for-specific-purposes-esp.html.

Flowerdew, L. (2002). Genre in the classroom: A linguistic approach. In A. Johns (Ed.), *Genres in the classroom* (pp. 91–102). Hillsdale, NJ: Erlbaum.

Howatt, A. P. R., & Widdowson, H. G. (2004). *A history of English language teaching* (2nd edition). Oxford, England: Oxford University Press.

Hutchinson, T., & Waters, A. (1987). *English for specific purposes. A learning-centred approach*. Cambridge, England: Cambridge University Press.

Hyon, S. (1996). Genre in three traditions: Implications for ESL. *TESOL Quarterly, 30*(4), 693–722.

Jordan, R. R. (1997). *English for academic purposes: A guide and resource book for teachers*. Cambridge, England: Cambridge University Press.

Maleki, A. (2008). ESP teaching: A matter of controversy. *English for Specific Purposes World, 7*(17). Retrieved from http://www.esp-world.info/Articles_17/PDF/ESP%20Teaching%20Iran.pdf

Munby, J. (1978). *Communicative syllabus design.* Cambridge, England: Cambridge University Press.

Orr, T. (Ed.). (1997, November). *Proceedings 1997: The Japan Conference on English for Specific Purposes.* University of Aizu, Fukushima, Japan. Retrieved from http://files.eric.ed.gov/fulltext/ED424774.pdf

Richterich, R. & Chancerel, J. L. (1980). *Identifying the needs of adults learning a foreign language.* Oxford: Pergamon

Strevens, P. (1977). Special-purpose language learning: A perspective. Survey article. *Language Teaching and Linguistics: Abstracts, 10*(3), 145–163.

Swales, J. (1990). *Genre analysis: English in academic and research settings.* Cambridge, England: Cambridge University Press.

Section III:
ESP and EAP in CLIL and ELT

Chapter 9

Program implementation without pedagogical standardization: A case of English language program teachers utilizing disparate classroom language policies

Brian G. Rubrecht

Meiji University, Japan

Abstract: The SOCEC Program was a short-lived content and language integrated learning (CLIL) program meant to teach Japanese university student participants English and commerce- and business-related material through the medium of English. While multiple explanations were proffered for why the program was eventually terminated (Rubrecht, 2020), one potentially undermining yet unexplored factor was the program's lack of a standardized classroom language policy (CLP) regarding first and second language (L1/L2) use. Specifically, one of the two native English instructors (NEIs) in charge of the program's flagship courses implemented a strict L2-only policy, while the other NEI (and other program course instructors) allowed varying degrees of L1 use. Results showed that while both NEIs presented rational arguments for their CLP of choice, a majority of students expressed strong preferences for at least some degree of bilingual support in their classroom learning. These results led first to two interrelated determinations, namely, that the less proficient or less motivated program participants were the ones who expected or desired Japanese-language assistance (to varying degrees) in their language classes and that the NEIs had essentially decided their CLPs *a priori* without first understanding these program students' characteristics, including their language use preferences or needs.

Keywords: Classroom policy, CLIL, SOCEC programme, implementation

***

1. Introduction

Conceptualizing the language teacher construct is a complicated affair (Borg, 2006). All instructors come to the language teaching situation with their own views and beliefs (Ford, 2009), many of which arise from their teacher training and personal teaching and learning experiences (McMillan & Rivers, 2011; Richardson, 1996). Because each second and foreign language (2L/FL) teaching and learning context has its own unique obstacles and challenges, it is precisely to these beliefs and experiences that teachers turn when they select the methodological methods and pedagogical practices (MM/PP) to be used as they perform their teaching duties.

Much of the literature that examines teachers' MM/PP choices explains their decisions – and the educational outcomes of those decisions – within independent teaching situations, that is, situations where single classes have no direct relation to other classes being taught within an educational institution. What has gone unexamined, however, are individual teachers' MM/PP decisions made in the typically standardized team-teaching endeavor of teaching in language programs. Of particular concern is when some instructors within a program allow students' first language (L1) use in the classroom while others only allow the second language (L2) to be used.

To fill this perceived gap in the literature, the current chapter details a preliminary research study regarding the disparate classroom language policies (CLPs) used by two native English instructors (NEIs) operating within a single small-scale English language program at a Japanese university. The chapter begins by providing background information about language programs before discussing the particular language program under investigation. The L1/L2 debate in 2L/FL teaching and learning is then briefly reviewed, with the above-mentioned English language program examined as an instance of program implementation that lacked pedagogical standardization. The rationales the NEIs used when selecting their CLPs are investigated, as are students' views of these CLPs and L1/L2 use in university-level language classes. The chapter ends by presenting and discussing conclusions drawn from the research data and directions for future research.

2. Background to Language Programs

Much can be discussed about language program types and purposes, as their use is documented from the 1960s (Tzoannopoulou, 2015). Some programs teach degree-seeking students while others are nestled within the curricula of study laid out by educational institutions. Language for specific purposes (LSP) or English for specific purposes (ESP) programs assist learners in becoming functional in a specific area or domain, although improved target language (TL) proficiency remains a highly relevant aim (Dudley-Evans & St. John, 1998). English for academic purposes (EAP) and English for specific academic purposes (ESAP) programs both tightly integrate content and language (Arnó-Macià & Mancho-Barés, 2015), the focus being to prepare learners for participation in academic settings (e.g., studying abroad).

More recently, programs grounded in content-based instruction (CBI) and content and language integrated learning (CLIL) have emerged. These program types see content subjects taught through the medium of another language (Dalton-Puffer et al., 2010; Tzoannopoulou, 2015) and are readily suited to some version of team-teaching instruction (Sandholtz, 2000). English as a second or foreign language (ESL/EFL) contexts see both CBI and CLIL utilized (Arnó-Macià & Mancho-Barés, 2015; Tzoannopoulou, 2015), but the former is noted to be more language-driven, the latter more content-driven (Räsänen, 2008).

The program discussed in this chapter is considered CLIL (see Coyle et al., 2010), as such program participants "learn language through content and learn content through language" (Yasuda, 2019, p. 51). The balance between the two need not be equal. Classroom structures can be highly contextualized and thus quite variable, even at the classroom level (Yasuda, 2019).

All language program stakeholders and participants desire positive educational outcomes, but all bring with them their conscious or unconscious theories on how languages are taught and learned and how they may best bring about what they perceive to be positive outcomes (see Briesmaster & Briesmaster-Paredes, 2015; Johns, 2006). No single pedagogical approach is applicable to all language teaching situations (Johns, 2006). Without explicit directives (e.g., from the institutional level), each individual instructor must decide all aspects of the teaching and learning endeavor (e.g., classroom policies, language assessment procedures), and these decisions may not match those made by other instructors within a program. As there is little discussion in the literature regarding program instructors adopting disparate MM/PP, the current chapter represents a preliminary exploration of this issue by discussing the School of Commerce English Concentration (SOCEC) Program and, specifically, one of the two program NEIs who taught via a contrasting CLP, namely, by enacting a strict English-only policy for his program classes. The results of this investigation are meant to add insight into how CLP should be determined, particularly within programs.

3. The SOCEC Program

3.1. SOCEC Program Background

The specifics behind the birth and termination of the SOCEC Program, as well as questionnaire results detailing program student characteristics, cannot be relayed in full here (see Rubrecht, 2018; Rubrecht, 2020), but briefly explained, it was a 4-year English program nestled within the School of Commerce at Meiji University in Tokyo, Japan. Established in the late 2000s, its main goal was to provide motivated and highly English-proficient students (including returnees and international students) the opportunity to learn about commerce- and business-related topics in English.

SOCEC Program participants were required to enroll in and pass various English courses, the most important of which were the twice-weekly intensive SOCEC classes (hereafter, S-classes) students took in their freshman and sophomore years. S-classes were taught exclusively by NEIs (a different instructor for each year). In these classes, students studied issues and topics related to commerce and business alongside related areas useful for promoting international communication and exchange. In order to accumulate program credits, students also enrolled in other English classes, some of which were taught by the same or different NEIs, others by native Japanese instructors. Successful program participants received a Certificate of Completion at graduation. The program ceased accepting applicants from the 2017 academic school year.

3.2. Program Construction and Issues

Though CLIL in nature, it forwent an interdisciplinary team-teaching model (Gladman, 2015; Stewart & Perry, 2005) in favor of a more mixed-type one (Sandholtz, 2000) because the MM/PP could neither be prescribed nor dictated, as Japanese university instructors are typically granted (and expect) a *de facto* "free hand" in deciding all facets of their own classes (Ford, 2009). Because of this, the Program Coordinator/freshman S-class NEI (hereafter, Teacher A, who was also the researcher) was only able to provide input and advice to the sophomore S-class NEI (Teacher B) about program pedagogical practices and methodological approaches. Content matters were also discussed so that there would be no overlap across the two years. In discussing program matters, it was discovered that of all program teachers, only Teacher B used a stringent English-only CLP.

4. The L2 Versus L1-Inclusion Debate

Before explaining Teacher B's divergent L2-only CLP, a brief overview of the L1/L2-use debate is warranted. Due to space restrictions, the overview is far from exhaustive. Readers should note that all 2L/FL instructors necessarily fall somewhere along the spectrum between absolute L1 exclusion to varying levels of L1-use acceptability (Nagy & Robertson, 2009; Macaro, 2001). They all also have their own reasons for their chosen CLP.

4.1. Arguing for L2 Use Only

Reasons instructors give for adopting an L2-only policy include:

1. It is tradition

The monolingual principle espousing L1 avoidance emerged in the 1880s, became the foundation of twentieth-century classroom language teaching principles (Howatt, 1984, as cited in Cook, 2001), and continues on today.

2. Language acquisition requires ample comprehensible input

This is a long-used argument (e.g., Ellis, 1984; Krashen, 1982; Wong-Fillmore, 1985) because of the desire to provide learners with frequent and natural TL exposure (Newman, 2010) and because negotiating meaning maximizes both L2 input and output (Ford, 2009).

3. The instructor lacks L1 fluency

Instructors lacking proficiency in the students' L1 may be hesitant to allow its use in class (Ford, 2009).

4. It is university-level learning

Instructors may view university as the appropriate time and place to assess and apply all pre-tertiary-level L2 learning (Ford, 2009).

5. It has face validity

A reason rarely if at all mentioned, strict L2-only policies allow institutions, policymakers, and individual instructors to adopt a veneer of legitimacy by appearing to take students' learning seriously, since their job is to have students learn the L2, but this stance may be used to disingenuous ends, for instance, to cover up teachers' lack of knowledge or experience (see McMillan & Rivers, 2011).

4.2. Arguing for L1 Inclusion

Over the past few decades, the *vox populi* L2-only arguments have been scrutinized and challenged. Apologists for this position often cite the following reasons:

1. The L1 serves a necessary cognitive function

The L1 plays "important cognitive, communicative, and social functions in L2 learning" (McMillan & Rivers, 2011, p. 252), as "FL teaching is the only subject where effective instruction requires the teacher to use a medium the students do not yet understand" (Borg, 2006, p. 5). This makes L1 use part of the natural psychological process required for language acquisition (Anton & DiCamilla, 1998; Cook, 2001; García, 2009) and 2L/FL development (Ghorbani, 2011), especially because its use has been found to allow learners to:

1. extend their zone of proximal development (Storch & Wiggleworth, 2003);

2. activate L1 schema, making it a cognitive scaffolding and structural device (Swan, 1985) that makes for improved task planning, preparation and organization (Anton & DiCamilla, 1998; Arnó-Macià & Mancho-Barés, 2015; Cohen & Brooks-Carson, 2001; Storch & Wigglesworth, 2003; Swain & Lapkin, 2000), rather than making it, as is often assumed, a linguistic crutch (Ghorbani, 2011); and

3. reduce their anxiety and affective filter levels (Horwitz, Horwitz, & Cope, 1986), thereby allowing for truer L2 input processing and acquisition (Briesmaster & Briesmaster-Paredes, 2015).

2. L1 inclusion fosters the democratization of learning

L2-only policies perpetuate hegemonic and old colonial-era thinking regarding L2 language and culture (McMillan & Rivers, 2011; Phillipson, 1992, as cited in Ford, 2009), fail to recognize bilingualism as an advantageous cognitive and social resource (García, 2009), and prevent learners from developing positive beliefs regarding what it means to be bilingual (Fuller, 2009). Native TL instructors using the L1 can become living models of language learning successes and failures and evince authentic scenarios of multi-language use (Ghorbani, 2011) and can use their students' L1 for rapport-building purposes (McMillan & Rivers, 2011), since code-switching is a natural communication feature among bilinguals (Cook, 2005).

3. Argument from efficiency

The L1 can be used as a time-saving device to explain facets of the L2 (Weschler, 1997), features of a specific activity (Ghorbani, 2011), or for task explanation and clarification (Cook, 2001).

4. Classroom L2 language can never be truly authentic anyway

Classroom language is its own genre (see Willis, 1996, as cited in Cook, 2001), and there is a long-running debate about TL language authenticity, especially with regard to learning materials (see the early and modern reviews on the subject by Adams (1995) and Al-Surmi (2012), respectively). At base, some view classroom TL as hopelessly and inevitably little more than a facsimile of the real thing.

5. The Different S-Class CLPs

This section relays information about the CLPs used by the two NEIs in their respective S-classes[1], namely, what they were, why they chose them, and what the students' impressions were about those CLPs. Data were limited to personal reflection (for Teacher A, the freshman S-class instructor), discussions and email correspondence (for Teacher B, the sophomore S-class instructor), and brief open-ended interviews (with the students)[2]. Data were gathered once students had completed all S-class lessons.

5.1. Teacher A's S-classes

Teacher A was cognizant of how the differences between high school and university can lead to students experiencing anxiety, underachieving, and dropping out (see Lowe & Cook, 2003). As such, he volunteered to teach the S-class freshmen. He eased them into university life by first using a series of introductory handouts before starting an English-language commerce textbook. The year ended with group video projects used to various ends (e.g., English speaking practice, comprehension assessment).

Classroom policies (e.g., for attendance, participation) were strict but fair and were meant to instill early on positive life habits. English use was strongly encouraged. He often told students things like, "You can speak in Japanese after class. Use class time to learn and practice English." and "Your university studies only last four years. Make your time here count and practice speaking in English."

The students (and teacher) were allowed to use Japanese, but students' Japanese utterances were often followed by teacher requests for their English equivalents (to check if the Japanese were due to a lack of knowledge or laziness). English was mandatory only for commonly-used questions and phrases (explained and practiced the first week), such as "How do you pronounce this?" and "I'm not sure what to do." Teacher A found Japanese advantageous for contrasting English and Japanese, for efficiency purposes, and for rapport building (to reduce student anxiety). He accepted Japanese in class as being "inevitable" (see Lucas & Katz, 1994; Turnbull, 2018) because classes were held "at a Japanese university located in Japan" and because he thought everyone would sooner or later slip up and accidentally speak in Japanese. Thus, he believed punishing students for speaking in Japanese was unnecessarily demotivating and anxiety-inducing, making it counterproductive.

5.2. Teacher B's S-classes

Teacher B[3] devoted the first semester to textbook case studies whereby students looked at problems in international business dealings and negotiations and worked in groups to determine solutions, all to discover the importance of cultural differences, cultural sensitivity, and basic business common sense. In the second semester, students primarily worked in groups to create advertising campaigns for a fictitious international marketing company interested in expanding into the Japanese market. Year's end saw students giving various presentations.

Because he considered English to be the language of the classroom, Teacher B utilized an L2-only CLP for all his language classes. Forcing the S-class students to use English exclusively made them "confront their own linguistic and communicative weaknesses." Transgressors were penalized by being counted absent that day. Teacher B claimed that all S-class students unanimously approved of this CLP, that some students found the policy to be one of the best parts of their program experience, and that some students came to feel strange speaking to classmates in Japanese outside of class. He remarked that the students "wanted to use English communicatively, but in other classes, English was taught in Japanese or an English-only policy was not strictly enforced, so they often felt uncomfortable speaking with classmates in English."

Teacher B avoided giving corrective feedback to these "generally hesitant or shy" Japanese students because in stressing communication, he felt "the less I interfered with students' pronunciation and grammar the better." He reflected on the program at its end, saying:

> If I had to teach the class over again, I would keep the same language policy. In spite of the problems with language level, the students were able to communicate with each other, to solve case studies, and to make successful presentations, therefore I felt the class was a success.

Teacher B mentioned several general problems/challenges of the classes, particularly students not being uniformly English proficient or motivated enough to want to continue in the program[4], with some more interested in English conversation than learning business English. He also noted that his CLP gave rise to "a sort of pigeon version (of English) that was basically comprehensible to a Japanese speaker but would not get them very far internationally."

In overview, both teachers expressed comprehensible reasons for their CLP of choice. Teacher A encouraged English but allowed Japanese. For him, Japanese was a multifaceted resource that should not (and could not) be expunged from the classroom. Teacher B's CLP was inflexible because, to him, English classrooms equal English-only spaces.

5.3. Students' Views on S-class CLPs

In total 15 program students (some of whom were enrolled in the researcher's other English classes) agreed to brief anonymous open-ended interviews[5], which were limited to the following four questions

> Q1. What is your opinion about instructors using Japanese when they teach English?
>
> Q2. How much (if at all) should instructors should use Japanese when teaching English?
>
> Q3. What is your opinion about the different S-class CLPs used?
>
> Q4. What are your general impressions about learning English, especially at university?

Interviews were conducted mainly but not exclusively in English. Students were instructed to answer honestly. Students were told that there were no "right" answers, that no answer would be thought of as offensive or disparaging to the researcher, and that interview participation would in no way affect their grades or university standing. Responses were analyzed, categorized, and tallied.

5.3.1. Q1 Responses

Nine students found Japanese use in their English classes as acceptable, the most-often-cited reason being that if universities are for student learning, then teachers need to do everything necessary to help them learn, which could include using Japanese for explanations. One student even found

Japanese explanations of concepts "normal." Four students viewed Japanese as unnecessary, either because it is tertiary-level learning or because English-only lessons provide valuable English listening practice. Two students answered ambivalently.

5.3.2. Q2 Responses

This breakdown reveals their opinions about how much instructors should use Japanese in English classes:

Always: 0

Frequently: 3

Occasionally: 6

Sparingly: 5

Never: 1

Although Q1 responses showed some students to see Japanese use in English classes as unnecessary, Q2 responses revealed that all but one interviewee found at least some Japanese use acceptable. Multiple students mentioned the difficulty of discussing commerce- and business-related material as it connects to Japan without using some Japanese. The lone "Never" respondent was a highly proficient and motivated international student who appeared aware that her exposure to English in Japan was limited. She expressed dissatisfaction with her obviously less-motivated classmates and their unnecessary use of Japanese in class. No students wanted Japanese-only instruction.

5.3.3. Q3 Responses

Nine students were "happy" or "grateful" the freshman S-class allowed Japanese use, 11 students found the sophomore S-class English-only policy (and its associated punishments) either "strict" or "too strict," and one student (the international student mentioned above) lamented that both years were not English only. While four students mentioned that it is "natural" or "to be expected" that their second year should be more challenging, 11 students voiced various concerns, for example, that the connection between the two years of study was "unclear" or "shallow" (3 students) and that the S-class teachers' personalities were very different (9), which made some students' transition to sophomore S-classes difficult (7). Six students expressed gratitude that the stricter CLP was in second and not first year (e.g., it was a sign of advancement, they had time to prepare).

5.3.4. Q4 Responses

Responses to this purposefully general question were mixed. With respect to CLP, nine comments showed favor to Japanese use (e.g., "Japanese use is for the benefit of students," "I am put at ease when concepts are easy to understand."), seven comments revealed English-only benefits (e.g., "I want to hear pronunciation from native speakers," "Nuances exist in English, so I can pick up things if they are said in English."), and one comment was ambivalent (i.e., "It depends on the type of English and the purpose for which that English is being taught."). Five students pointed out the merits of both CLPs.

Judging from these responses, particularly those from Q2 and Q4, it appeared that the students interviewed generally had preferences for some degree of bilingual support, a finding noted elsewhere for Japanese contexts (Critchley, 1999).

6. Determinations

From the above, two interrelated determinations were made about using disparate language CLPs within the SOCEC Program. First, it was the less proficient/motivated students who expected/desired Japanese use in their S-classes. This determination came from the student interview data, the researcher's familiarity with the students (his having taught them directly), and the questionnaire data gathered previously (Rubrecht, 2018). As explained in that study, circumstances required the easing of program entry restrictions, which meant that a majority of students were not the highly proficiency and motivated target program students. In fact, it was found that over the ten-year period that the questionnaires were administered, 93 students (83%) were motivated to learn English for conversational purposes and not for future job preparation (16; 14%). Given that SOCEC was a CLIL program meant to help prepare students for work in commerce- and business-related fields, this finding was disconcerting. Proficient and motivated students still entered the program, but they were few in number, especially in the program's final years, and few desired to have English become an integral part of their lives.

This mixed student cohort caused Teacher B difficulty. The less proficient students had trouble keeping up with his advanced curriculum taught exclusively in the L2. Interview data revealed that the weaker students generally espoused the benefits of L1 use in learning, and they were the ones who explained why Japanese was sometimes necessary and even "natural" for learning English.

Judging from students' interview responses indicating their differing opinions about the acceptability of Japanese in their university English classes as well as their mentioning the lack of cohesion between the S-classes, the second determination is that the students' classroom language use preferences and needs were scarcely considered by the S-class instructors, particularly Teacher B. As previously-mentioned, university teachers in Japan enjoy a "free hand" in determining class aspects like CLPs[6]. With this freedom, each S-class instructor could decide whether or not to allow the L1 in their S-classes[7]. Teacher A, with his L1-inclusive CLP, was in a better position to adjust the amount and timing of students' Japanese use because he could assess their proficiency and progress as he guided them through their various assignments and activities. He compensated somewhat for the students' lower-than-desired proficiency levels[8] by allowing more classroom Japanese than he would have liked, but there were limits to this, as there were content aspects of this CLIL program that had to be covered (i.e., there was more to these S-classes than just English teaching and learning). Teacher B, on the other hand, having forbidden L1 use completely, made no CLP adjustments. Student proficiency and motivation levels made no difference, and students caught using Japanese were unerringly penalized.

Regarding students' interview responses about their opinion of the different S-class CLPs used, few students (4) favourably viewed the move from an easier/more student-level-appropriate CLP (Teacher A's) to a more difficult/challenging one (Teacher B's), more (9) were "happy" or "grateful" that the freshman S-classes allowed Japanese, and even more (11) mentioned that Teacher B's English-only CLP was strict in a negative sense. These responses appear to indicate that the students had CLP preferences in terms of both type and timing.

7. Conclusion and Discussion

Considering these two determinations, several conclusions about disparate language program CLPs can be proffered. First, CLPs should not be decided or implemented without having first considered participants' characteristics, including their proficiency and motivation levels, past learning experiences, and language learning goals. Language programs (and teaching in general) are less about a specific approach, method, or technique and more about appropriate content selection and teaching approach. Students' perceptions of teaching and learning also carry weight (Zamani & Ahangari, 2016) because they have been determined to be connected to university course expectations, satisfaction, and commitment (Horwitz, 1988). Language classes not meeting student expectations can lead to their losing confidence in the pedagogical approaches used, thereby limiting their ultimate achievement (Horwitz, 1987).

The SOCEC Program failed to attract proficient and motivated students (Rubrecht, 2018), which meant that the program required reevaluation[9], but for too long program continuation was deemed to be of greater importance than matching the program content and language levels to the participating students. This failure to make appropriate program changes marked a disservice to the program participants, as program teachers and coordinators could not accurately predict or properly assess student progress, and it undermined the predetermined goals of the program as a whole, which brought the program's very existence into question.

Because appropriate methods inherently surpass specific ones (Kenny, 2016), effective teaching requires teachers to be flexible and adaptable (Al-Seghayer, 2017; Ehrman, Leaver, & Oxford, 2003). With the program students' characteristics known, Teacher B's pervasive and intransigent CLP could not be considered appropriate, and his claim that the students unanimously agreed, year after year, to his default English-only CLP seems incongruous, given that (a) these were "generally hesitant or shy" students, (b) there were various hegemonic factors at work (Teacher B being a white Western male NEI), and (c) students were asked to vote on the sophomore S-class CLP during the first lesson of the school year[10]. Knowing these factors, even had students dissented to Teacher B's chosen CLP, they likely would not have voiced their opinions.

Teacher A assessed the students yearly and made adjustments to his CLP, but since his default CLP involved L1 inclusion, his adjustments were simply a matter of degree and, depending on the activity, timing. He covered all of the planned yearly content. Teacher B, with CLP adjustment options nonexistent, had no choice but to speak English more slowly and use easier vocabulary than intended. In this way, he preserved his policy but he did so at the expense of his teaching plans.

Second, in order to avoid potentially negative outcomes brought about by divergent CLP use, program creators and coordinators should be tasked with considering and establishing a standardized or near-homogenous CLP (and other MM/PP) appropriate for their programs and student participants. They must clearly communicate to program instructors the CLP to be used and the reasoning behind their choice. This is concluded because the beliefs students develop at pre-tertiary levels about how languages are learned are challenged at university (Rubrecht, 2008). Students could become confused about the "true" or "correct" role of the L1 in the face of teachers' conflicting pedagogical approaches as they try to reconstruct their beliefs. In other words, programs are meant to be integrated cohesive educational systems. Disparate CLP may lead students to adopt study methods unsuitable to their proficiency level or to the learning task at hand, since it can be imagined that some activities are more welcoming and deserving of L1 usage (e.g., vocabulary meaning checks) than others (e.g., English speech contest practice).

The third conclusion is that an inflexible L2-only CLP is likely inappropriate and indefensible for practically all 2L/FL teaching and learning situations. It was clearly unsuitable for the sophomore S-classes, as it led to their production of apparently internationally incomprehensible pigeon English, and an examination of recent literature has increasingly shown that the learners' L1 is an important resource and tool for learning that must not and cannot be ignored.

The "L2 = good, L1 = bad" precept for learning environments has been denounced for being based on long-outdated pedagogic traditions rather than on research-based training or principles of language learning theory (Ford, 2009). It is a twentieth-century holdover, as increased student L2 exposure through L2-only instruction has not been found to lead to improved learning outcomes (Macaro, 2005) or to increased L2 linguistic quality (Kim & Elder, 2005), and there is ample evidence to suggest it may actually be counterproductive (Turnbull & Dailey-O'Cain, 2009). With the exception of the most advanced students, L2 learners will inevitably draw upon their L1 knowledge and utilize other resources they have built up through that L1 (see Cook, 2001; Macaro, 2005), making the argument for L2-only environments over-simplistic, unimaginative, unjustifiable, and, according to Turnbull & Dailey-O'Cain (2009), simply "untenable" (p.182). Most educators now realize that it is no longer a question of whether or not the L1 belongs in the classroom, but rather, when its use is most appropriate (Ford, 2009).

Considering all that has been discussed thus far, Teacher B's use of his L2-only CLP may hardly be seen as justifiable. And yet, Teacher B cannot be faulted out of hand for having pedagogical beliefs, as such beliefs are developed and strengthened through many years of formal schooling and personal experiences (see Pajares, 1992; Richardson, 1996). Legitimate calls for an L2-only environment may exist, but the S-classes certainly would not be such an example, which is why teachers must remain flexible and be willing to reexamine their beliefs.

Now, two decades into the new millennium, with L1 exclusion practices being found commonsensically sound but largely indefensible, it is becoming increasingly important for teachers to keep up with the recent literature and stay current in the field of 2L/FL teaching and learning so they can remain up-to-date with the latest research on the subject. Those who do not risk becoming ineffectual (see Ramazani, 2014), which ultimately jeopardizes students' learning. Although his discussion centered on digital pedagogy rather than language policy, Patterson's (2018) words are just as applicable when asserting the need for instructors to teach by staying knowledgeable in their field:

> This stuck-in-the-past approach...seems very unprofessional in the extreme, as no other profession comes to mind that would tolerate the application of out-of-date methodologies and practices by its practitioners, especially when these are at odds with current best practices. ... Yet in language teaching, this stuck-in-the-past approach is evident with some teachers and universities using materials and approaches that are older than the students they teach. Furthermore, teachers with this old-school approach are doing a real disservice to their current students, as these past-based teaching approaches are inadequately preparing students for their future. (p. 10)

Allowing L1 use in the classroom does not mean it is to be used unnecessarily (Yavuz, 2012), nor does it mean students will have reduced TL exposure (Tang, 2002). If used judiciously and in a theoretically-principled manner, the L1 use can be used to support language T/L processes (Butzkamm, 2003; Cook, 2001; Dailey-O'Cain & Liebscher, 2009; Macaro, 2001, 2005; McMillan & Turnbull, 2009; Turnbull & Arnett, 2002), which is why much current research investigates and advocates translanguaging in students' language learning endeavors.

Put simply, translanguaging views learners' different languages as parts of an integrated language system, meaning that learners do not *acquire* the TL so much as they *add the TL to their linguistic repertoire.* Thus, either the L1 or the L2 may be used to further develop learners' skill with and knowledge of the TL. Taking such a translanguaging approach and thereby accepting that the L1 has a use in the language classroom – allows for the abandoning of the L2-only "double monolingual" educational goal and the accepting of learners as aspiring bilinguals instead of as failed L2 speakers (see Cook, 1999; Turnbull, 2018; Turnbull & Dailey-O'Cain, 2009). Had Teacher B taken a translanguaging approach, his sophomore students, being free from L1-use punishments, might have taken more communicative risks. Their spoken English may still have been grammatically imperfect, but they might have been able to sidestep developing their worrisome pigeon English as they learned to become competent bilinguals.

8. Future Directions

As can be seen, the three conclusions of this study all have the shared common feature of illustrating the importance of teachers forgoing if necessary their personal MM/PP and CLP preferences and teaching in ways that are in accord with program goals, student characteristics, and recent literature-based research results. However, this was a limited small-scale study, and several possible avenues of future research have been identified.

The first avenue could explore students' perceptions of CLPs prior to, during, and after program enrollment as a means to identify and reduce potentially demotivating mismatches between their learning expectations and their teachers' MM/PP decisions. Second, research could also examine instructors' views about adjusting or changing completely their preferred CLP when teaching within a program, should the situation call for it. Language educators have been found to change their beliefs, going from using L2-only pedagogical practices to those that view the L1 as a valuable resource (e.g., Auerbach, 1994; Ford, 2009). Should one or more program instructors be directed to make CLP changes, their views behind the CLP to be adopted and their perceptions of how effective they ultimately were at implementing them could be investigated.

Finally, future research could investigate the relationship between CLP used and students' learning outcomes, which the current study was unable to do. In the case of CLIL programs, this would entail inspections of both content- and linguistic-based outcomes. It is acknowledged that assessing such relationships would not be without its challenges. Nevertheless, if teachers are to be truly effective at the task of teaching, they must be the ones to evaluate their teaching methods, students' characteristics, and educational outcomes. In the end, if we as language instructors wish to strive to teach our students, we must gauge our own understanding as well as theirs.

References

Adams, T. W. (1995). What makes materials authentic. (ERIC Reproduction Service No. ED391389)

Al-Seghayer, K. (2017). The central characteristics of successful ESL/EFL teachers. *Journal of Language Teaching and Research*, *8*(5), 881-890. doi:http://dx.doi.org/10.17507/jltr.0805.06

Al-Surmi, M. (2012). Authenticity and TV shows: A multidimensional analysis perspective. *TESOL Quarterly*, *46*(4), 671-694. doi:https://doi.org/10.1002/tesq.33

Anton, M., & DiCamilla, F. (1998). Socio-cognitive functions of L1 collaborative interaction in the L2 classroom. *The Canadian Modern Language Review*, *54*(3), 314-342.

Arnó-Macià, E., & Mancho-Barés, G. (2015). The role of content and language in content and language integrated learning (CLIL) at university: Challenges and implications for ESP. *English for Specific Purposes*, *37*(1), 63-73. doi:http://dx.doi.org/10.1016/j.esp.2014.06.007

Auerbach, E. R. (1994). The author responds.... *TESOL Quarterly*, *28*(1), 157-161. doi:10.2307/3587204

Auerbach, E. R. (2000). Creating participatory learning communities: Paradoxes and possibilities. In *The sociopolitics of English language teaching* (pp. 143-164). Clevedon: Multilingual Matters.

Berk, R. A. (2005). Survey of 12 strategies to measure teaching effectiveness. *International Journal of Teaching and Learning in Higher Education, 17*(1), 48-62.

Borg, S. (2006). The distinctive characteristics of foreign language teachers. *Language Teaching Research, 10*(1), 3-31. doi:10.1191/1362168806lr182oa

Bradford, A., & Brown, H. (Eds.) (2018). *English-medium instruction in Japanese higher education*. Bristol: Multilingual Matters.

Briesmaster, M., & Briesmaster-Paredes, J. (2015). The relationship between teaching styles and NNPSETs' anxiety levels. *System, 49*, 145-156. doi:http://dx.doi.org/10.1016/j.system.2015.01.012

Butzkamm, W. (2003). We only learn language once. The role of the mother tongue in FL classrooms: Death of a dogma. *Language Learning Journal, 28*(1), 29-39. doi:10.1080/09571730385200181

Cohen, A. D., & Brooks-Carson, A. (2001). Research on direct versus translated writing: Students' strategies and their results. *The Modern Language Journal, 85*(2), 169-188. doi:10.1111/0026-7902.00103

Cook, V. (1999). Going beyond the native speaker in language teaching. *TESOL Quarterly, 33*(2), 185-209. doi:https://doi.org/10.2307/3587717

Cook, V. (2001). Using the first language in the classroom. *Canadian Modern Language Review, 57*(3), 402-423. Retrieved from http://www.viviancook.uk/Writings/Papers/L1inClass.htm

Cook, V. (2005). Basing teaching on the L2 user. In E. Llurda (Ed.), *Non-native language teachers: Perceptions, challenges and contributions to the profession* (pp. 47-61). New York: Springer.

Coyle, D., Hood, P., & Marsh, D. (2010). *Content and language integrated learning*. Cambridge: Cambridge University Press.

Critchley, M. P. (1999). Bilingual support in English classes in Japan: A survey of student opinions of L1 use by foreign teachers. *The Language Teacher, 23*(9), 10-13, 3.

Dailey-O'Cain, J., & Liebscher, G. (2009). Teacher and student use of the first language in foreign language classroom interaction: Functions and applications. In M. Turnbull & J. Dailey-O'Cain (Eds.), *First language use in second and foreign language learning* (pp. 131-144). Bristol: Multilingual Matters.

Dalton-Puffer, C., Nikula, T., & Smit, U. (2010). Charting policies, premises and research on content and language integrated learning. In C. Dalton-Puffer, T. Nikula, & U. Smit (Eds.), *Language use and language learning in CLIL classrooms* (pp. 1-19). Amsterdam: John Benjamins.

Dudley-Evans, T., & St. John, M. J. (1998). *Developments in English for specific purposes: A multi-disciplinary approach*. Cambridge: Cambridge University Press.

Ehrman, M. E., Leaver, B. L., & Oxford, R. L. (2003). A brief overview of individual differences in second language learning. *System, 31*, 313-330. doi:10.1016/S0346-251X(03)00045-9

Ellis, R. (1984). *Classroom second language development*. Oxford: Pergamon Press.

Ford, K. (2009). Principles and practices of L1/L2 use in the Japanese university EFL classroom. *JALT Journal, 31*(1), 63-80.

Fuller, J. M. (2009). How bilingual children talk: Strategic codeswitching among children in dual language programs. In M. Turnbull & J. Dailey-O'Cain (Eds.), *First language use in second and foreign language learning* (pp. 115-130). Bristol: Multilingual Matters.

García, O. (2009). Emergent bilinguals and TESOL: What's in a name? *TESOL Quarterly, 43*(2), 322-326.

Ghorbani, A. (2011). First language use in foreign language classroom discourse. *Procedia: Social and Behavioral Sciences, 29,* 1654-1659. doi:10.1016/j.sbspro.2011.11.408

Gladman, A. (2015). Team teaching is not just for teachers! Student perspectives on the collaborative classroom. *TESOL Journal, 6*(1), 130-148. doi:10.1002/tesj.144

Horwitz, E. K. (1987). Surveying student beliefs about language learning. *Learner Strategies in Language Learning, 15*(3), 119-129.

Horwitz, E. K. (1988). The beliefs about language learning of beginning university foreign language students. *The Modern Language Journal, 72*(3), 283-294.

Horwitz, E. K., Horwitz, M. B., & Cope, J. (1986). Foreign language classroom anxiety. *The Modern Language Journal, 70,* 125-132.

Howatt, A. (1984). *A history of English language teaching.* Oxford: Oxford University Press.

Johns, A. (2006). Languages for specific purposes: Pedagogy. In K. Brown (Ed.), *Encyclopedia of Language and Linguistics* (2nd ed., pp. 684-690). Elsevier. doi:https://doi.org/10.1016/B0-08-044854-2/05295-0

Kenny, N. (2016). Is there a specific method for teaching ESP? *The Journal of Teaching English for Specific and Academic Purposes, 4*(2), 253-260.

Kim, S., & Elder, C. (2005). Language choices and pedagogic functions in the foreign language classroom: A cross-linguistic functional analysis of teacher talk. *Language Teaching Research, 9*(4), 355-380. doi:https://doi.org/10.1191/1362168805lr173oa

Krashen, S. (1982). *Principles and practice in second language acquisition.* Oxford: Pergamon Press.

Lowe, H., & Cook, A. (2003). Mind the gap: Are students prepared for higher education? *Journal of Further and Higher Education, 27*(1), 53-76.

Lucas, T., & Katz, A. (1994). Reframing the debate: The roles of native languages in English-only programs for language minority students. *TESOL Quarterly, 28*(3), 537-561.

Macaro, E. (2001). Analysing student teachers' codeswitching in foreign language classrooms: Theories and decision making. *The Modern Language Journal, 85*(4), 531-548. doi:https://doi.org/10.1111/0026-7902.00124

Macaro, E. (2005). Codeswitching in the L2 classroom: A communication and learning strategy. In E. Llurda (Ed.), *Non-native language teachers: Perceptions, challenges and contributions to the profession* (pp. 63-84). New York: Springer.

McMillan, B. A., & Rivers, D. J. (2011). The practice of policy: Teacher attitudes toward "English only". *System, 39,* 251-263. doi:10.1016/j.system.2011.04.011

McMillan, B. A., & Turnbull, M. (2009). Teachers' use of the first language in French immersion: Revisiting a core principle. In M. Turnbull & J. Dailey-O'Cain (Eds.), *First language use in second and foreign language learning* (pp. 15-34). Bristol: Multilingual Matters.

MEXT. (2011). *The revisions of the courses of study for elementary and secondary schools.* Retrieved from http://www.mext.go.jp/en/policy/educati on/elsec/title02/detail02/__icsFiles/afieldfile/2011/03/28/1303755_001.pdf

MEXT. (2014). *English education reform plan corresponding to globalization.* Retrieved from http://www.mext.go.jp/en/news/topics/detail/__icsFiles/a fieldfile/2014/01/23/1343591_1.pdf

Nagy, K., & Robertson, D. (2009). Target language use in English classes in Hungarian primary schools. In M. Turnbull & J. Dailey-O'Cain (Eds.), *First language use in second and foreign language learning* (pp. 66-86). Bristol: Multilingual Matters.

Newman, E. (2010). Peaceful coexistence of L1 and L2 in a language classroom. *Teacher Talk.* Retrieved from http://azargrammar.com/teacherTalk/blog/20 10/05/peaceful-coexistence-of-l1-and-l2-in-a-language-classroom/

Pajares, M. F. (1992). Teachers' beliefs and educational research: Clearing up a messy construct. *Review of Educational Research, 62*(3), 307-332.

Patterson, R. (2018). An e-Vangelical approach to professional development and 21st-century teaching. *CUE Circular, 8,* 8-11.

Phillipson, R. *Linguistic imperialism.* Oxford: Oxford University Press.

Ramazani, M. (2014). Mismatches in beliefs between teachers and students, and characteristics of effective English teacher: An Iranian context. *Procedia: Social and Behavioral Sciences, 98,* 1518-1527. doi:10.1016/j.sbspro.2014.0 3.573

Räsänen, A. (2008). Redefining "CLIL": Towards multilingual competence. In A. A. Greere & Räsänen (Eds.), *LANGUA Year 1 Report.* Retrieved from http://www.lanqua.eu/files/Year1Report_CLIL_ForUpload_WithoutAppend ices_0.pdf

Richardson, V. (1996). The role of attitudes and beliefs in learning to teach. In J. Sikula (Ed.), Handbook of research on teacher education (2nd ed., pp. 102-119). New York: Simon & Schuster Macmillan.

Rubrecht, B. G. (2008). Shifting goals, instructor roles, and Japanese university students' English study methods. In M. Mantero, P. C. Miller, & J. Watzke (Eds.), *ISLS readings in language studies, Vol. 1: Language across disciplinary boundaries* (pp. 539-553). Laguna Beach, CA: International Society for Language Studies, Inc.

Rubrecht, B. G. (2018). A decade of the SOCEC Program: Lessons taught, lessons learned. *The Bulletin of Arts and Sciences Meiji University, 537,* 37-54.

Rubrecht, B. G. (2020). Examining the pitfalls behind a failed Japanese University ESP Program. In N. Kenny, E. E. Işık-Taş, H. Jian (Eds.), *English for Specific Purposes Instruction and Research: current practices, challenges and innovations (pp 105-123)* Cham, Switzerland: Palgrave Macmillan.

Sandholtz, J. H. (2000). Interdisciplinary team teaching as a form of professional development. *Teacher Education Quarterly, 27*(3), 39-54.

Stewart, T., & Perry, B. (2005). Interdisciplinary team teaching as a model for teacher development. *TESL-EJ, 9*(2), 1-17.

Storch, N., & Wigglesworth, G. (2003). Is there a role for the use of the L1 in an L2 setting? *TESOL Quarterly, 37*(4), 760-770. doi:https://doi.org/10.2307/3588224

Swan, M. (1985). A critical look at the Communicative Approach (2). *ELT Journal, 39*(2), 76-87.

Swain, M., & Lapkin, S. (2000). Task-based second language learning: The uses of the first language. *Language Teaching Research, 4*(3), 253-276. doi:https://doi.org/10.1177/136216880000400304

Tang, J. (2002). Using L1 in the English classroom. *English Teaching Forum, 40*(1), 36-43.

Turnbull, B., & Arnett, K. (2002). Teachers' uses of the target and first languages in second and foreign language classrooms. *Annual Review of Applied Linguistics, 22*, 204-218. doi:https://doi.org/10.1017/S0267190502000119

Turnbull, B. (2018). Is there a potential for a translanguaging approach to English education in Japan? Perspectives of tertiary learners and teachers. *JALT Journal, 40*(2), 101-134.

Turnbull, M., & Dailey-O'Cain, J. (2009). Concluding reflections: Moving forward. In M. Turnbull & J. Dailey-O'Cain (Eds.), *First language use in second and foreign language learning* (pp. 182-186). Bristol: Multilingual Matters.

Tzoannopoulou, M. (2015). Rethinking ESP: Integrating content and language in the university classroom. *Procedia: Social and Behavioral Sciences, 173*, 149-153.

Weschler, R. (1997). Uses of Japanese in the English classroom: Introducing the Functional-Translation Method. *Kyoritsu Women's University Department of International Studies Journal, 12*, 87-110.

Willis, J. (1996). *A framework for task-based language learning*. London: Harlow.

Wong-Fillmore, L. (1985). When does teacher talk work as input? In S. M. Gass & C. G. Madden (Eds.), *Input in second language acquisition* (pp. 17-50). MA: Newbury House Publishers.

Yasuda, S. (2019). Conceptualizing integration in CLIL: More than just learning content and language. *JALT Journal, 41*(1), 49-65.

Yavuz, F. (2012). The attitudes of English teachers about the use of L1 in the teaching of L2. *Procedia: Social and Behavioral Sciences, 46*, 4339-4344. doi:10.1016/j.sbspro.2012.06.251

Zamani, R., & Ahangari, S. (2016). Characteristics of an effective English language teacher (EELT) as perceived by learners of English. International Journal of Foreign Language Teaching & Research, 4(14), 69-88.

Notes

1. Space limitations dictate that other program-related classes cannot be discussed.
2. Due to school-level decisions that considered the S-classes to be part of an isolated program, these classes were ineligible for semester-end class evaluation administration, meaning a valuable data source was unavailable (see Berk, 2005).

3. Teacher B retains anonymity. Also, quotations are from email correspondence with him, dated March 5, 2018, six weeks after the final sophomore S-class was taught.
4. These were recognized problems (Rubrecht, forthcoming).
5. Difficulty was encountered in arranging post-S-class interviews because juniors and seniors do not study at the same campus as freshmen and sophomores.
6. There are exceptions (Bradford & Brown, 2018; Turnbull, 2018) that the Japanese Ministry of Education, Culture, Sports, Science and Technology (MEXT) would like to see become the rule (see MEXT 2011, 2014).
7. Their CLP beliefs were well ensconced prior to their being hired at the university.
8. Their proficiency was low relative to the advanced S-class content.
9. Reevaluations were eventually conducted, which led to the program's termination.
10. Negotiation of CLP is not unheard of (see Auerbach, 2000, as cited in Ford, 2009).

Chapter 10

Examining L2 learners' source text reading strategies for an MA module assignment in a UK university

Takeshi Kamijo

Ritsumeikan University, Japan

Abstract: L2 learners in content-based academic courses must apply strategies of reading their source texts to writing tasks (McCulloch, 2013; McGrath et al., 2016). As they read their source texts, L2 learners critically scrutinize the perspectives of relevant researchers and understand intertextuality within the research genre (Swales, 1990). Thus far, little research has been conducted to examine the reading of source texts by L2 learners. The present exploratory study investigated how two selected successful L2 learners used think-aloud methods to read self-selected reviews of scholarly literature for a Master of Arts (MA) module assignment at a UK university. This study applied the cognitive reading framework (Weir & Khalifa, 2008) and employed revised coding categories by McCulloch (2013) to analyse the data. The results revealed that the two learners read the selected literature reviews to understand the debates among the researchers and to structure their assignment arguments. The think-aloud findings indicated the critical and evaluative reading strategies of the learners, including the elaboration of content, the creation of inferences, awareness of the text structure, and the use of paraphrased descriptions, which suggested the learners' comprehensive representations of the source texts.

Keywords: reading strategies, MA module assignment, think-aloud methods, cognitive reading model, elaboration

***

1. Introduction

1.1. Definition and research into L2 reading strategies

The comprehension of a text comprises an active constructive process in which readers attempt to use cognitive and metacognitive strategies to understand the written document (Allen, 2003; Pressley & Afflerbach, 1995). Singhal (2001) classifies six cognitive reading strategies in an L2 reading strategy model that is based on a global processing approach: note-taking and the formal practice of reading, summarizing, paraphrasing, predicting, and using contextual cues. Reviewing extant studies on both L1 and L2 reading, Allen (2003) categorised cognitive reading strategies such as relating the text to the reader's life, determining facts that are important or unimportant, summarizing information, filling in details, drawing inferences, and asking questions. Evans (2008) modified Allen's model and applied it to an L2 English for Academic Purposes classroom context at a Japanese university. These reading strategies suggest that cognitive reading strategies utilise global processing to increase text comprehension, whereas metacognitive strategies are applied to reinforce the use of reading strategies through monitoring and evaluation (Anderson, 2003; Oxford, 2011). Metacognitive knowledge is also considered important for reinforcement, which refers to the understanding of cognitive reading strategies, how the strategies are used, and when and why they are applied in the reading of a text (Iwai, 2011; Oxford, 2011). These definitions of cognitive and metacognitive reading strategies are widely relevant to L2 learners in English as a Foreign Language (EFL) and English as a Second Language (ESL) contexts.

Numerous researchers in EFL and ESL contexts have, for the past 40 years, focused on think-aloud protocols from available research methods to investigate the use of reading strategies by L2 learners. Hosenfeld (1977) applied the think-aloud method to investigate the reading strategies of 20 successful and 20 unsuccessful foreign language learners and found that successful readers retained the meaning of a passage in their mind while reading, read in broad phrases, skipped unimportant words, and displayed a positive self-concept. In contrast, unsuccessful readers did not understand the meaning of sentences. Block (1986) also utilised the think-aloud method to scrutinize the reading strategies of nine English learners in the United States and found that successful readers integrated information, were aware of the text structure, and monitored their strategies. Upton (1997) used the think-aloud method to investigate the reading strategies of Japanese L2 learners, and Zhang (2001) employed a similar approach in a study of Chinese L2 learners. Both research investigations found that the more capable and successful learners used global processing strategies, monitoring, and evaluation. Through the application of explicit coding schemes to assess reading strategies, researchers found that proficient readers tend to apply global reading strategies and to monitor and evaluate their reading strategies with metacognitive awareness (Lau, 2006).

Some researchers later began to adopt think-aloud protocols and data analysis to investigate the reading strategies used by L2 learners to carry out writing tasks (Esmaeili, 2002; Plakans, 2009; Plakans & Gebril, 2012). Plakans (2009) investigated the integrated reading and writing strategies of 12 learners by using reading-to-write tasks for which the learners were asked to read two source texts based on a theme and then to write an argumentative essay related to this theme. Strategies identified through the think-aloud protocols of the participants were goal setting, cognitive processing, global strategies, and metacognitive awareness, as well as mining or scanning texts for key words or phrases. Hijikata et al., (2013) employed think-aloud methods with two Japanese university L2 learners to examine their reading of academic source texts associated with their course-writing tasks. Applying global, local, and metacognitive strategy coding categories, the researchers found that the proficient learner used more global strategies, while the less effective learner used more local strategies. These cognitive and metacognitive reading strategy categories were similar to the results obtained by studies on the reading strategies applied by conventional L2 learners.

1.2. Critical and evaluative reading strategies for academic writing

L2 learners registered for university courses that specify academic content, however, need to use reading strategies differently. Content-based courses in higher education require L2 learners to focus on discussions of relevant sources on which argumentative assignments are based. Therefore, L2 learners must use specific reading strategies for writing tasks that require assimilation of the academic reading material that forms the content of their coursework (Grabe, 2009; Grabe & Zhang, 2013; McCulloch, 2013; McGrath et al., 2016). In order to do written argumentative assignments based on the course syllabus, L2 learners need to select relevant texts and critically assess them to develop their own arguments. In other words, L2 learners must skim and scan a number of potential source texts to grasp the main ideas. They must also select relevant source texts and read their contents critically, understanding the academic research genre of the texts to formulate the arguments for their assignments (Hijikata et al., 2013; Weir and Khalifa, 2008; Swales, 1990).

McCulloch (2013) has criticised previous studies with regard to reading strategies that utilise passages in experimental settings. She emphasizes the need for a natural setting in which researchers investigate the reading strategies of L2 learners for the purpose of writing. McCulloch employed think-aloud protocols to investigate the reading strategies that two L2 postgraduate participants used for their dissertation drafts. Think-aloud sessions were held during week three of the semester. The participants reported the think-aloud processes they employed in reading randomly selected source texts for their draft dissertations. Six main coding categories were identified: locating source texts; reading source texts; taking notes; referring to an emerging draft dissertation; referring to the participants' own research data; and employing general study strategies. The coding category used most frequently by the two participants was the reading of source texts, and 13 subcategories emerged within this classification. Among these, the study identified the participants' responses to source texts, elaboration of source content, the making of inferences about sources, and intertextual awareness as the major subcategories. In 2013, McCulloch's study has contributed to the understanding of L2 learners' reading strategies of source texts for writing, as the data of the four subcategories may be related to these learners' use of critical and evaluative reading comprehension for writing tasks.

Despite the implications, however, the two participants in McCulloch's study did not necessarily select important literature for the think-aloud sessions. The study did not show whether or not the selected articles were used as the participants' key source texts for critically evaluating content and establishing arguments in their draft dissertations. Additionally, the study did not indicate how such reading strategies as elaborating and making inferences might be related to the participants' critical and evaluative reading of the source texts. Accordingly, the present study investigated the reading strategies of the selected two L2 learners, based on their application of think-aloud protocols to their self-selected review articles. The two learners' used research review articles as key source texts for establishing the arguments in their assignment essays. The reading strategy categories proposed by McCulloch (2013) were revised and applied to the data analysis. The model of critical and evaluative reading processes by Weir and Khalifa (2008) was also used to analyse the think-aloud data of the two L2 learners. The following two questions were posited:

1. What were the two L2 learners' characteristics of the reading strategies analysed through the think-aloud protocols of their self-selected review articles?

2. To what extent were the reading strategies reported through the think-aloud protocols related to the critical and evaluative reading?

2. Methods

2.1. Participants

The participants in the study were two L2 learners who were enrolled in Master's of Arts (MA) programmes in the Teaching of ESL (TESOL) and in English Language Teaching (ELT) at a university in the United Kingdom. Initially, six postgraduate L2 learners were interviewed, and two students were found to be successful in their grading of MA assignment essays with distinction levels between 70 and 80 percent. Hence, these two learners were selected for further data examination. The selected two participants were female students from China who had no previous overseas educational experience prior to their MA. Both participants had tested at the advanced English language proficiency level, and both had accrued around seven to eight years of experience in ELT. Both participants also displayed sufficient background knowledge with regard to their selected assignment themes, and both had enrolled in the programme in September 2017, had submitted one of their assignments in early January 2018, and had received feedback and grades in late January.

2.2. MA Module and assignment

Learner 1 was studying for an MA in TESOL, and her assignment pertained to second language learning principles. Learner 2 was reading for an MA in ELT, and her assignment was related to education measurement. The primary purpose of both their assignments was to conduct a review of theories related to their focus topics and also to refer to their teaching experiences and other scholarly evidence in the presentation of their arguments for the assignment. The learners were required to select source texts for their specific topics, to critically read the texts and, subsequently, to present their arguments in the assignments, because well-balanced and theoretical evaluations and their application to practice are crucial for postgraduate studies in TESOL and ELT.

2.3. Data collection: Interviews and think-aloud sessions

Two 40-minute interviews were conducted with Learner 1 in November 2017 and in February 2018. Learner 2's first 40-minute interview was held in November 2017, and her second interview was divided into one 20-minute session and another 30-minute session that occurred in late February 2018 and in early March 2018. Twenty-minute think-aloud sessions were provided to the two participants before the second phase of interviews. The data collected from the think-aloud sessions are presented in this study. The data obtained from the two 40-minute interviews that were held after the 20-minute think-aloud sessions are not reported in the present study.

Each participant brought the two source texts she had used for the assignment essays to conduct the concurrent think-aloud narration of the introductory portion of the selected texts. Learner 1 selected a research review article by Bitchener (2012), while Learner 2 chose a research review article by Sternberg (2012). Before the think-aloud sessions, the author confirmed the relevance of the texts with the two participants. Both the learners used the selected research review articles as key source texts, which were essential for establishing arguments for their assignments.

The present author directed them not to prepare in any manner before the think-aloud sessions. Hence, they had not read the two source texts since they had submitted their assignment essays, which amounted to a period of one to two months. The present instructed the participants on think-aloud procedures and demonstrated a sample think-aloud exercise on a 300-word text at the start of the think-aloud sessions.

2.4. Data analysis

The author modified McCulloch's (2013) reading strategy categories for the data analysis of the think-aloud protocols. The source text reading strategy categories by McCulloch (2013) include responses to source texts, elaboration of source content, the making of inferences about sources, and intertextual awareness. After the initial data collection and analysis, these categories were modified. The revised coding categories comprise demonstrating awareness of text structure, elaborating on content, making inferences, paraphrasing, and direct quote.

Table 10.1 Coding Categories for Data Analysis

Category	Description
Awareness of text structure	Utilizing paraphrased words and phrases to develop an understanding of the academic genre structure and of the debate suggested by researchers in the research-based source texts.
Elaborating	Applying paraphrased words and sentences to add new meaning and to express personal understanding and interpretations.
Inferencing	Making implications about the author's viewpoints and perspectives.
Paraphrasing	Using reworded sentences to describe the content.
Direct quote	Applying direct quotes from the text to describe the content.

Next, global-based critical and evaluative reading processes by Weir and Khalifa (2008) were used for data analysis. Weir and Khalifa (2008) define these processes of text representation, which include inferencing and elaborating, building a mental model of a text, and constructing a text-level structure (pp. 6–7). Inferencing is a creative process through which readers add information not explicitly mentioned and elaborate content in a text to develop coherent understanding of it. Additionally, evaluative and critical reading requires readers to build a representation of a text. Readers construct their own understanding of the text into a mental model by actively linking their previously obtained knowledge to the text content. Weir and Khalifa (2008) also assert that readers use their knowledge of the text genre and construct an organised representation of the text. Readers grasp how the different parts of a text can be put together and which parts of it are more important to the readers' purpose.

Concerning the two L2 learners' evaluative reading of source texts, the learners' think-aloud data are analysed based on the above four key categories and the development of a mental model and a text-level structure.

3. Results

This section includes four extracts from Learner 1's think-aloud protocols and three extracts from Learner 2's think-aloud data respectively.

3.1. Data from Learner 1/Research review article

Learner 1 reported the structure and content of the selected research review article about L2 written corrective feedback (Bitchener, 2012) through the think-aloud protocol. The reading processes for this research review article and the key reading strategy categories she used are explained below. In extract 1, she indicated the author's expressions and subsequently elaborated on them.

> **Extract 1:**
>
> Firstly, he mentions **the controversy** whether written corrective feedback can contribute to second language acquisition and to writing **that is, I mean,** the effectiveness of L2 writing and because there is research literature into **different claims** and one**, just like I mentioned, one is for** written corrective feedback and **the other is against** written corrective feedback.

Learner 1 used a quote from the text to describe the theme as 'the controversy whether written corrective feedback can contribute to second language acquisition and to writing.' She then elaborated on the content, using such phrases as 'that is, I mean, the effectiveness of L2 writing' and 'just like I mentioned, one is for—and the other is —.' Learner 1 paraphrased the author's terms in her own words and added her interpretations. Also, she understood that the text's author intended to review a scholarly debate between researchers.

In extract 2, the think-aloud protocol showed her awareness of text discourse and inferences about the author's viewpoint.

Extract 2:

And then he just mentioned that, and <u>also he talks about</u> his structure of this article and <u>the first section of this article</u>, that is, he distinguishes learning and acquisition because <u>he thinks that it is very important</u> to discuss what is meant by learning and what is meant by acquisition, because second language learning and linguistics make distinction about learning and acquisition.

Learner 1 indicated her awareness of the text discourse, as she referred to the phrase 'also he talks about' and 'the first section of the article.' Moreover, through the part of the sentence that says, 'he thinks that it is very important,' she inferred the author's intent to define the important distinction between acquisition and learning in the beginning text. Learner 1 added her interpretation that the definition of learning and acquisition is important in the theory of second language learning and linguistics.

In extract 3, she used an inference about the author's opinion concerning the theme and reconfirmed it in the following sentence.

Extract 3:

And then he continues to examine the theoretical perspective about the potential of written corrective feedback to facilitate L2 learning and acquisition, so <u>from this part, actually I can see</u> that the author is for written corrective feedback, <u>actually</u> he is not against that.

Learner 1 indicated 'the potential of written corrective feedback to facilitate learning and acquisition,' which is quoting from the text, and she added the expression 'from this part, actually I can see—,' suggesting her inference about the author's viewpoint. In addition, she used a sentence: 'actually he is not against that' to confirm her inference about the above author's opinion. Learner 1 recognised that the author attempted to argue for the use of written corrective feedback through a review of the relevant literature.

In extract 4, she elaborated on the text's contents and made further inferences about the author's viewpoint.

Extract 4:

And the third section or the third part of this article discusses the potential of, sorry, it says about the research literature on written corrective feedback, so <u>that is how researchers have done some research about written corrective feedback</u>. And section-4 just considers the mediating factors that have been, I mean, shown in [time] series and how learners' engagement with written corrective feedback, so I mean, <u>actually learners' engagement with written corrective feedback is very important</u>.

In the above extract, Learner 1 used the term 'research literature,' which she took from the text. Then, she explained in her own words, as she paraphrased: 'how researchers have done some research about written corrective feedback.' After that, Learner 1 mentioned 'learners' engagement with written corrective feedback is very important,' which suggested she elaborated on the content, as she added her interpretation about the essential role of learners' engagement. She understood that the author used the theoretical framework of mediation and learners' engagement to support the role of written corrective feedback.

3.2. Summary of the results/Learner 1

The results of Learner 1's think-aloud protocol data gathered from the reading of the research review article showed her use of critical and evaluative reading strategies. She employed some quotes from the text but gave paraphrased and more elaborate expressions on the content to add her own explanations and to reconfirm understanding. Learner 1 attempted to redefine the author's explanations by linking her own knowledge to the text's content, developing her mental model of the text. Also, she was well aware of text structure, as the author intended to define the terms and review the relevant research studies, using the theoretical implications of mediation and learner engagement to support his claims. In this sense, she also had a text-level representation.

3.3. Data from Learner 2/Research review article

Learner 2 explained the research review article (Sternberg, 2012), which she chose for establishing the argument concerning the theme of a child's educational intelligence in her argumentative essay. In extract 5, she described some researchers who were concerned with the early stage of educational intelligence studies.

Extract 5:

Speraman is the person when modern study of intelligence is dated back to, because he studied intelligence and purpose of that is that it could be understood in terms of a general ability. However when we mention modern testing intelligence, some other researchers will be included like Binet and Simon. These two professors decided most widely used scale of testing intelligence.

Learner 2 referred to Speraman, a major scholar, who defined a child's educational intelligence as a general ability. She continued, saying, 'However we mention modern intelligence testing, some other researchers will be included—.' This is a paraphrased sentence, suggesting that Learner 2 recognised the major researchers who developed educational intelligence testing based on Speraman's definition.

In extract 6, she came up with other researchers to explain the further development of research into the measurement of a child's educational intelligence.

Extract 6:

Meanwhile another person that should be mentioned in the early testing of intelligence is Wechsler, and he also decided another widely accepted measurements. For this, Wecheserler's measurements of intelligence mainly focus on overall IQ, and in this measurement, they [include] many tests of global measurements of performances. For this, Binet and Wechester of measurements of intelligence, they focus on measuring intelligence on the judgement and good sense.

Learner 2 utilised quotes from the text, such as 'In the early testing of intelligence' and 'judgment and good sense.' Moreover, she applied paraphrased expressions related to several researchers' major research contributions, such as 'Meanwhile another person that should be mentioned'; 'For this, Wechesler's measurements—'; and 'For this, Binet and Wechester of measurements—.' Learner 2 also used paraphrased expressions such as 'another widely accepted measurement' and 'many tests of global measurements of performance.' This indicated how research into wide-scale and global educational intelligence measurements had developed.

In extract 7, she indicated the limitations of previous studies, stating that measuring a child's educational intelligence had become controversial as it includes different variables.

Extract 7:

However, another researcher Galton, he argued intelligence is not only for this, but should include other skills, like visual and auditory ones. And now we can find the argument about measuring intelligence, that is, IQ is quite variable. And some researchers Flynn showed that average IQ could be increased every decade, and in this article, the author will discuss different aspects of intelligence in difference fields like biological, race difference not only for theories of intelligence.

Learner 2 continued mentioning the researchers' work through her own expressions, as Galton and Flymn challenged the generalised view of the measurement of a child's educational intelligence. She added a sentence: 'And now we can find the argument about measuring intelligence, that is, IQ is quite variable.' She understood the researchers' debates on the measurement of a child's educational intelligence and added her interpretations about the importance of different variables related to the measurement of educational intelligence.

Learner 2 concluded that the author of the text would discuss the key different features concerning a child's educational intelligence in addition to theories.

3.4. Summary of the results/Learner 2

The results of Learner 2's think-aloud protocol data collected from the reading of the research review article indicated her active strategies and an understanding of researchers' scholarly discussion. When she explained the text, she used some direct quotes from it, but applied paraphrased and elaborated expressions to elucidate the development of arguments extended by the authors and to outline the research outcomes. Similar to Learner 1, she attempted to redefine the author's review of the literature according to her own understanding so that she could relate her background knowledge to the text's new content. Also, Learner 2 demonstrated through her protocols that she had a text-level representation of the researchers' debate. Especially in extract 11, after her description of the work of different researchers, she summarised the contentions and stated that arguments on the educational intelligence of children could be observed.

4. Summary, Discussion, and Conclusions

Researchers have previously investigated the reading strategies of L2 learners in terms of their cognitive and metacognitive categories. Many studies in EFL and ESL contexts have found that proficient L2 learners tend to use global processing and to apply metacognitive strategies to reinforce their use of strategies. The L2 reading strategies employed as part of the content of education courses, however, are considered different from conventional reading approaches. In particular, L2 learners must select source texts and critically evaluate them to establish arguments in their assignment essays along with supporting evidence. McCulloch (2013) has classified the categories of source text reading strategies used for academic writing into responses, elaboration of content, creation of inferences, and intertextual awareness. Weir and Khalifa (2008) have defined this process, which comprises global-level stages of building a mental model and constructing a text-level structure.

The present study revised McCulloch's (2013) source text reading strategy categories and the critical and evaluative reading processing model posited by Weir and Khalifa (2008). The results revealed that Learner 1 used elaboration of content and made inferences in her reading of the research review article, as she attempted to confirm her understanding and to add her personal interpretations of the text. Also, she constructed a mental model of the text as well as a text-level representation of this text. Learner 2 paraphrased, elaborated, and constructed a text-level structure of the research review article. She clearly understood the discourse and organization of this article. The results also suggest that she had a mental model of the text and a discourse-level representation of the text as the relevant researchers' debate. The results of these critical and evaluative reading strategy categories are aligned with the goal-based reading strategies suggested for L1 academic reading (Field, 2004; Kintsch and van Dijk 1978).

There are two limitations of the present study: first, participants were restricted to two learners due to the exploratory nature of this research project; second, the data were only collected from the think-aloud protocols of the participants. Future research should gather data from a larger number of participants and should use multiple methods such as think-aloud protocols, interviews, and questionnaires for compiling the data.

Nevertheless, the present study has contributed to the exploration of an understudied issue: the critical and evaluative source text reading strategies used by L2 learners to formulate arguments for their assignments. Similar research studies should further be conducted to develop a more comprehensive understanding of evaluative source text reading strategies used in content-based academic reading.

References

Allen, S. (2003). An analytic comparison of three models of reading strategy instruction. *International Review of Applied Linguistics, 41,* 319–338.

Anderson, N, J. (2003). Metacognitive reading strategies increase L2 performance. *The Language Teacher, 27,* 20-22.

Bitchener, J. (2012). A reflection on the language learning potential of written CF. *Journal of Second Language Writing, 21,* 348–363.

Block, E. (1986). The comprehension strategies of second language readers. *TESOL Quarterly, 20,* 463–494.

Esmaeili, H. (2002). Integrated reading and writing tasks and ESL students' reading and writing performance in an English language test. *Canadian Modern Language Journal, 58,* 599–622.

Evans, S. (2008). Reading reaction journals in EAP courses. *ELT Journal, 62,* 240–247.

Field, J (2004). *Psycholinguistics: the Key Concepts,* London: Routledge.

Grabe, W. (2009). *Reading in a second language: Moving from theory to practice.* Cambridge: Cambridge University Press.

Grabe, W., & Zhang, C. (2013). Reading and writing together: A critical component of English for Academic Purposes teaching and learning. *TESOL Journal, 4,* 9 24.

Hijikata, Y., Nakanishi, Y., & Shimizu, M. (2013) Japanese EFL Students Reading Processes for Academic Papers. *Journal of Education and Learning, 2,* 70–83.

Hosenfeld, C. (1977). A preliminary investigation of the reading strategies of successful and nonsuccessful language learners. *System, 5,* 110–123.

Iwai, Y. (2011). The Effects of Metacognitive Reading Strategies: Pedagogical Implications for EFL/ESL Teachers. *Reading Matrix, 11,* 150-159.

Kintsch, W., & van Dijk, A. (1978). Toward a Model of Text Comprehension and Production, *Psychological Review 85,* 363–394.

Lau, K. L. (2006). Reading strategy use between Chinese good and poor readers: A think-aloud study. *Journal of Research in Reading, 29,* 383–399.

McGrath, L., Berggren, J., & Mezek, S. (2016). Reading EAP: Investigating high proficiency L2 university students' strategy use through reading blogs. *Journal of English for Academic Purposes, 22,* 152–164.

McCulloch, S. (2013). Investigating the reading-to-write processes and source use of L2 postgraduate students in real-life academic tasks: An exploratory study. *Journal of English for Academic Purposes, 12,* 136–147.

Oxford, R. (2011). *Teaching & Researching: Language Learning Strategies.* New York: Routledge.

Plakans, L. (2009). The role of reading strategies in integrated L2 writing tasks. *Journal of English for Academic Purposes, 8,* 252–266.

Plakans, L., & Gebril, A. (2012). A close investigation into source use in integrated second language writing tasks. *Assessing Writing, 17,* 18–34.

Pressley, M., & Afflerbach, P. (1995). *Verbal protocol of reading: The nature of constructively responsive reading.* Hillsdale, NJ, US: Lawrence Erlbaum Associates, Inc.

Singhal, M. (2001). Reading proficiency, reading strategies, metacognitive awareness, and L2 readers. *The Reading Matrix, 1*, 1–23.

Sternberg, R. (2012). Intelligence. *WIREs (Wiley Interdisciplinary Reviews) Cognitive Science, 3*, 501–511.

Swales, J. (1990). *Genre Analysis: English in academic and research settings.* Cambridge: Cambridge University Press.

Upton, T. (1997). First and second language use in reading comprehension strategies of Japanese ESL students. *Electronic Journal for English as a Second Language, 3*, 1–23.

Weir, C., & Khalifa, H. (2008). A cognitive processing approach towards defining reading comprehension. *Cambridge ESOL Research Notes,* 31, 2-10.

Zhang, L. J. (2001). Awareness in reading: EFL students' metacognitive knowledge of reading strategies in an acquisition-poor environment. *Language Awareness, 10,* 268–288.

Chapter 11

Investigating the system of TRANSITIVITY in passive *that-clauses* of research abstracts

Leonardo Pereira Nunes, Bárbara Malveira Orfanò

Federal University of Minas Gerais, Brazil

Abstract: This chapter investigates verbs within the system of TRANSITIVITY in passive *that-clauses* retrieved from research abstracts belonging to the Corpus of Academic English (*CorIFA*), a learner corpus being compiled at the Federal University of Minas Gerais, Brazil. By drawing on Systemic Functional Linguistics (Halliday & Matthiessen, 2014) and Corpus Linguistics methodologies, we compared linguistic data from such texts to elements in an English *Lingua Franca* reference corpus comprised of abstracts published in high-impact journals across various disciplines. Findings reveal higher frequencies of passive *that-clauses* with verbs realizing mental processes in *CorIFA*, indicating that learners linguistically convey a less conscious position regarding the phenomena observed when they structure passives. Investigating how these students use passive constructions in abstracts in comparison to a *Lingua Franca* corpus can yield interesting insights that shall improve the design of academic writing pedagogical materials for Brazilian graduate and undergraduate students.

Keywords: learner corpus, *Lingua Franca* corpus, research abstracts, system of TRANSITIVITY, passive *that-clauses*.

***

1. Introduction

As an area within the realm of English Language Teaching (ELT), English for Academic Purposes (EAP) has been a very relevant domain for research and language teaching within higher-level education in many countries around the globe (Hyland, 2006). Despite the fact that its scope is somewhat wide, it basically entails the teaching of English to aid learners with their university studies and academic research (Flowerdew & Peacock, 2001).

Since the greatest amount of scientific literature worldwide is produced in English (Benesch, 2001; Hyland, 2006), the ability to write academic English proficiently has become of utmost importance. This scenario includes Brazil, which is our research and teaching context.

In order to offer pedagogical subsidies in the teaching of Brazilian learners of academic English, the *Corpus of Academic English* (hereafter *CorIFA*) is being compiled by members of a learner corpus research group and EAP teachers/lecturers of the Federal University of Minas Gerais (UFMG).

CorIFA comprises a variety of academic texts produced by the university's graduate and undergraduate students from many academic fields of knowledge taking EAP subjects. Among the genres taught in the discipline are research abstracts. These texts are prominent in academia in general as they function as screening devices and previews for readers and reviewers (Swales & Feak, 2009).

In this work, we have conducted a corpus-driven quali-quantitative investigation of verbs in passive *that-clauses* in research abstracts taken from *CorIFA* in the light of the system of TRANSITIVITY within Hallidayan Systemic Functional Linguistics (SFL) (Halliday & Matthiessen, 2014). For such, we have compared the data retrieved from *CorIFA* with the same type of clauses found in an English *Lingua Franca* reference corpus comprising research abstracts taken from high-impact academic journals within the 'softer' and the 'harder' sciences.

The main contribution of this study is to provide insights as to how Brazilian tertiary students' interlanguage has an impact on passive constructions in research abstracts, and how this gathered knowledge could be applied in devising EAP teaching materials for such learners.

2. The system of TRANSITIVITY in SFL

From a systemic-functional perspective, a text "is a rich, many-faceted phenomenon" which can be explored from various standpoints (Halliday & Matthiessen, 2014, p. 3). The clause, being its main unit of analysis, can carry several types of meanings that are grammatically integrated.

Within the clause, one specific kind of meaning (representational) operates as shown in Table 11.1:

Table 11.1 Representational meaning within the clause [adapted from Halliday and Matthiessen (2014, p. 83)]

Metafunction	Clause as...	System	Structure
experiential	representation	TRANSITIVITY	Process + Participants + Circumstances

The experiential domain of texts entails how worldly events, or 'goings-on', are construed in the clauses, conveying representational meaning. Through the system of TRANSITIVITY, the clause grammatically structures the flow of events through the following elements: process, participants and circumstances.

Table 11.2 shows two instances of how the clause construes experiential meaning via these three elements in such a system:

Table 11.2 Examples of grammatical realizations within the system of TRANSITIVITY (adapted from Halliday and Matthiessen (2014, p. 225)

Clause	He	is living	up there now
	The fruiting rod	was replaced	-
Functions in the system of TRANSITIVITY	Participant	Process	Circumstance

According to the examples, verbs are the linguistic elements which realize processes within the clause, and therefore have been the sole feature of investigation in the system of TRANSITIVITY in this study. The next section covers how verbs realise different types of processes to construe several meanings within the clause.

2.1. Types of processes realised by verbs

In SFL, six processes construe experiential meanings. These processes are typologically displayed according to their similarities, as shown in Figure 11.1:

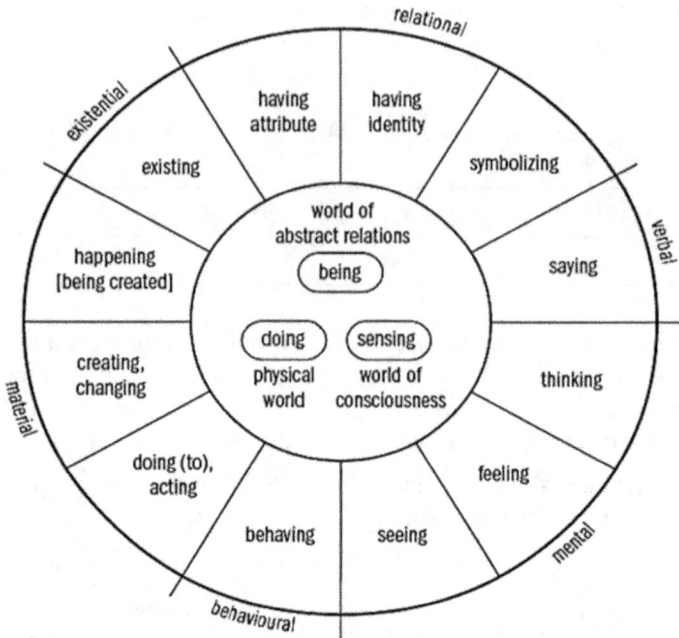

Figure 11.1 The grammar of experience: types of process in English[1]

As presented in Figure 11.1, not only is each one of the six processes (material, behavioural, mental, verbal, relational and existential) set apart according to their distinctive core semiotic nature but they are also spatially organised together based on their topological similarities.

Halliday and Matthiessen (2014, p. 214) state that there is a distinction within experiential meanings in that they either take place externally in the world or internally within the individuals. This is to say, on the one hand, that verbs basically construe outer experiences in *material* processes. On the other hand, they can build inner realities in *mental* processes.

As to the external meanings built around material processes, experiences can either be categorised and taxonomically related to one another by means of *relational* processes within the clause (Halliday & Matthiessen 2014, p. 214).

---

[1] From: Halliday's Introduction to Functional Grammar, M.A.K. Halliday & Christian M.I.M Matthiessen, Copyright © 2014 and Imprint. Reproduced by permission of Taylor & Francis Group. Reproduced with permission of the Licensor through PLSclear.

Also, a process can grammatically construe experience by means of attributing existence to a sole entity (or Participant), therefore being *existential*.

Regarding internal meanings, and at the boundaries around mental processes, experiences can be construed through verbs which either build interactions between sayer and addressee in *verbal* processes (Halliday & Matthiessen, 2014, p. 217) or which convey physiological and psychological states and actions in *behavioural* processes (Halliday & Matthiessen 2014, p. 301).

Table 11.3 shows examples of clauses taken from the English *Lingua Franca* corpus with verbs realizing each one of the six processes shown in Figure 11.1. Each example has been labelled with its corresponding academic field.

Table 11.3 Types of processes in instances taken from the English *Lingua Franca* corpus in several domains of knowledge

Process type	Example
Material	(…) we **conducted** new data collection during 3-year fieldwork in the Aripuanã River, where the species **was discovered**. [*Biology*]
Existential	There **has been** considerable effort to produce soft, flexible, and stretchable electronic skin (E-skin) devices. [*Physics*]
Relational	These results **suggested** that GSP had prostatic protective nature via regulating the androgen-MAPK/AKT-ICAM pathway. [*Chemistry*]
Verbal	The researchers **told** half of the participants that they would do a recall task after reading an English text; the rest **were** not **told** what the postreading task would involve. [*Applied Linguistics*]
Mental	Native English speakers **are thought** to have an advantage (…) while second language users must invest more time, effort and money into formally **learning** it. [*Applied Linguistics*]
Behavioural	If nestlings were to **defecate** when parents were absent, however, feces could accumulate in the nest. [*Biology*]

We can perceive that verbs realizing the two main outer and inner processes (material and mental) may either be in active or passive voice structures. As the aim of this study is to query verbs occurring in passive voice structures in two sub-corpora, verbs realizing processes in active voice structures have not been considered for investigation.

2.2. *That*-clauses in academic texts

Gray (2015, p. 11) advocates that *that*-clauses are "productive structures in academic prose" in that they are somehow thorough not only in presenting claims but also in carrying the writer's position. As to these types of clauses in verb-controlled passive constructions with the pronoun *it* as subjects, Charles (2006b) provides evidence of their wide use to report information in theses within the humanities and the sciences.

Similar to the latter study, this work has queried verbs in passive *that*-clauses with *it* as a pronoun. Nevertheless, as previously stated, the main academic genres hereto analysed are research abstracts produced by Brazilian learners of English from various academic backgrounds. These have been compared with texts of the same genre taken from articles published in scientific journals from several fields of knowledge.

Occurrences of verb types in clauses with such a structure have been investigated to somehow measure the extent to which these elements realize the six semiotic processes categorised in the system of TRANSITIVITY within a systemic-functional framework of language.

3. Corpus and methodology

This chapter presents a corpus-driven study relying on the results yielded from the data. As mentioned previously, the first, the Corpus of Academic English[2], is being compiled at the Federal University of Minas Gerais - Brazil. This corpus represents our learner data. The second, the English *Lingua Franca* corpus, is used as a reference *corpus* for this study. The main corpus comprises texts written by Brazilian undergraduate and graduate university students from different subject fields who are attending one of the five disciplines of English for Academic Purposes (EAP).

The disciplines are organized according to students' proficiency level ranging from B1 to C1 level (intermediate to advanced) according to the Common European Framework of Reference for Languages (CEFR). In each level, students learn a specific written academic genre: summary, statement of purpose, abstracts, essays, literature reviews, and research papers. Thus, *CorIFA* comprises the texts that are submitted by students taking EAP classes as part of their assignment[3]. Table 11.4 illustrates the genres that are contemplated in the learner data.

---

[2] *CorIFA* (2016) is coordinated by Professor Deise Prina Dutra under the Learner Corpus Research Project at the Faculty of Languages and Literature-UFMG. For more information about *CorIFA* check the website: https://sites.google.com/site/corpusifa/home. Viewed 5 January 2020.

[3] The texts included in the corpus have been authorized by students who signed a consent form agreeing to participate in the research project.

Table 11.4 Academic genres in CorIFA

Discipline	Proficiency level	Written genre
EAP 1	B1	Statement of Purpose/Summary
EAP 2	B1+	Abstract
EAP 3	B2	Essay
EAP 4	B2+	Literature review
EAP 5	C1	Research paper

The data is gathered using *Google Forms*. First, students fill in a form with personal and academic information (metadata) and sign a consent letter allowing their texts to be used for research purposes. After that, texts are extracted and saved as *.docx* to be further analysed by researchers. For this specific study, the files were uploaded on *Sketch Engine*, thus facilitating its comparison to the *Lingua Franca* corpus. At the present moment, *CorIFA* has approximately 530,000 words encompassing six sub-corpora related to different academic written genres. In this study, we use a sub-corpus of 78,000 words comprising the research abstracts written by this group of Brazilian learners.

The reference corpus called *English Lingua Franca* corpus consists of abstracts taken from journals belonging to three main areas: Life Sciences, Exact Sciences and Human Sciences.

The researchers consulted faculty members from the Federal University of Minas Gerais and identified the journals that this specific community consider relevant for their area and therefore submit their research papers. The texts come from high-impact journals in the disciplines of Physics, Chemistry, Biology and Applied Linguistics. For each discipline, we compiled a corpus of 54,000 words. The abstracts were copied from the journals, pasted in different documents and cleaned manually. After that, they were saved as .txt files and uploaded on *Sketch Engine* for analysis. At the present moment, the entire corpus has 215,351 words and it is compared to the main corpus throughout the analysis.

The analysis starts with the identification of passive *that-clauses* constructions with the pronoun *it* as a subject in the learner corpora. In this phase, we use the tools available in the *Sketch Engine*[4] website. It is important to

---

[4] Basically, the Sketch Engine website (2020) allows users to build, upload and search different corpora using its tools: concordance, wordlists, collocation lists and etc. For more information see the website: https://www.sketchengine.eu/. Viewed 5 January 2020.

note that the *Sketch Engine* can also be considered a platform with different corpus tools allowing researchers to analyse different linguistic phenomena. First, using the Corpus Query Tool (CQL) from Sketch Engine concordance lines were generated in order to analyse the occurrences of the passive constructions under scrutiny. Figure 11.2 shows the CQL used for this analysis.

[word="it"][tag="V.*"][tag="V.*"][word="that"]

Figure 11.2 CQL used in both corpora

The lines were analysed and the examples that did not correspond to it + passive *that*-clauses were excluded from the analysis. The CQL tool allowed us to identify the examples of passive constructions in the data as can be seen in Figures 11.3 and 11.4.

Then, the verbs that are used in combination with the passive *that*-clauses were identified and categorized according to the six semiotic processes within the SFL's system of TRANSITIVITY presented in section 2.1. This is to determine the most prevalent meanings construed in the abstracts written by learners in contrast with the ones found in the *Lingua Franca* corpus. These results have been compared and analysed having in mind how information is conveyed depending on the verbs used in each corpus.

Investigating the system of TRANSITIVITY 171

Figure 11.3 Set of concordance lines for passive *that*-clauses in the *CorIFA*

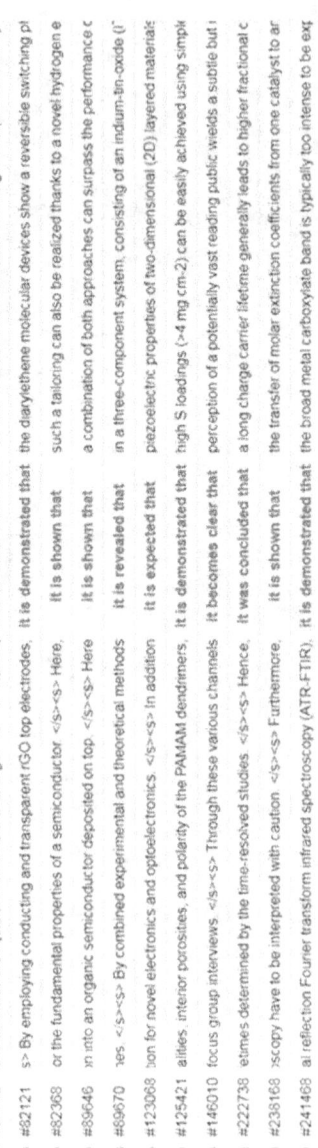

Figure 11.4 Set of concordance lines for the passive *that*-clauses in the English *Lingua Franca* corpus

4. Results and discussions

Figure 11.5 shows the statistics as to the types of processes found in the *CorIFA*:

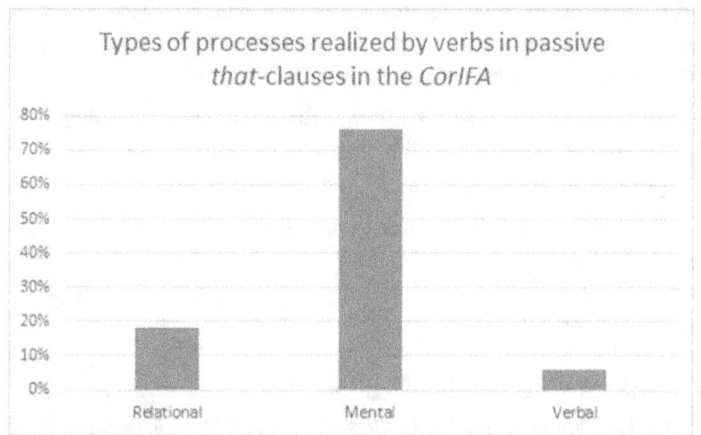

Figure 11.5 Types of processes realized by verbs in passive *that*-clauses in the *CorIFA*

At this initial stage of the analysis, we find that 76% of the occurrences in the passive constructions are made with verbs realizing mental process, 18% with verbs realizing relational processes and 6% realizing verbal processes. Table 11.5 shows the verbs that are used in each process type in the learner data.

Table 11.5 Verbs realizing processes in passive *that*-clauses in *CorIFA*

Process type	Verbs
Relational	Show demonstrate
Mental	observe verify assume conclude notice evaluate
Verbal	Argue

By observing Figure 11.5 and Table 11.5 we can argue that verbs realizing mental processes in passive constructions are significantly more frequent in *CorIFA*, which might be an indication that this group of learners when writing their abstracts make use of linguistic features that keep the author distant from the propositions present in their research. This entails the fact that their findings, instead of being more closely thought about and reflected upon by the author through his/her inner experiences, are merely described or reported through outer experiences. This is because the use of the passive in the structures under investigation (it + *that*-clauses with verbs realizing mental processes) allows the writer to delete the conscious agent and thus remain distant from the findings they discuss.

The verbs *observe, verify* and *notice* are the most used verbs by learners. The three verbs are cognates in Brazilian Portuguese, which might be an indication that this group is still relying on their L1 when writing texts in English.

Below is a concordance line with a verb realizing a mental process in *CorIFA*:

Extract 1 - Instance of verb realizing mental process in passive *that*-clauses in *CorIFA*

*In Functional Magnetic Resonance Imaging **it was observed that**, with cannabis prenatal exposition, it happened a significant increase in the neural activity in the bilateral prefrontal cortex and right premotor cortex. </s>*

In this example, we have the writer omitting the conscious subject(s) by using the pronoun (*it*) followed by a verb realizing a mental process (*was observed*), therefore conveying a less active position in the investigation of the phenomenon. This might indicate a weaker sense of authorship for certain academic communities.

Figure 11.6 shows the statistics as to the types of processes found in the English *Lingua Franca* corpus:

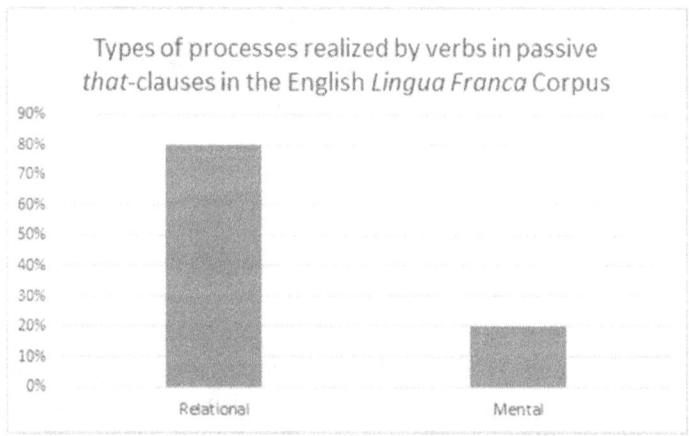

Figure 11.6 Types of processes realized by verbs in passive that-clauses in the English *Lingua Franca* corpus

We find that 80% of the occurrences of verbs in the passive it + *that*-clauses realize relational processes and 20% realize mental processes. Table 11.6 shows verbs that are used in each process type in the reference corpus data.

Table 11.6 Verbs realizing processes in passive *that*-clauses in the English *Lingua Franca* corpus

Process type	Verbs
Relational	show demonstrate reveal
Mental	expect conclude

Contrary to the data retrieved from *CorIFA*, the occurrences of verbs realizing mental processes in the reference corpus are significantly surpassed by verbs realizing relational processes. This shows that scholars who are proficient in academic English and thus write research abstracts which are accredited by their peers make wider use of linguistic elements in passive structures to associate facts and highlight features (see Figure 11.1 for *having attribute*) rather than reflect and discuss phenomena (see Figure 11.1 for *thinking*). This may be an indication that such researchers are more actively conscious of the object of study they investigate, and therefore show more intellectual authority by making less use of verbs realizing mental processes in passive *that*-clauses.

Below is an extract of a verb realizing a material process in the English *Lingua Franca* corpus:

Extract 2 - Concordance line with verb realizing material process in passive *that*-clauses in the English *Lingua Franca* corpus

Utilizing the high degree of surface functionalities, interior porosities, and polarity of the PAMAM dendrimers, **it is demonstrated that** *high S loadings (>4 mg cm-2) can be easily achieved using simple processing methods. </s>*

In this clause, we have the writer relating two propositions (method and result) by using the pronoun (*it*) followed by a verb realizing a relational process (*is demonstrated*), therefore showing the ability to associate propositions.

5. Conclusions

This chapter has discussed passive *that*-clauses retrieved from abstracts written by a group of *EAP* Brazilian students and from abstracts written by academic English proficient scholars. Relying on the backdrop of research on the system of TRANSITIVITY within Hallidayan Systemic Functional Linguistics (SFL), we observed how information is conveyed depending on the verbs used within passive structures.

The results indicate that in *CorIFA* verbs realizing mental processes (*observe, verify, assume, conclude, notice and evaluate*) are more prevalent than in the English *Lingua Franca* corpus. It strongly suggests that this group of learners, when writing their abstracts, organize their discourse using passive structures in combination with verbs that convey a less active position about the phenomenon under investigation in their research. This indicates that this group seems to be unaware of the linguistic resources available and how they can be used for creating authorship in academic writing.

The English *Lingua Franca* corpus, on the other hand, presents a different framework towards the use of verbs in the passive *that*-clauses. Verbs from the relational domain are more prevalent in this corpus (*show, demonstrate* and *reveal*). When explaining their research in academic abstracts, scholars tend to organize their argument by making associations between different facts related to their research. This skill allows writers to engage with their readers in a more convincing way, giving their research more credibility.

In terms of how the results can yield benefits to the classroom, one can claim that usually teachers focus more on teaching the structure of the passive. However, as the results demonstrate in the analysis section, accuracy alone will not entirely fulfil the requirements of a good academic abstract. Being able to highlight and report the results of any research using 200 words is not an easy task and requires specific writing skills that go beyond grammar rules. In this sense, when dealing with passive structures in academic texts, EAP teachers need to bear in mind that it is also necessary to incorporate the underlying meaning construed by verbs used in combination with the passive construction in their classes. This knowledge will provide specific linguistic support to EAP students who wish to convey a message that complies with the expectations of their respective academic peers. The results can subsidize teachers in preparing their classes, choosing and designing EAP materials, therefore providing Brazilian learners of English better chances in participating in a more globalized academic community.

References

Benesch, S. (2001). *Critical English for Academic Purposes*. Mahwah, NJ: Erlbaum.

Charles, M. (2006b). The construction of stance in reporting clauses: A Cross-disciplinary Study of Theses. *Applied Linguistics* [online] **27**(3), 492–518. [Viewed 4 January 2020]. Available from: doi: 10.1093/applin/aml021

CorIFA. (2016). CorIFA: Inglês para Fins Acadêmicos / UFMG [Corpus of Academic English: English for Academic Purposes / Federal University of Minas Gerais]. [online]. *CorIFA*. [Viewed 5 January 2020]. Available from: https://sites.google.com/site/corpusifa/home

Flowerdew, J. and Peacock, M. (2001). Issues in EAP: A preliminary perspective. In J. Flowerdew, and M. Peacock. (Eds). *Research perspectives on English for Academic purposes*. pp. 8-24. Cambridge and New York: Cambridge University Press.

Gray, B., (2015). *Linguistic Variation in Research Articles: When Discipline only Tells Part of the Story*. Amsterdam: John Benjamins.

Halliday, M.A.K. and Matthiessen, C.M.I.M., (2014). 4th ed. *Halliday's Introduction to Functional Grammar*. London: Routledge.

Hyland, K. (2006). *English for academic purposes: an advanced resource book*. London: Routledge.

Sketch Engine. (2020). Learn how language works [online]. *Sketch Engine*. [Viewed 5 January 2020]. Available from: https://www.sketchengine.eu/

Swales, J. M. and Feak, C. B. (2009). *Abstracts and the writing of abstracts*. Ann Arbor MI.: The University of Michigan Press.

Chapter 12

Designing research for academic writing in the field of psychology

Joanna Moraza Erausquin

Universidad Nacional de Educación a Distancia (UNED)

Abstract: The teaching and learning of languages for specific purposes is a discipline that usually involves writing professional texts and many applications have been developed in the last few years to make this process easier. This paper focuses on the writing of specific texts in the practice of the Psychology discipline. It examines some qualitative and quantitative methodologies in order to identify the most challenging texts for professionals so that students can work with real templates. The first results show a series of difficulties that psychologists must face when writing common and more difficult texts. A number of linguistic features are analysed since they occur frequently in the pieces of text under discussion. Considering these characteristics, students are guided in the writing of professional texts. The templates will be available in both Spanish and English, so that students may contrast both types of texts providing that each language may exhibit different linguistic options. Furthermore, they can also serve for teachers as materials in bilingual programs in the degree of Psychology.

Keywords: English for specific purposes, writing specific texts, Linguistics, Psychology.

***

1. Introduction

The learning and teaching of languages for specific purposes is nowadays an increasing discipline, although there has been very little in research until recently (Douglas, 2000). Following Kaplan (2011), English is one of the most relevant languages used for specific purposes (mostly in science and technology). This is in partly due to the consequences of World War Two, where most of the American infrastructure was spread over other countries. Consequently, the United States of America (USA) obtained the leadership in research and science and most of the information, papers or documents were written in English (Kaplan, 2011). This also explains why English has been called the international language for scientific expertise (Wood, 2001).

Over the last few years, the use of the English *language in scientific* research papers has become more and more prevalent. As a language of science, the English language allows scientists to communicate between themselves but also to describe different phenomena among the scientific community in a more formal way. For this purpose, scientists try to use the most objective and efficient way to explain the appearance, characteristics and function of the phenomena (Reeves, 2005). The language of science, as well as other specific languages, has its own features that correspond to certain terminology using abstract words, technical and scientific taxonomies, and complex syntax structures, ranging from passive sentences to intricate embedded sentences (Li and Li, 2015). These particular features of scientific language may be found in a range of fields like politics, law, physics, social sciences, and others where an academic register is required.

Considering linguistic variety in different fields, language for specific purposes (LSP) could be defined as a discipline that requires teaching and learning of these variations through a particular domain, or through linguistic variants of professional settings (Gunnarsson, 1997).

The acquisition of a specific language also demands further communication skills training. Writing is usually considered the most difficult skill to acquire due to its additional requirements to use (specific vocabulary, a style-sheet and formal language). Findings in previous studies such as in Barker (2000) suggest that, in effect, students have some difficulty with writing in academic English since it requires a generic structure, some intellectual content, surface-level features and access to the feedback they may receive from senior lecturers. Furthermore, writing scientific manuscripts requires a very high cognitive burden. There were some problems in distinguishing the content as well as the formal structure or the backward design of the manuscript (Shah et al., 2009). Although most approaches to teaching writing for specific purposes do not take the subject of formal structure into account, some approaches do so such as the product-oriented approach, the process-oriented approach, the genre-oriented approach and the creative-oriented approach.

To support academic writing learning, many experts in the field have designed textbooks to provide students with both materials and tasks that are oriented to write academic pieces of text. To illustrate, the APA style Manual 7th edition, created by the American Psychological Association (APA from now onwards), has just been launched and it is one of the most prestigious, rigorous and important manuals used by researchers, students and professionals all over the world. This manual addresses issues like scholar writing and publishing principles, elements and format in papers, journal article reporting standards, grammar and style, tables and figures, apart from their well- known reference style.

Following León's (2005) manual, there are also some tips for scientific and academic writing considering the previous APA advice. The author emphasizes the hierarchical structure of different types of writings, such as PhD dissertations, final master papers, assessment questionnaires and research articles in both Psychology and Education fields. A hierarchical study is included explaining, step by step, the whole process of attending structural features. León also emphasises the need of a periodical revisions before papers being submitted, recommending checking at least one per day, until reaching a final review.

These textbooks are just some examples of many existing materials available for the learning audience. Nowadays, nearly every university has its own writing guidebook or handbook in order to guide their students through this path. Immersed as we are in the digital era, applications for automatic writing have emerged to respond to this challenge.

The *arText* program (Sistema-artext.com, 2015) was born a few years ago for this purpose. This application has a variety of templates in the fields of public administration, medicine and tourism. Each template counts with the specific structure, phraseology and in general the linguistic features of several specific texts concerning each domain.

Even though in the last few years the research conducted in this field blossomed and many manuals and applications were produced. Yet, there is still a need to continue conducting research on this topic. The main aim of this paper is to share the first results of an on-going study that combines applied linguistics with specific text writing in the field of Psychology. Based on the results of the study presented here and after a linguistic analysis of the specific features of the most common pieces of texts in the field of Psychology, some templates will be implemented in the next few years the *arText* system.

2. Method

For the creation of the templates that will help with the writing of some of the most difficult and challenging texts in Psychology, some quantitative and qualitative methodology have been pursued.

In the initial stage, teachers, professionals, and students in the degree of Psychology were contacted in order to gather information about the types of texts that are more usually found in the teaching and practice of the Psychology discipline. In particular, they were asked to complete some questionnaires: a quantitative questionnaire and a qualitative questionnaire.

A qualitative questionnaire was submitted to the consideration of nine participants who came from different learning settings in the field of Psychology; Three university professors, two graduate students and four professionals. The information gathered by this study together with the bibliography collected served to define a second quantitative questionnaire delivered in the next stage. Then, a larger number of participants were asked to complete it. In particular, the sample was collected from university and official colleges which were contacted through a psychologists' directory. Regarding the inclusion criteria, participants had to be related to the field of Psychology at the moment of answering the questionnaire.

The second quantitative questionnaire was sent to those who agreed to participate in the study in an anonymous fashion. This questionnaire sample was finally completed by 76 participants who also included personal information concerning the following domains:

- Level of education
- Nationality
- Area of specialisation

2.1. Questionnaires

The first qualitative questionnaire mainly consisted of the following three multiple-choice questions:

1. Which of the following texts related to psychology do you usually write?
2. In your opinion, which are the most difficult ones to be written?
3. From the above difficulties, which are the ones you have found or dealt with?

The second quantitative questionnaire included the types of texts and the types of difficulties that, according to references, are more common when writing. Participants had to score them in a ranking from the most to the least difficult text or difficult task when writing academic texts in the field of Psychology.

3. Results

In what follows, results obtained by both questionnaires are examined in turn. In the first place, results obtained with the qualitative test by participants were examined. Then, the information gathered in the second quantitative test was examined according to participants' answers regarding their difficulties.

Results I: Qualitative Questionnaire

Considering the findings in the first questionnaire, the type of texts written by teachers, students and professionals, were not the same. For this reason, slightly different questions were included. In particular, regarding teachers' questions, there were ten questions for teachers whereas the questionnaire for students and professionals only included nine questions. Once the first questionnaire was completed, the first results were examined. They led to some conclusions and supported some claims about academic writing training, which were taken into account to design the second questionnaire.

The information gathered from the first qualitative questionnaire is illustrated in the following two tables. Table 12.1 consists of the summarised answers by university teachers whilst Table 12.2 includes the answers obtained from students and professionals. In order to preserve the participants' identity, numbers are used.

Table 12.1 Qualitative questionnaire (University teachers' answers)

Questions	1	2	3
1. What kind of psychology-related texts do you write or read daily/more frequently?	Journal articles	Papers, abstracts, blogs	Books
2. Which are the most relevant texts for you in the field of psychology (example. articles, reports, etc.)?	Journal articles	Papers	The academic text (book) The scientific paper Poster to congress Communication to congress Clinical report Disclosure paper The self-help book Degree and Master final assessment The doctoral dissertation

3. Any magazine/manual or publication media you can mention? And in Spanish?	Cognition, Cognitive Science, Behavioural and Brain Sciences, Journal of Memory and Cognition, etc. The only ones I know in Spanish are from my country, Chile: Onomázein and Revista Signos	Standard cognitive journals. The Conversation. Several blogs around research methods (e.g., Andrew Gellman). Nothing in Spanish, sadly	APA Publications Manual, 6th ed.
4. Do you know if they are written by psychologists or by professionals from other fields (example. medicine)?	Mostly by psychologists, linguists, and cognitive scientists	Mostly by psychologists. Andrew Gellman is a statistician, primarily	Mostly by psychologists.
5. In your opinion, which are the most difficult to write? Why? What difficulties do they entail?	Papers. They deal with complex topics and you need to follow a logical chain of arguments, plus the formal requirements of structure and length.	Papers can be hard to write because of length restrictions or formal requirements	Research papers. The reason is that they must follow very strictly to the formatting rules of the APA 6º
6. Do you use any help (dictionary/ manual/editor/ corrector) when writing texts?	Not really	I write in RMarkdown or LaTeX where possible (or Google docs if collaborating)	Dictionaries, APA Manual, How to write scientific texts (León, 2015), Spanish Dictionary of Doubts (Seco)
7. Based on the texts you daily read, which are the texts presenting more mistakes? And what errors would you highlight?	They don't usually have any mistakes in that sense of the word. You might criticise their methods, but those are not 'mistakes'	Statistical errors in published papers	Students' degree final assessments. There are so many errors. Lack of clarity, conciseness, hierarchy in the text, etc.
8. Are there any guides dedicated to the writing of texts?	I know of a couple of books on academic writing, and there's also workshops and courses	There must be, but I haven't read them	Yes (León, 2015)
9. Which kind of texts do usually students write?	Essays	A huge variety	Degree and Master final assessments, internship reports.
10. Which kind of texts should psychology students know how to write because of their relevance?	Essays, to move from there to articles	Papers first and foremost. Popular science too	Students should write neat, clear, concise and according to APA 6 rules

Table 12.2 Qualitative questionnaire (Students and professionals' answers)

Questions	1	2	3	4	5	6
1. What kind of psychology-related texts do you write or read daily/more frequently?	Research papers and some chronics such as Psychology Today	Texts related to clinical psychology	Texts related to educational needs: high capacities, hyperactive, etc.	Research papers and thematic handbooks or manuals	Texts related to psychotherapy with gender-based violence	Papers and books, both research and disclosure
2. Which are the most relevant texts for you in the field of psychology (example. papers, reports, etc.)?	No answer	Research papers	Papers related to emotions or daily news	Research papers and thematic handbooks or manuals	There are many of them	All of them
3. Any magazine/manual or publication media you can mention? And in Spanish?	I could mention only the ones in English	Databases such as Psycinfo or Psicodoc	Journal such as Convive, Papeles del psicólogo, DSM V	El error de Descartes	The ones published by the Official College of Psychologists or Mosaico journal	There are many. According to my specialisation those include both psychology and linguistics journals and books
4. Do you know if they are written by psychologists or by professionals from other fields (example. medicine)?	Mostly by psychologists but also by sociologists and psychiatrists	They are very reliable sources of information as they are written by professionals, go through a committee and are validated by professionals in the field of psychology.	In general by psychologists in collaboration with other professionals	They are usually written by psychologists, psychiatrists, neurologists, etc. In the case of El error de Descartes the author is a neuroscientist Antonio Damasio.	As far as I know they are written by psychologists	They are written by psychologists, philosophers, linguists, anthropologists and neuroscientists

5. In your opinion, which are the most difficult to write? Why? What difficulties do they entail?	All of them have their difficulties	PhD dissertations for their difficulties	DSMV because its lack of consensus	No answer	I don't know, I have never published	Specialized articles have the difficulty of reviewing and knowing the literature well before starting to write, in addition to tell the story clearly and simply. Outreach papers have the difficulty of getting down to the level of the general public and making them motivating
6. Do you use any help (dictionary/ manual/ editor/corre ctor) when writing texts?	I type in English and I sometimes use an online dictionary or the laptop corrector	For translations I use Google translator, but after you need to correct it because it is not very precise	Yes	Yes, online	I have never publishe d so until know I don´t use anything	Apart from the Spanish-English dictionary, no.
7. Based on the texts you daily read, which are the texts presenting more mistakes? And what errors would you highlight?	I only read research papers and I found no mistakes	The texts that appear in Google are not reliable. It is necessary consulting reliable databases	I detect very few mistakes	Some manuals, they are not updated enough	I would need more time to answer this question	Of the ones published, no. But in my students'; of course (as they are learning). In fact, part of my subject is a Scientific Writing Workshop where I teach them how to write better

8. Are there any guides dedicated to the writing of texts?	No answer	No idea	Yes, online, I use their suggestions	Yes	No idea	We use several chapters of the Student Handbook of the School of Psychology
9. In your opinion, which kind of texts you must know to write?	It depends on the speciality. For psychotherapists clinical reports, for researchers research papers and for teachers handbooks.	Research papers	Reports, papers or meeting scripts	Reports, papers or text reports	I should know how to write psychological reports on gender-based victims and papers related to this topic.	The ones I mostly write. Both research and outreach papers and books

Looking at Tables 12.1 and 12.2 above, some contrasting answers emerge. First of all, mainly psychologists chose texts related to the psychological area as the most difficult ones since they could have been written by experts in the medicine field or similar areas. According to the answers provided by the teachers that participated in the study, the texts that presented most writing difficulties were academic papers. However, other questioned participants registered other different answers. In general, most participants admitted using several ways to help themselves to write academic texts correctly.

Results II: Quantitative Questionnaires

Above all, the information obtained in the first stage of the study helped to elaborate the quantitative questionnaire submitted in the second stage, which mainly consisted of the following three multiple-choice questions, already mentioned above, but repeated here for convenience:

1. Which of the following texts related to psychology do you usually write?

2. In your opinion, which are the most difficult ones to be written?

3. From the above difficulties, which are the ones you have found or dealt with?

The first results show that there are two distinct domains to be taken into account, the professional field and the academic field. In Figure 12.1 results of questions one and two are compared in the professional field. Instead, in Figure 12.2 the results for the academic field can be observed.

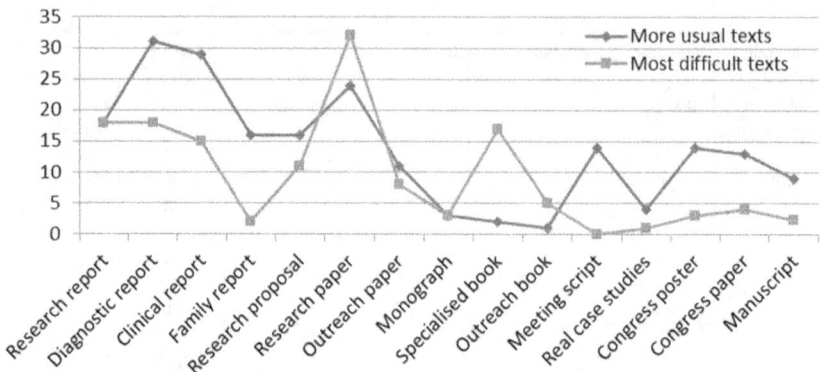

Figure 12.1 Quantitative questionnaires results (Professional Field)

As illustrated by Figure 12.1, the five most usual texts rendered in the professional field were the diagnostic report (40, 8%), the clinical report (38,2%), the research paper (31,6%), the research report (23,7%) and the family report and research proposal (both of them 21,1%). On the other hand, the five texts that were considered more difficult to write were: the research paper (42, 1%), the research report (23, 7%), the diagnostic report (23, 7%), the specialised book (22,4%) and the clinical report (19,7%).

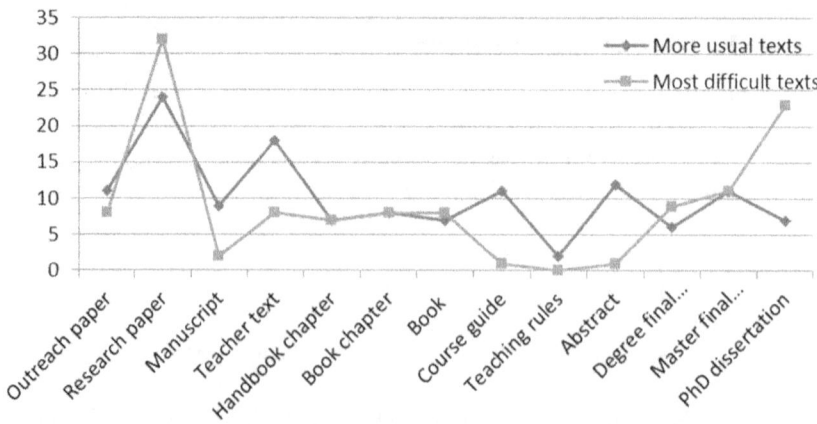

Figure 12.2 Quantitative questionnaires results (Academic Field)

In contrast to Figure 12.2, Figure 12.2 illustrates that the five more common texts found in the academic field were the research paper (31, 6%) that matches with the most difficult one too (42, 1%), followed by teacher's text (23, 7%), the abstract (15, 8%), the outreach paper (14, 5%) and degree final assessment (14, 5%). Furthermore, the five most difficult ones, apart from the research paper (42, 1%) mentioned before were the PhD dissertation (30, 3%), the master final assessment (14, 5%), the degree final assessment (11, 8%) and the teacher's text (10, 5%). Finally, Figure 12.3 depicts the result of the whole sample (n=76) including all answers in a more general score figure.

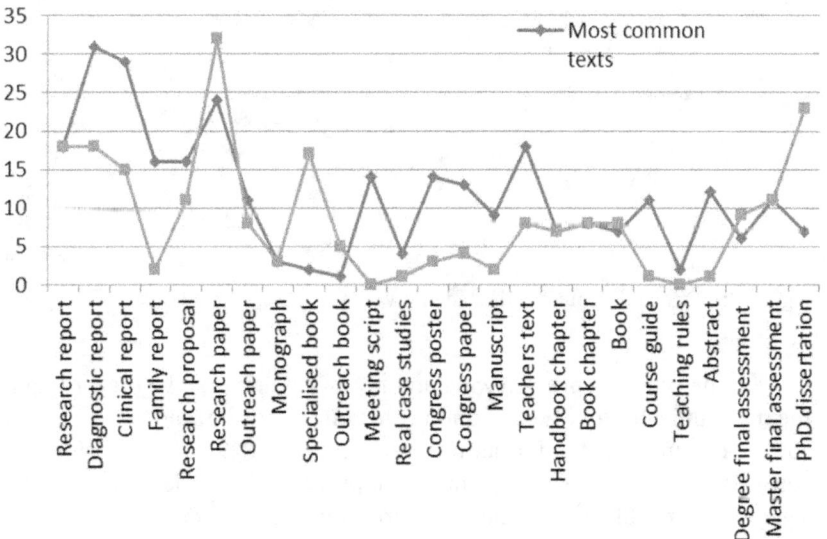

Figure 12.3 Quantitative questionnaire (Results Collapsed)

According to Figure 12.3 above, the five texts rendered as the most common ones in the field of Psychology were the diagnostic report (40, 8%), the clinical report (38, 2%), the research paper (31, 6%) and, finally, the research report and the teacher's text (23, 7%, each).

On the other hand, those results did not match with the texts that were found to be more difficult. Note that the texts that were considered more difficult to write were: the research paper (42, 1%), the PhD dissertation (30, 3%), the diagnostic report and the research report (23, 7%, each) and the specialised book (22, 4%). As a result, this second questionnaire has brought to light a series of difficulties concerning the writing of texts in Psychology, which should be considered in the training of academic writing and in ESP.

In the quantitative questionnaire, participants were also asked to render their view about the type of difficulties they may find when writing academic texts. Figure 12.4 below illustrates these difficulties. They are ordered from the most to the least difficult aspects according to participants' answers.

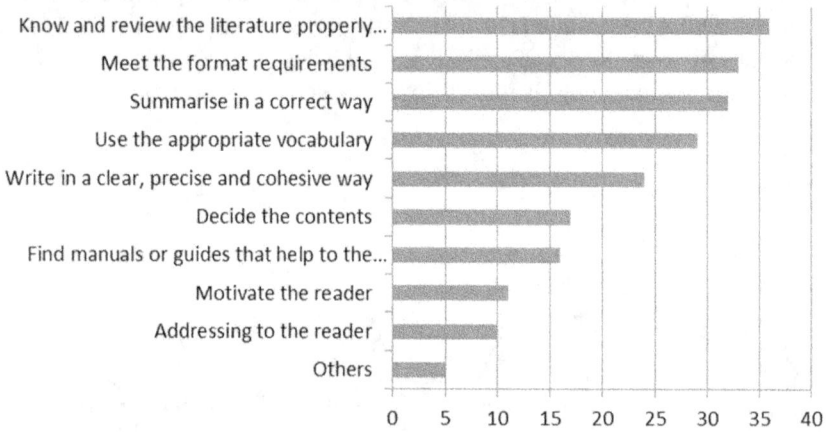

Figure 12.4 Difficulties found with academic writing

Given the scores above, knowing and reviewing literature before writing is the most difficult step when attempting to write a specific academic text (over 35%). Next, meeting the format requirements (over 32%), summarising in a correct way (over 31%), and using the appropriate vocabulary (above 27%) were the more difficulties found when writing academic texts.

4. Discussion

The present chapter shows the first results of a study that has combined both quantitative and qualitative methodology in order to get a basis for the creation of templates that may help to solve some of the difficulties above mentioned.

Reading and reviewing bibliography are a must to reach the level of accuracy that requires this type of specific writing. Most of the people already know about the topic they want to write about, but finding, reading and quoting specialised sources on the subject will give essays more rigour.

Meeting the format demands is, as the results have displayed, is not an easy task even for the most experienced researchers and professionals. Every journal or publication medium has its own particularities when accepting and publishing different papers, monographs, reports or another kind of documents. Reading and being aware of those specificities are essential before drafting our text. As mentioned before, many are the universities and teachers that have created their own manuals to give a response for some difficulties people have to face when writing these types of texts. Following Flowerdew and Costley (2016), some steps need to be taken when preparing academic writing to meet common challenges: i) selecting relevant bibliography, ii) reading teachers' materials to understand the sources, iii) taking notes from lectures or texts; iv) drafting topics and questions to practice the development of academic arguments; and, v) summarising and evaluating the sources.

Properly summarising is another task to be considered. According to Hahn and Mani (2000), a summary may imply an abstraction of key words from one or more information sources. The analysis of the source text allows to, discriminate the important points of a text and to synthesize the output (Hahn and Mani, 2000). Skimming the text to quickly get a general idea of meaning, together with scanning, to find specific information may also be very helpful. In addition, another effective strategy includes examining paragraphs and passages to avoid looking at individual sentences. In this way, one may identify cue phrases, like titles and headings, or discourse connectors as relevant information using standard sentence patterns (Mani, 2001).

As mentioned before, there are different publishing formats and one needs to suit them by using an appropriate vocabulary or by writing in a cohesive and clear way, which may be a challenge for novice writers. Lexical features are also essential for each type of text. Hence, learning specific vocabulary is required as much as highlighting some relevant ideas, in order to make a draft, one can also use some standard formulas to make the text coherent on the same grounds.

As for contents, some aspects will have to be previously analysed, such as the targeted audience, the medium of appearance and the author´s objectives. If there is an existing format, the contents will be subjected to this format. As an example, taking a look into the structure of a research paper the author will need to write an abstract, an introduction, the description of the method used or proposition of a theory, the results and a discussion of those results, as well as quoting and references (Monippally and Pawar, 2008).

Although these first results reflect a pattern in which are the most difficult texts in Psychology, and the difficulties perceived by the sample, some limitations have been found so far. On one hand, the results of the first qualitative questionnaire show that some questions were not clear enough for some participants on the sample. As a consequence, these questions were not answered and a more concise questionnaire should be submitted in future studies. On the other hand, the only criteria used when selecting the sample on the quantitative phase, was to be related with the domain under study.

This means that the sample was very asymmetrical in the years of experience in the field or the specialisation area of the participants.

These limitations together with the conclusions gathered, lead us to think that future studies are necessary in order to continue obtaining advantageous discoveries in the language for specific purposes domain. Even if some manuals and automatic writing applications are already created to provide guidelines and help writers, more research for implementing and updating them is completely necessary given the results. The creation of templates in new fields such as Psychology or similar, could be a way to improve these tools, but there is still a long way to run.

Finally, taking into account the results provided by the previous samples, some of the most challenging texts will be selected and analysed, considering a number of linguistic features in three main domains or spheres: textual sphere, lexical sphere and discursive sphere. The analysis of each sphere was carried out considering different linguistic theories such as Macrostructures theory (van Dijk, 1980), Communicative Theory of Terminology (Cabré, 1999) and Rhetorical Structure Theory (Mann and Thompson, 1987).

References

Barker, G. (2000). *Barker, 2000 First year students' perceptions of writing difficulties in science "I didn't expect it to be so different to school"*. Department of Communication, Language and Cultural studies. Victoria University.

Cabré, M. (1999). *La terminología: representación y comunicación elementos para una teoría de base comunicativa y otros artículos*. Barcelona: Universitat Pompeu Fabra Institut Universitari de Lingüística Aplicada.

Douglas, D. (2000). *Assessing Languages for Specific Purposes Cambridge language assessment series The Cambridge applied linguistics series*. Ernst Klett Sprachen, pp.4-5.

Flowerdew, J. and Costley, T. (2016). *Discipline-specific writing*. Routledge.

Gunnarsson, B. (1997). *LANGUAGE FOR SPECIAL PURPOSES Encyclopedia of Language and Education, Volume 4: Second Language Education*, G.R. Tucker and D. Corson Kluwer Academic Publishers. pp.105-117.

Hahn, U. and Mani, I. (2000). *The Challenges of Automatic Summarization*. [PDF] Available at: https://www.researchgate.net/publication/2955348 [Accessed 11 Jan. 2020].

Kaplan, R. (2011). *The Dominance of English as a Language of Science: Effects on Other Languages and Language Communities Volumen 84 de Contributions to the Sociology of Language [CSL]*. Ulrich Ammon, Walter de Gruyter, pp.3-19.

León, O. (2005). *Cmo Redactar Textos Cientficos En Psicologa y Educacin Catálogo General Ciencias Sociales Y Juridicas*. Netbiblo.

Li, X. and Li, L. (2015). *Characteristics of English for Science and Technology*. Proceedings of the 2015 International Conference on Humanities and Social Science Research.

Mani, I. (2001). *Automatic Summarization*. John Benjamins Publishing, p.33.

Mann, W. and Thompson, S. (1987). *Rhetorical Structure Theory: A theory of text organization. Reprinted from The Structure Discourse.* [ebook] Marina del Rey. California. Available at: https://www.sfu.ca/rst/05bibliographies/bibs/ISI_RS_87_190.pdf [Accessed 12 Jan. 2020].

Monippally, M. and Pawar, B. (2008). *Academic Writing: A Guide for Management Students and Researchers Response Books.* SAGE Publications India, pp.34-42. https://apastyle.apa.org. (2020). *Publication Manual of the American Psychological Association, Seventh Edition (2020).* [online] Available at: https://apastyle.apa.org/products/publication-manual-7th-edition/ [Accessed 9 Jan. 2020].

Reeves, C. (2005). *The Language of Science Intertext (London) Intertext (London), England) Intertext - Routledge Intertext Series.* Psychology Press.

Shah, J., Shah, A. and Pietrobon, R. (2009). *Scientific Writing of Novice Researchers: What Difficulties and Encouragements Do They Encounter?.* HHS Public Access.

Sistema-artext.com. (2015). *arText - un sistema de ayuda a la redacción de textos en español de ámbitos especializados.* [online] Available at: http://sistema-artext.com/#about [Accessed 10 Jan. 2020].

Van Dijk, T. (1980). *MACROSTRUCTURES An Interdisciplinary Study of Global Structures in Discourse, Interaction, and Cognition.* [PDF] Hillsdale, New Jersey: LAWRENCE ERLBAUM ASSOCIATES, PUBLISHERS. Available at: http://www.discourses.org/OldBooks/Teun%20A%20van%20Dijk%20-%20Macrostructures.pdf [Accessed 12 Jan. 2020].

Wood, A. (2001). *Research Perspectives on English for Academic Purposes Cambridge Applied Linguistics.* Matthew Peacock, John Flowerdew, Cambridge University Press, pp.8-25.

Chapter 13

Lexical hedging and boosting strategies in the abstracts written by undergraduate ELT students

Arzu Ekoç

Yildiz University, Turkey

Abstract: No matter what piece of writing it is, showing some degree of certainty/uncertainty is inevitable. In this sense, hedges are used to detach oneself from commitment to the proposition in order to decrease possible criticisms while boosters are used to increase commitment to the proposition. There is a growing interest in these interactional metadiscourse markers and in the reviewed literature, hedging and boosting strategies of academics, researchers and postgraduate students have been under great scrutiny. However, teaching hedging and boosting strategies to undergraduate students is the issue which relatively gets less attention. Also, writing a good abstract is very important for university students as submission of an abstract is an academic requirement for conference presentations, articles, book chapters and so on. The aim of this study is to underpin the use of lexical hedging and boosting strategies in undergraduate ELT students' abstracts. They were targeted because they were prospective teachers of English so they would teach their students the conventions of second/foreign language writing in the future and have the potential to continue their postgraduate degrees or attend conferences. ELT students in their sophomore year in the academic year of 2017-2018 were asked to write abstracts that summarize their presentations and submit them to their lecturer before they had their presentation as part of Oral Expression and Public Speaking course. 25 abstracts were chosen randomly and the frequency count of occurrence of lexical hedging and boosting strategies across all of the data was determined manually. Hyland's (2000b) categorization of hedges was used and the categories were expanded to include some items such as passives and personal pronouns that were not included in the list. From the results of this study, it can be suggested that students utilized hedging and boosting degrees to a certain extent but it is also evident that interactional metadiscourse markers need to be included in undergraduate writing lessons to show students, as novice writers, how to tone down their statements and reduce the risk of opposition or strengthen their claims.

Keywords: hedges, boosters, metadiscourse, undergraduate students, writing

***

1. Introduction

Writing is considered as a challenging skill to master in L2 language, even in L1 language as "in order to fulfil their goals writers need to carefully choose among the available metadiscoursive tools and skilfully balance their use" (Hatipoğlu and Algı, 2018, p. 957). No matter how experienced writers are or what piece of texts they are writing, writers need to tone down their risky propositions and refrain from criticism or show their certainty and put their emphasis while conveying their attitudes to readers. These devices are known as hedges and boosters. In Hyland's (2000a) terms:

> Hedges such as *might, probably* and *seem* signal a tentative assessment of referential information and convey collegial respect for the views of colleagues. Boosters like *clearly, obviously* and *of course* allow writers to express conviction and to mark their involvement and solidarity with an audience (p. 179).

These devices are useful to balance conviction with caution. As Hatipoğlu and Algı (2018, p. 958) underline "L2 writers often struggle to appropriately express their doubts or to balance their degree of certainty". In order to alleviate this problem, hedges and boosters have attracted increasing attention in various contexts. In order to add to the growing bulk of research, this chapter undertakes a descriptive study investigating the use of hedges and boosters in undergraduate ELT (English Language Teaching) students' presentation abstracts written for Oral Expression and Public Speaking course. This study is trying to shed light on whether there is any significant difference in the frequency of hedging and boosting strategies employed by undergraduate ELT students. Some degree of conscious attention is necessary for undergraduate students based on the idea that novice researchers should learn the conventions that are specific to their disciplinary community. Learning to write in different genres is inevitable for students' future life. Therefore, many undergraduate programmes offer academic writing courses for students in their freshmen year. Abstract is one of those genres that students should become familiar with since they are going to write abstracts for their theses, research papers, conference proposals and so on in their future career. As Pho (2008, p. 231) underpins "acquiring the skills of writing an abstract is therefore important to novice writers to enter the discourse community of their discipline".

Taking the fluid nature of categorization into consideration, this study employs Hyland's (2000b) list of hedges and boosters. The findings have pedagogical implications in teaching academic writing to Turkish ELT students and offering related course materials.

1.1. Hedging and boosting strategies

Mansouri et al. (2016, p. 299) state that "metadiscourse is a specific means of facilitating communication and making relationship between the members of a particular discourse community". As Hyland (2004) puts it:

> It is based on a view of writing as a social engagement and, in academic contexts, reveals the ways writers project themselves into their discourse to signal their attitudes and commitments (p. 133).

Similarly, Gholamit and Ilghamit (2016) state that:

> As an umbrella term, metadiscourse includes the heterogenous array of cohesive and interpersonal features which writer uses to relate text to context and assist readers to connect, organize, and interpret content in a way which he or she prefers (p. 349).

In the taxonomy of metadiscourse by Hyland (2004), hedges and boosters are considered as interactional resources that involve the reader in the argument. Hyland (2004, p. 139) defines hedges as marking "the writer's reluctance to present propositional information categorically" and boosters as expressing "certainty" and emphasising "the force of propositions". In Vazquez and Giner's (2009, p. 219) terms, "they are both two sides of the same coin in the sense that they both contribute to the persuasive import of academic communication". Authors must employ these interactional resources to interact with their readers.

In the reviewed literature, there is a growing bulk of research on hedges and boosters. Hedging and boosting devices were identified in different contexts. Some scholars have studied these devices in research articles. For instance, Gao (2004) analysed hedges in Chinese and English scientific articles from the perspective of contrastive pragmatics and found out that there were significant differences between Chinese and English scientific articles in use of hedges. Vazquez and Giner (2009) analysed the use of boosters in a corpus of articles from three different disciplines (Marketing, Biology and Mechanical Engineering) and they suggested that boosting devices needed further emphasis to study persuasion in academic writing. Yagiz and Demir (2014) analysed the hedging frequencies in 100 articles published in English that equally belong to non-native writers (Turkish) and native writers of English (Anglo-sphere). As for hedging frequencies, it appeared that native writers "use more hedges in an attempt of weakening their statements or for other rhetorical purposes when compared to non-native writers" (Yagiz and Demir, 2014, p. 266). Some other scholars investigated these devices in different parts of theses. For instance, Kondowe (2014) investigated dissertation abstracts of PhD candidates in the field of literature using Hyland's (2005) metadiscourse taxonomy. He suggested that lessons on hedging and boosting should be included in the research writing subjects of novice writers. Atmaca (2016) analysed 10 M.A. theses and 10 Ph.D. dissertations and it was seen that hedges used in the Ph.D. dissertations nearly double those in the M.A. theses. Hatipoğlu and Algı (2018) examined the frequency and categories of modal hedges by Turkish L2 students' argumentative paragraphs in English. Akbas and Hardman (2018) examined ninety discussion sections of dissertations to identify and classify hedging and boosting devices. Taking these studies into consideration, it appears that there are a growing number of studies in post-graduate students' writings while undergraduate students' writings have taken relatively less attention. There are relatively fewer scholars who dealt with undergraduate students' use of hedging and boosting devices. Bayyurt (2010) investigated essays in Turkish and English written by Turkish university students to discover the way how they use hedges and intensifiers. It was seen that students used hedges more frequently than intensifiers in both Turkish and English essays. There need to be more studies on undergraduate students' writings in different genres. To close this research gap, this study attempts to examine hedging and boosting devices that help undergraduate students to show detachment or certainty in the abstracts written for their presentations.

1.2. Abstract writing

As Pho (2008, p. 232) underlines "abstracts are thus an important genre to study, for both reading and writing purposes". The features of an abstract can be ordered as such:

- Abstracts are accompanied with a title that takes the attention of the readers for further reading.

- It must be concise and within word limits.

- There shouldn't be a big gap between the abstract and presentation/thesis/paper. Abstract should represent the completed or proposed work.

- Authors should spend time and effort to write a well-organized abstract.

- It is important to add appropriate keywords at the end of an abstract that help readers differentiate one abstract from another. It saves the reader's time.

As Akbas (2012) states:

> abstracts clearly stand out as a consequence of the rhetorical functions of briefly introducing what has been done in the research and what the striking points are (p. 12).

Therefore, as Beyea and Nicoll (1998, p. 274) note "when writing and submitting an abstract, the challenge is to be as comprehensive as you can in as few words as possible".

Regarding all those features, abstract is not only important for experienced writers but also for novice writers. As Plakhotnik (2017, p. 52) underlines "simple definition of an abstract could be deceiving and could mislead novice researchers into neglecting the value or the function of their manuscript abstracts". As they are shorter than other genres, they may seem easy to write but it is not the case specifically for novice authors. As Hyland (2000b, p. 64) maintains, abstract is "a selective representation rather than an attempt to give the reader exact knowledge" of article's, presentation's and thesis' content. In Klimova's (2015, p. 909) terms, writing an abstract is "one of the most important things for students since they have to summarize and highlight the most important thoughts/ideas of their text". Students have to synthesize their information in a limited space with word limits. Students should learn the features of an abstract as they are likely to write an abstract for their bachelor projects, master thesis, dissertation, conferences, research papers and proposals. Writing for undergraduate students not only requires language skills but also more than that. As Klimova (2015) underpins:

> It also requires the mastering of other skills, such as metacognitive skills since learners need to set an objective for their writing, plan it

carefully, think over its layout and logical structure, revise it... In the process of writing they have to use cognitive skills; they have to analyse their sources and then synthesize them in a compact piece of writing (p. 909).

Knowing how to write a good abstract is essential as there is a huge amount of information in almost each field. Abstract writing is very useful for prospective English teachers, as they may have to write abstracts for conferences, postgraduate degrees, proposals and so on. It could also be a good practise for their writing skills as students will try to condense the significant information in a limited space.

Researching abstracts is growing in popularity as abstracts carry gatekeeping position and they are the points where readers stop or continue reading. As Ebrahimi and Chan (2015) maintain:

It also has a persuasive function in capturing the reader's attention by drawing him to significant information, thus, persuading him to read the entire research... (p. 382)

In the reviewed literature, some studies have focused on the schematic structure of abstracts while some have focused on the use of linguistic features in abstracts. As Akbas (2012) underpins:

That function of the abstract in highlighting interaction between a writer and a particular group of people is mostly dependent on a range of rhetorical strategies and discourse conventions of that specific community (p. 12).

Abstracts have been analysed in terms of functional moves and metadiscourse devices. For instance, Samraj (2002) analysed twenty abstracts' moves from two disciplines "Conservation Biology" and "Wildlife Behaviour". Although there are some subtle differences, it appeared that abstracts from two disciplines are not so different from each other in terms of rhetorical moves. As for the differences, situating the research move was found commonly in Conservation Biology abstracts while the purpose move is slightly higher in Conservation Biology. Montesi and Urdiciain (2005, p. 515) held 62 interviews with researchers from six European universities to identify different types of problems in abstracts in the areas of Education and Agriculture and they classified these problems under different categories, namely "terminology, over-condensation, lack and excess of information, expectations and coherence, structure, register and layout". Ufnalska and Hartley (2009, p. 71) discussed three methods for evaluating abstracts, indicating their pros and cons and suggested that the readability of abstracts can be enhanced by their typographic settings and abstracts should not be printed in smaller typefaces as they "are read much more often than whole articles". Furthermore, it was suggested that separating "the components of abstracts under subheadings (to create structured abstracts) can make them more readable" (p. 71). There are also some scholars focusing on metadiscourse devices in abstracts. For instance, Gillaerts and Van de Velde (2010) investigated hedges, boosters and attitude markers in 72 research article abstracts in Journal of Pragmatics taken from different volumes with five years intervals each and they revealed that the use of hedging and boosting devices has undergone significant changes in the past 30 years. Hu and Cao (2011, p. 2795) investigated 649 abstracts collected from 8 journals of applied linguistics and tried to see whether "hedging and boosting strategies differ between applied linguists publishing in Chinese- and English medium journals and between authors of empirical and non-empirical academic articles". They supported some previous findings from previously published studies and revealed that "scholars publishing in English-medium academic journals tend to adopt a more tentative stance than their counterparts publishing in some other language" (Hu and Cao, 2011, p. 2804). Onder-Ozdemir and Longo (2014, p. 59) scrutinized 26 theses from USA students and 26 from Turkish students and showed that "Turkish students used metadiscourse transitions, frame markers and hedges more than USA students".

2. Method

The corpus of this paper consists of the abstracts produced for the presentations in the Oral Expression and Public Speaking course. Before their presentations, the students submitted their abstracts to the lecturer to give information about the content of their presentation. They were sophomore students in the Department of English Language Teaching. Their age varied between 19-21. A total of 25 abstracts were chosen from students' submitted abstracts. The total number of words in the corpus was 5584. This study is restricted to interactional metadiscourse primarily focusing on hedges and boosters. The identification of hedges and boosters can be seen as problematic in the literature. Therefore, Hyland's (2000b) list of hedges and boosters was used. Some more categories such as impersonalization strategies such as passives, inanimate subjects and personal pronouns were added to the pool of hedges and boosters that were examined. An initial manual analysis was done to identify the hedges and boosters that were evident in the abstracts. Given the highly contextual and strategic nature of hedges and boosters, only lexical hedging and boosting strategies were chosen. The corpus was searched manually on the Word document for all the hedging and boosting strategies in the list and for more delicate categories such as passives and inanimate subjects, potential signals were identified and then, hedges and boosters were added to the list.

3. Results

Table 13.1 Undergraduate Students' Use of Lexical Hedges

Undergraduate Students' Use of Lexical Hedges	
Frequency	Percentage
Almost (2)	0.036 %
Argue (2)	0.036 %
Certain (3)	0.054 %
Extent (2)	0.036 %
I/We claim (1)	0.018 %
Could (1)	0.018 %
General (1)	0.018 %
Generally (6)	0.107 %
Mainly (1)	0.018 %
May (7)	0.125 %
Might (1)	0.018 %
Most (6)	0.107 %
Often (3)	0.054 %
Possible (4)	0.072 %
Quite (2)	0.036 %
Rarely (1)	0.018 %
Rather (2)	0.036 %
Seem (1)	0.018 %
Should (18)	0.322 %
Shouldn't (4)	0.072 %
Sometimes (4)	0.072 %
Suggest (2)	0.036 %
Tend (2)	0.036 %

Tendency (2)	0.036 %
Usually (2)	0.036 %
Would (7)	0.125 %
Passives (52)	0.931 %
Inanimate subjects (11)	0.196 %
We (32)	0.573 %
Total (182)	3.260 %

The list is dominated by passives (n=52), first person plural personal pronoun "we" (n=32), modal verbs such as "should" (n=18), may (n=7) and inanimate subjects (n=11). From Table 13.1, it was evident that some hedges were expressed impersonally in the corpus as the students wanted to underline the detachment they wish to attach to their arguments. Another reason why students used impersonalisation strategies such as passives and inanimate subjects can be explained with the fact argument that they consciously or unconsciously reinforce "the predominant view of science as impersonal, inductive enterprise" (Hyland, 2000b, p. 94). It is evident that students employed passives as a hedging strategy to explain the gaps in the reviewed literature, the aim of their study, data procedure and the results. In the following examples, the ways students employed passives in their abstracts can be seen.

> Many methods have been tested and implemented until this time and many of them have been failed in some way.

> Data were gathered via an open-ended questionnaire which was about emotional state of them and the effectiveness of peer feedback.

> In this research, it is aimed to bring the issue -how peer pressure affects classroom environment, how peer pressure is interrelated with other disruptive elements, and how other discouraging factors provide an environment for peer pressure in classroom- to light.

Undergraduate students employed 18 instances of "should" in their abstracts. It was sometimes combined with the first-person plural personal pronoun. Such uses may refer to shared responsibility.

> This study suggests that even if it may seem hard, we should consider teaching visual representation of speech sounds (or phones), phonetic

alphabet (phonetic transcription). The sooner it stars the more effective it will be.

We should approach the issue with a solution that handle the situation at the most basic and cover it completely.

There are many instances of modal verbs such as "may" in the abstracts. In this way, in Hyland's (2000b) terms:

They seek to head off the possible negative consequences of overstatement and so anticipate rejection of their claims (p. 92)

In the following extracts, such examples can be seen.

Over time students may struggle then eventually there will be a point where they will become detached from the class.

Some individuals may argue that this is impossible to handle, but with the aid of technology this utopian like system can become a reality.

There are also introductory verbs such as "seem, suggest" evident in the study. In the following typical cases, it can be seen that verbs such as "suggest, observe, report" were more easily combined with inanimate subjects "allowing agency to be attributed to abstract rhetors" (Hyland, 2000b, p. 94). Also, the booster "show" was combined with an inanimate subject. It added tentativeness to the claims.

My findings mainly suggest the idea of achieving the skills of a language by exposure is better than being taught the language according to widely used procedures.

This article will also show the homophobia, low intellectual intelligence and insensibleness among the teachers according to their behaviours during the lecture.

Hedges such as "quite, rarely, almost, generally" were salient in the abstracts and helped the authors to limit the scope of the accompanying statement. Such cases can be seen in these examples:

English is one of the main lessons in almost every country. Despite the fact that students are taught English for years in schools and that they face with English almost every field in their lives, they have difficulties with communicating.

When people think of ways to effectively and innovatively teach, they rarely look for how test taking can be improved but rather how it can be replaced.

Generally, both in high and elementary schools, English learning is not beneficial for students because there are many reasons behind this problem.

In addition to hedges, boosters are also important to promote "the worth and importance of what the writer has to say" (Hyland, 2000b, p. 91). Table 13.2 shows the most frequently occurring items that have acted as boosters in students' abstracts.

Table 13.2 Undergraduate Students' Use of Boosting Hedges

Undergraduate Students' Use of Boosting Hedges	
Frequency	Percentage
Actually (2)	0.036 %
Always (5)	0.089 %
Certainly (1)	0.018 %
Certain that (1)	0.018 %
Couldn't (1)	0.018 %
Of course (1)	0.018 %
Demonstrate (1)	0.018 %
Determine (1)	0.018 %
In essential (2)	0.036 %
Expect (2)	0.036 %
In fact (1)	0.018 %
The fact that (2)	0.036 %
Impossible (2)	0.036 %
Inevitable (1)	0.018 %
We know (1)	0.018 %

More than (21)	0.376 %
Must (1)	0.018 %
Obvious (1)	0.018 %
Quite (2)	0.036 %
Show (5)	0.089 %
Sure (2)	0.036 %
True (1)	0.018 %
Will (27)	0.483 %
I (20)	0.358 %
Total (104)	1.863 %

From Table 13.2, it is understood that students used "will" (n=27) highly in their abstracts. They utilized "will" mostly in the concluding parts of their abstracts to explain what they aimed to achieve in their presentations. Some instances can be seen in the following extracts:

> Those are the questions I tried to answer on my research. I will try to answer these with the help of some previous researches and my own interview and data from OECD (The Organisation for Economic Co-operation and Development).

> At the end of the presentation listeners will learn about methods about oral presentations and how to improve their or their student's oral skills, how to use these methods.

The results reveal that "must" has rarely been used in the abstracts. This may stem from the fact that they didn't choose to strengthen their claims. It was seen that undergraduate students wrote cautiously when presenting their claims.

The results also show that students employed "always" (n=5), "true" (n=1), "impossible" (n=2) and similar adjectives and adverbs to strengthen their claims in their abstracts. They didn't totally avoid them.

> However, consequences are always low in our country though expectations are high.

It's certainly impossible to measure sole effects of the peer pressure independent from all other harmful elements that disrupts students to bring about its full potential.

It is also noticeable that undergraduate students used first-person singular pronoun "I" (n=20) in their abstracts. First-person singular pronoun "I" was treated as a booster in this study as it shows confidence in the statements. In Gholamit and Ilghamit's (2016, p. 359) terms, "self-mention markers are the explicit presence of author in the discourse". They also underline that:

> Previously in the traditional academic writing, researchers were obliged to use an impersonal and objective tone of voice in representing the text (Gholamit and Ilghamit, 2016, p. 359).

In contrast to traditional academic writing conventions, the participants in this study employed "I" in their abstracts. There can be several reasons why they used first-person singular pronoun. One possible reason is that they didn't regard it as a face-threatening act and therefore, they didn't soften their claims. Another possible reason is that the novice writers may not be aware of the disciplinary conventions as Akbas and Hardman (2018) note:

> Novice writers of any discourse community are both novice with regard to their academic performance and managing authorial strategies to meet the expectations of experienced members of the academic community (p.833).

In line with this thought, they need more instruction that will guide them to meet the expected conventions. The undergraduate students in this study didn't prefer to use strong verbs, but they employed epistemic lexical verbs such as show (n=5) and demonstrate (n=1) as boosters in their abstracts. As Akbas and Hardman (2018, p. 832) argue "this was likely to have a conscious linguistic choice by the writer of the text". A stance of conviction is expressed by using such epistemic lexical verbs in the following examples:

> In this study, I show that more payment makes teachers more successful and motivated.

> Moussaoui's study (2012) demonstrated that implementing peer evaluation has enabled the learners to not only enhance their written drafts, but as well advance their ability of critical thinking via examining their friends' papers.

Overall, when the frequency of hedging devices in students' abstracts was compared with the frequency of the boosting devices in students' abstracts, the frequency count of hedging devices was higher than boosting devices. As Hyland (2000b) argues that:

> These choices are to some extent influenced by individual factors, such as self-confidence and experience, and we often regard them as largely unreflective and automatic aspects of writing. Once again, however, all acts of communication carry the imprint of their contexts (p. 91).

As Yagiz and Demir (2014, p. 266) underpin "in English, we know that the writer can remove the "active doing" from the meaning and, thus, soften a threat to the reader's face considerably". In this case, this can be understandable as students are novice writers who are trying to learn the conventions of the disciplinary community. This finding is in line with the reviewed literature. The scholars who compared hedging and boosting devices in terms of frequency counts observed that writers used hedging devices more often than boosting devices (Bayyurt, 2010; Serholt, 2012).

4. Conclusion

Due to the significant role of hedging and boosting devices in academic writing, the present research intended to examine the frequency of hedging and boosting devices in undergraduate students' abstracts in the field of English language teaching. Based on similar studies, materials can be developed for novice writers to utilize in writing their abstracts. In addition to brevity and clarity inherent in abstracts, students should learn how to write while interacting with the reader. Abstract as a genre offers a suitable arena for students to practise that sort of interaction with the reader. As Gholamit and Ilghamit (2016) suggest:

> Syllabus designers could include genre awareness courses and train the students the features which they can apply in their writings to make their academic discourse acceptable to the members of the discourse community (p. 359).

The results point to some pedagogical implications. This aspect of writing should not be neglected. EAP instructors should also be aware of hedging and boosting strategies before they teach them to learners. Use of authentic materials can be used in academic writing courses to make students aware of metadiscourse and its functions. As McEnery and Kifle (2002, p. 185) underline students "may have a limited repertoire of devices at their disposal" so with a close analysis of those devices, they should become familiar with ways to show detachment and commitment to the statements. Exercising different degrees of caution and certainty should be part of academic writing lessons.

One limitation for this study can be the restricted number of abstracts that were selected for this study. A larger sample of participants should be used in further research. Also, it is restricted to only one-dimension, non-native country context. For further research, a comparative study can be done with undergraduate students in the other parts of the world. Furthermore, only one genre is dealt with here so similar studies should be done in other genres. In addition to frequency counts, interviews can be conducted with the participants to understand their choices and degree of awareness of hedging and boosting strategies. The results of this study also call for further studies of hedges and boosters in the abstracts of students in different disciplines.

References

Akbas, E. (2012). Exploring Metadiscourse in Master's Dissertation Abstracts: Cultural and Linguistic Variations across Postgraduate Writers. *International Journal of Applied Linguistics & English Literature, 1* (1), 12-22.

Akbas, E. and Hardman, J. (2018). Strengthening or Weakening Claims in Academic Knowledge Construction: A Comparative Study of Hedges and Boosters in Postgraduate Academic Writing. *Kuram ve Uygulamada Eğitim Bilimleri, 18* (4), 831-859. DOI: 10.12738/estp.2018.4.026

Atmaca, C. (2016). Comparison of hedges in M.A. theses and Ph.D. dissertations in ELT. *ZfWT, 8* (2), 209-325.

Bayyurt, Y. (2010). Author positioning in academic writing. In S. Zyngier & V. Viana (Eds.), *Avaliaçoes e perspectivas: Mapeando os estudos empiricos na area deHumanas* [Appraisals and perspectives: Mapping empirical studies in the Humanities] (pp. 163-184). Rio de Janeiro: The Federal University of Rio de Janeiro.

Beyea, S. C. and Nicoll, L. H. (1998). Writing and submitting an abstract. *AORN Journal, 67* (1), 273-274.

Ebrahimi, S. F. and Chan, S. C. (2015). Research article abstracts in Applied Linguistics and Economics: Functional analysis of the grammatical subject. *Australian Journal of Linguistics, 35* (4), 381-397. DOI: 10.1080/07268602.2015.1070660

Gao, X. (2004). Contrastive analysis of hedges in a sample of Chinese and English molecular biology papers. *Psychological Reports, 95*, 487-493.

Gholamit, J. and Ilghamit, R. (2016). Metadiscourse markers in biological research articles and journal impact factor: Non-native writers vs. Native writers. *Biochemistry and Molecular Biology Education, 44* (4), 349-360. DOI: 10.1002/bmb.20961

Gillaerts, P. and Van de Velde, F. (2010). Interactional metadiscourse in research article abstracts. *Journal of English for Academic Purposes, 9*, 128-139. DOI: 10.1016/j.jeap.2010.02.004

Hatipoğlu, Ç. And Algı, S. (2018). Catch a tiger by the toe: Modal hedges in EFL Argumentative Paragraphs. *Kuram ve Uygulamada Eğitim Bilimleri, 18* (4), 957-982. DOI: 10.12738/estp.2018.4.0373

Hyland, K. (2000a). Hedges, Boosters and Lexical Invisibility: Noticing Modifiers in Academic Texts. *Language Awareness, 9* (4), 179-197. DOI: 10.1080/09658410008667145

Hyland, K. (2000b). *Disciplinary Discourses: Social Interactions in Academic Writing.* London: Longman.

Hyland, K. (2004). Disciplinary interactions: metadiscourse in L2 postgraduate writing. *Journal of Second Language Writing, 13,* 133–151. DOI: 10.1016/j.jslw.2004.02.00

Hyland, K. (2005). *Metadiscourse.* London: Continuum.

Hu, G. and Cao, F. (2011). Hedging and boosting in abstracts of applied linguistics articles: A comparative study of English- and Chinese-medium journals. *Journal of Pragmatics, 43,* 2795–2809. DOI: 10.1016/j.pragma.2011.04.007

Klimova, B. F. (2015). Teaching English Abstract Writing Effectively. *Procedia - Social and Behavioral Sciences, 186,* 908-912. DOI: 10.1016/j.sbspro.2015.04.113

Kondowe, W. (2014). Hedging and boosting as interactional metadiscourse in literature doctoral dissertation abstracts. *International Journal of Language Learning and Applied Linguistics World (IJLLALW), 5* (3), 214-221.

Mansouri, S., Najafabadi, M. M., Boroujeni, S. S. (2016). Metadiscourse in Research Article Abstracts: A Cross Lingual and Disciplinary Investigation. *Journal of Applied Linguistics and Language Research, 3* (4), 296-307.

McEnery, T. and Kifle, T. A. (2002). Epistemic modality in argumentative essays of second-language writers (pp. 182-196). In J. Flowerdew (Ed.) *Academic Discourse,* Pearson Education.

Montesi, M. and Urdiciain, B. G. (2005). Abstracts:problems classified from the user perspective. *Journal of Information Science, 31* (6), 515–526. DOI: 10.1177/0165551505057014

Onder-Ozdemir, N. and Longo, B. (2014). Metadiscourse Use in Thesis Abstracts: A Cross-cultural Study. *Procedia - Social and Behavioral Sciences, 141,* 59 – 63. DOI:10.1016/j.sbspro.2014.05.011

Plakhotnik, M. S. (2017). Writer's Forum— Tips to Understanding and Writing Manuscript Abstracts. *New Horizons in Adult Education & Human Resource Development, 29* (3), 51-55.

Pho, P. D. (2008). Research article abstracts in applied linguistics and educational technology: a study of linguistic realizations of rhetorical structure and authorial stance. *Discourse Studies, 10* (2), 231-250. DOI: 10.1177/1461445607087010

Samraj, B. (2002). Disciplinary variation in abstracts: The case of Wildlife Behaviour and Conservation Biology (pp. 40-57). In J. Flowerdew (Ed.) *Academic Discourse,* Pearson Education.

Serholt, S. (2012). *Hedges and Boosters in Academic Writing: A Study of Gender Differences in Essays Written by Swedish Advanced Learners of English.* Goteborgs University, Gothenburg, Sweden.

Ufnalska, S. B. and Hartley, J. (2009). How can we evaluate the quality of abstracts? *European Science Editing, 35* (3), 69-71.

Vazquez, I. and Giner, D. (2009). Writing with Conviction: The Use of Boosters in Modelling Persuasion in Academic Discourses. *Revista Alicantina de Estudios Ingleses, 22*, 219-237.

Yagız, O. and Demir, C. (2014). Hedging strategies in academic discourse: A comparative analysis of Turkish writers and native writers of English. *Procedia - Social and Behavioral Sciences, 158*, 260-268. DOI: 10.1016/j.sbspro.2014.12.085

Appendix

Hyland's (2000b, p. 188-189) list of hedges:

HEDGES			
About	Frequently	Perhaps	Speculate
Admittedly	(in) general	Plausible	Suggest
Almost	Generally	Possibility	Superficially
(not) always	Guess	Possible(ly)	Suppose
Apparently	Hypothesise	Postulate	Surmise
Appear	Hypothetically	Predict	Suspect
Approximately	Ideally	Prediction	Technically
Argue	(we) imagine	Predominantly	Tend
Around	Implication	Presumably	Tendency
Assume	Imply	Presume	In theory
Assumption	Indicate	Probable(ly)	Theoretically
Basically	Infer	Probability	Typically
My/our belief	Interpret	Provided that	Uncertain
I believe	Largely	Propose	Unclear
A certain X	Likely	Open to question	Unlikely
Certain extent	Mainly	Questionable	Unsure
I /we claim	May	Quite	Usually
Conceivably	Maybe	Rare(ly)	Virtually
Conjecture	Might	Rather	Would

Consistent with	More or less	Relatively	
Contention	Most	Seen (as)	
Could	Not necessarily	Seem	
Deduce	Normally	Seemingly	
Discern	Occasionally	Seldom	
Doubt	Often	(general) sense	
Essentially	Ostensibly	Should	
Estimate	Partly	Shouldn't	
Evidently	Partially	Somewhat	
Formally	Perceive	Sometimes	

Hyland's (2000b, p. 188) list of boosters:

BOOSTERS		
Actually	in fact	precise(ly)
Always	the fact that	prove
assured (ly)	we find	(without) question
Certainly	given that	quite
certainty	impossible(ly)	reliable(ly)
certain that	improbable(ly)	show
clear (ly)	Indeed	sure(ly)
Conclude	inevitable(ly)	surmise
conclusive(ly)	we know	we think
Confirm	it is known that/to	true
Convince	(at) least	unambiguous(ly)
convincingly	manifest(ly)	unarguably
couldn't	more than	undeniab(ly)
of course	Must	undoubted(ly)
decided(ly)	necessarily	unequivocal(ly)
definite(ly)	Never	unmistakab(ly)

demonstrate	no doubt	unquestionabl(ly)
determine	obvious (ly)	well-known
doubtless	particularly	will
is essential	Patently	won't
Evidence	Perceive	wouldn't
Expect	plain(ly)	wrong(ly)

Chapter 14

Analysing English Dative Alternation in the Interlanguage of students in CLIL context

Ivan Calleja Rituerto

Universidad Nacional de Educación a Distancia (UNED)

Abstract: This chapter offers a pilot study on the acquisition of the English dative alternation by Spanish young adult learners attending a course on English for Specific Purposes (ESP) in the field of catering. The experimental study examines the learners' interlanguage during the process of acquisition of dative structures with ditransitive verbs such as to *give, sell or send*. All participants attended a course with the methodology of Content Language Integrated Learning (CLIL) where from an implicit or explicit form they had access to the phenomenon of English dative alternation addressing personal relations and commercial or professional interchange. There were two groups of learners in the study: one experimental group who received immediate knowledge of the linguistic phenomenon under stake and a second group of learners for whom such a feedback was not provided, since they just develop implicit learning through a communicative approach. The chapter discusses difficulties from both linguistic and methodological perspectives. It also has clear implications for the teaching of closely related languages. It finally suggests that instruction should not only focus on cross-linguistic contrasts but also prioritize complex interface integration, which is essential in the acquisition of foreign languages.

Keywords: ESP, CLIL, catering, dative alternation, ditransitive verbs, catering

***

1. Introduction

Scholars have developed studies on the acquisition of foreign languages under the scope of English for Specific Purposes (ESP) over the last few decades, and it is still the subject of current research. The advances achieved in this field come from the interdisciplinary fields of Linguistics, Psychology, Education, Neurolinguistics, and, Cognitive Science.

The acquisition of a second language implies the learning and incorporation of a new linguistic system. A significant number of approaches and methods have analyzed the interrelation and influence between the source and the target languages and how the first language has an impact on the second language. The acquisition of a second language deals with the study and internalization of a linguistic system and its subsequent use by learners (Benati, 2016). Having ESP as background, in this paper, we focus on a grammatical aspect of the English language given a specific formal linguistic phenomenon: English Dative alternation.

Just as several disciplines develop the concepts that define their contents, ESP has been the focus of many studies that attempt to define its goals in comparison with other approaches such as English for Academic Purposes (EAP). Wright (1992) defines ESP as 'language learning which has its focus on all aspects of language on a particular field of human activity while taking into account the time constraints imposed by learners.' Other authors, such as Mackay and Mountford (1978), bring out the utilitarian purpose of ESP. This purpose entails "the needs of the learners, which could be academic, occupational, or scientific." These needs, in turn, determine the content of the ESP curriculum be taught and learned. Mackay and Mountford also defined ESP and the 'special language that takes place in specific settings by certain participants.' Dudley-Evans (1998) offers a universal definition of ESP. This study refers to the absolute characteristics of ESP centered on language use in terms of learning activities concerning grammar, lexis, register, skills, discourse, and genre.

In sum, the ESP approach is highly related to the CLIL approach, which entails the teaching of disciplinary content through a second language (L2). Following the learning perspective offered by Halliday (1980), learning a language consists of learning through language and learning about language. From a linguistic and methodological perspective, Dalton-Puffer (2007) refers to the CLIL classes expectations as 'efficient and effective language learning settings, which emerge as a reflection of the widespread opinion about traditional teaching methods such as the Grammar Translation Method or the use of grammar drills. The relationship between ESP and CLIL has gone through different stages: from considering them as opposing approaches to being part of the same continuum and sharing synergies and mutual inspirations.

2. CLIL and Catering Services

CLIL teachers need to pay special attention to the preparation of contents, materials, and activities related to professional practice. The training program discussed in this paper was related to catering services in the tourism industry. It was endorsed by the Spanish Ministry of Education (MEC) for young learners from vocational schools. The main goal was to motivate and stimulate trainees and trainers by enhancing their self-development and extending opportunities for lifelong learning and employability

Experts designed the course in hospitality and customer care management with the title of 'Communicating in English, at an independent user level, in catering services.' The target participants were students from vocational schools, workers in the catering, hotel and tourism industry, and potential employees seeking to improve their English competence. The main targets of this course were to:

- Understand essential communication and enhance spoken language in the catering industry (interviews with trainees, trainers, and caterers in the industry);

- Extract information from short and simple documents written in English in the field of catering in order to obtain information, process, and carry out the appropriate actions.

- Produce primary spoken language in the target language in everyday catering situations to improve service delivery and catering sales.

- Write documents in English, necessary for the marketing of the offer, and the management of the catering activities.

- Communicate face to face with one or more customers in English in simple conversations.

The resulting ESP course is designed for young adult learners, either at a vocational school or in a professional work situation. The fulfillment of the targets above may lead to different job opportunities. In particular, we can highlight the development of catering activities in both small bar-cafeterias and large- and medium-sized hotels or catering companies, such as restaurants in the public or private sector. As access criteria, students had to have a command of the Spanish language, basic knowledge of mathematics and computers, and an A2-level in the English language according to the

European framework of languages — the curricula of secondary school-certified these competences.

Considering the diversity of the students that attended this training module, it was necessary to have a general knowledge of their characteristics. In this way, the method and the didactic design of the sessions would have more possibilities of success in the achievement of the targets. For this purpose, we followed some didactic guidelines for the Curricular Development of Specific Vocational Training in the Autonomous Community of Andalusia (Spain), taking into account aspects such as personal information (parents' socioeconomic level, education, and professions) and academic profile (students' previous itineraries, information received and motivation regarding the training course).

The catering service course reported here took place in a private training center in Alcalá de Henares (Madrid).[1] The course took place from December to February during the academic year 2018-2019. Most students were working part-time at a fast-food restaurant, which supported them during their course attendance. Participants consisted of 12 students who had completed secondary school. It lasted 90 hours, three days a week (Monday, Tuesday, and Wednesday).

The development of the course contents was supported by a CLIL method, which highlighted its practical nature by considering tasks for the following contents:

- Greetings/Client reception.

- Taking notes. (Dealing with restaurant customers)

- Claims/ Suggestions. (Attending customers' complaints)

- Payment. (Assisting checking out)

As a CLIL proposal, the above contents were integrated using expressions and vocabulary specific to the fast-food catering service through Warm-Up activities at the beginning of each session and through Role Plays to dramatize real situations. These tasks could allow students to put into practice communicative situations in which they sometimes acted as servers and sometimes as customers/clients. Finally, to reinforce the training, a few

---

[1] We are grateful to the students and facilitators from the center in Alcalá de Henares (Madrid) for letting us conduct the research reported in this paper.

thematic videos and listening activities were used to offer students access to real situations where ESP played an important role.

In learning a second language, the phenomenon of language transfer takes place. Linguistics points this out as a problem that occurs when a speaker uses transferred native language patterns into a foreign language. In linguistics, knowledge is limited around two questions: What has been transferred, and how does such language transfer take place?

In the 1940s and 1950s, the concept of language transfer was coined. Its importance in the acquisition of an L2 is unquestionable. However, its presence as an object of study in linguistics and pedagogical research or L2 learning is scarce. Language transfer, strongly influenced by behaviorism, was considered in linguistics as the predominance of L1 habits in L2 learning and performance. Fries (1945), a well-known behaviorist, argued that the comparison between the mother tongue and the target language is essential for both L2 theory and pedagogy.

The role of the theory of language transfer has transformed in recent years. The importance of L1 transfer has moved from considerable opposition in the early 1970s and 1980s. Some researchers have placed L1 within the cognitive approach focused on language learning. This approach gives the learner the decision to discern what should be or not transferred from their L1 to L2 learning (Gass, 2000). Academics, such as Cohen & Brooks-Carson (2001), have pointed out in recent years that L1 transfer, besides being a complex mental operation, is also part of a repertoire of strategies that learners use in the L2 learning process. In this sense, Bialystok (1983) pointed out that learners can use the structures of their language to overcome the problems encountered in their learning. This idea radically changes the perception of the learner from a passive to an active subject who takes control of his or her learning process.

In what follows, the linguistic phenomenon to be attained by the learning process carried out in this study is explained first. Then, the two types of instruction of such phenomena are explained in order to see which of them is more appropriate when targeting contrastive evidence.

3. The Dative Alternation: A contrastive analysis

When a native learner ventures to learn a new language, there are likely to be one or more obstacles to overcome. One of the best ways to overcome it is to build a ladder or bridge to reach the goal: the L2. This way, to reach the target language is known as an interlanguage. At the beginning of the learning process, the stairs or bridges will still be very weak; however, as time goes by, they will become stronger and offer strong support so that the learner can reach higher levels of learning in the L2. The interlanguage is a linguistic system used by second language learners when learners attempt to communicate themselves in the target language. Most likely, students' L1 affects this kind of language as they use the linguistic knowledge of their mother tongue to understand the new one or to compensate for competency gaps. It is important to note that interlanguage is a different system since it comprises grammatically incorrect productions formed by elements from both L1 and L2 and which come from the speaker's perception and which differ from one learned to another since they create their own linguistic rules, the nature of which will depend on the context, teachers, and peers.

The Spanish and English language structure seems very far from each other because of their Romance and Germanic origins. Notwithstanding, they share vocabulary and grammar features because of the influence of Latin in the field of knowledge. This circumstance is of great interest, and its nature responds to different linguistic, educational, and cultural levels. Thus, in the material preparation for their lessons, language teachers must consider those linguistic aspects (morphological, phonetic, and syntactic), which may contain symmetries between the L1 and the target language. Sometimes this can become an ally of the teacher and the student for the teaching and acquisition of syntactic constructions. There are cases such as that of Dative Alternation in which, precisely, the symmetry that exists between Spanish and English concerning Prepositional Construction (PPC) causes the Spanish student difficulties in gaining **DA.**

Consider the following examples:

1) a. Mary sent a letter to Peter

   b. Mary sent Peter a letter

2) Helen bought a new car for Alex.

In both examples, a ditransitive verb allows for three participants: the agent, the theme and the receiver. However, the syntactic distribution varies. In example (1), the indirect object, the receiver "Peter", may go after the direct object "a letter", as in (1a) or before it, as in (1b). In the latter case, the dative follows the preposition "to". In example (2), the receiver "Alex" is introduced by the preposition "for". The dative alternation (DA) illustrated by the minimal pair in (1) is common in English but not in other languages like in Spanish where the dative preposition "a" (to, in English) is required regardless whether the dative phrase goes before or after the direct object, as illustrated by the Spanish counterpart in (3).

3) a. Mary envió una carta a Peter

   b. Mary envió *(a) Peter una carta

In effect, the starred bracket indicates that unlike English, the Spanish dative preposition cannot be omitted when the dative phrase goes before the direct object, cf. (1b) vs. (3b).

At the conceptual level, the dative alternation is defined by Wolfe-Quintero (1993) as "a lexical alternation between several types of clauses that are related to one another both grammatically and semantically." The structure of these clauses refers to the lexical structure or argument structure. Dative lexical structures can be related to one another because they refer to the movement of some object to an animate goal, and they are associated with particular verbs, like give, the prototypical dative verb. Following Morales (2008), "We speak of dative constructions and not of dative because the use of the pronoun is associated with a noun phrase which, preceded by the preposition 'a,' can optionally appear in the sentence. The Spanish preposition 'a' is linked to the dative pronoun, since on many occasions when the speaker does not use the pronoun, the preposition that appears is necessarily another one. Finally, the complement of the preposition must agree in number and a person with the atomic pronoun."

Bresnan (2007) sees the question of predicting DA as "one very natural approach to the problem is predicting different dative structures from different meanings. Advanced by Green (1974) and Oehrle (1976, 1978), this idea was taken up in an influential work on language learnability by Gropen et al. (1989, pp. 110–1117). They argued that there are two ways of viewing the same giving event: causing a change of state (possession) or as causing a change of place (movement to a goal). They hypothesized that the different ways of conceptualizing the giving event are associated with different structures, the possession meaning with the double object structure and the movement meaning with the prepositional dative structure. A similar phenomenon of dative alternation in Spanish has been attested but this involves clitic doubling phenomena, as was discussed in detail by Demonte (1994,1995). The phenomena of clitic doubling are however beyond the scope of this paper.

For the sake of our study, we focus on the English dative alternation counterpart, as challenging linguistic phenomena for Spanish-speaking leaners. Following Aguirre (2015), we may assume that such a difficulty may be overcome in the interlanguage of Spanish learners over time. Yet, we may test the type of teaching instruction that may favor the earlier acquisition of this phenomenon. The main hypothesis to be tested is that explicit knowledge has a positive impact on the acquisition of the second language. Hence, the main research question is formulated as follows:

3.1. Research question

Are there any differences between using explicit or implicit instruction in the successful development of the target linguistic phenomenon within the ESP-based course in the study?

In order to address this main question, the two types of instruction (implicit and explicit) have to be explained in full detail to test their impact on the ESP approach carried out in our study.

4. Two types of instruction

4.1. Explicit instruction

Explicit instruction is one of the bases and references of traditional second language teaching methods. In this sense, we can take as a reference to the grammar-translation method. However, this type of instruction is not exclusive to outdated or disused methodologies; on the contrary, explicit instruction is now part of many educational curricula and methodologies and techniques applied in the classroom in many contexts: language academies, training courses, English for Specific Purposes (ESP). According to Archer and Hughes (2010), explicit instruction is a structured, systematic, and valid methodology for teaching academic skills. They refer to explicitness, which includes both instructional design and delivery procedures. In this kind of instruction, students attend explanations and demonstrations of the target language. Furthermore, there are practice and subsequent feedback until learners master independence.

4.2. Implicit instruction

On the other side is the implied instruction. In Ellis's terms, "implicit learning is the acquisition of knowledge about the undergoing structure of a complex stimulus environment by a process which takes place naturally, simply and without conscious operations." Some cognitive theories focus on learners' language abilities and competencies (Ellis, 2002a, p.146). In this regard, emergentism claims that language acquisition is an implicit process in which various input plays a vital role, and language properties emerge when cognitive learning mechanisms interact with data from the learner's context. This apparent polarization of the two teaching approaches does not imply the absence of complementarity at different moments of the teaching-learning process.

5. The Method

As mentioned above, the pilot study reported in this paper involved 12 participants. All of them were studying the module of professional English for the service of restoration at the center of Professional Formation SEM in Alcala de Henares (Spain). All participants were working in a well-known fast-food restaurant. The classes were held three days a week (Monday, Tuesday, and Wednesday) during five-hour sessions with an intensive course format. The rest of the week, the students kept working at the same restaurant. As for education, all of them had completed secondary school.

The study's research material consisted of a multiple-choice-question test with 36 items, as illustrated in the Appendix. This test served as both pretest and post-test for paired data analysis. The experimental items and distractors were counterbalanced so that students could not identify the type of grammaticality about which they were tested. The test included 18 experimental items and 18 distractors. The experimental items consisted of nine examples of Dative alternation with an indirect object going before a direct object, i.e. *I will give Peter a bicycle for his birthday;* and, nine examples of prepositional indirect objects, i.e. *Their friends brought a new book for Harry*. The distractors consisted of nine inalienable possession sentences, i.e. *Mary touched his foot*, and nine passive sentences, i.e. *The award was given to Spielberg*.

For our research interests, the test included three crucial experimental items which contain ditransitive verbs (give, sell, send), as illustrated in (4), where the indirect object is freely fronted before the direct object. Note that their Spanish counterparts are impossible in Spanish.

4) a. I will give Peter a bicycle for his birthday

b. Rita sold John a car.

c. Mike will send Sylvia a package next week.

The implementation of an explicit and an implicit methodology for the teaching and subsequent acquisition of these structures will allow us to discover significant differences, if any, between one type of teaching and another.

Students had to render their grammatical judgments after reading all the items. They were asked to mark each option as correct, incorrect, or leave it unanswered if they were not sure about it. Their level of English varies, depending on the Spanish education system, between A2 and B1, on the CEFR. As we are a small sample of the population, we have used percentages to quantify the results. In the class design, students were explicitly taught about the DA phenomenon which was illustrated by several sentences, like the ones illustrated below:

5) a. The waiter gave the menu to the customer.

   b. The waiter gave the customer a menu.

6) a. Alex sent the bill to the supplier.

   b. Alex sent the supplier the bill.

7) a. The cook sold his recipes to the new kitchen assistant.

   b. The cook sold the new kitchen assistant his recipes.

The verbal core was composed of the ditransitive verbs give, send, and sell. The frame of the semantic content belonged to the customer service context, including specific vocabulary from the communicative situation that took place.

6. Results

In what follows, the results of the pilot study are discussed regarding the type of instruction delivered in each group. First of all, the correct responses provided by all 12 participants were counted before splitting the groups in two. Table 14.1 below includes the correct response by all subjects in the pretest.

Table 14.1 Pre-test Score (All subjects)

Students	Pre test score
1	77,7
2	77,7
3	66,6
4	66,6
5	66,6
6	66,6
7	55,5
8	55,5
9	55,5

10	55,5
11	55,5

Figure 14.1 below also illustrates the correct answer concerning DA by all participants in the pretest.

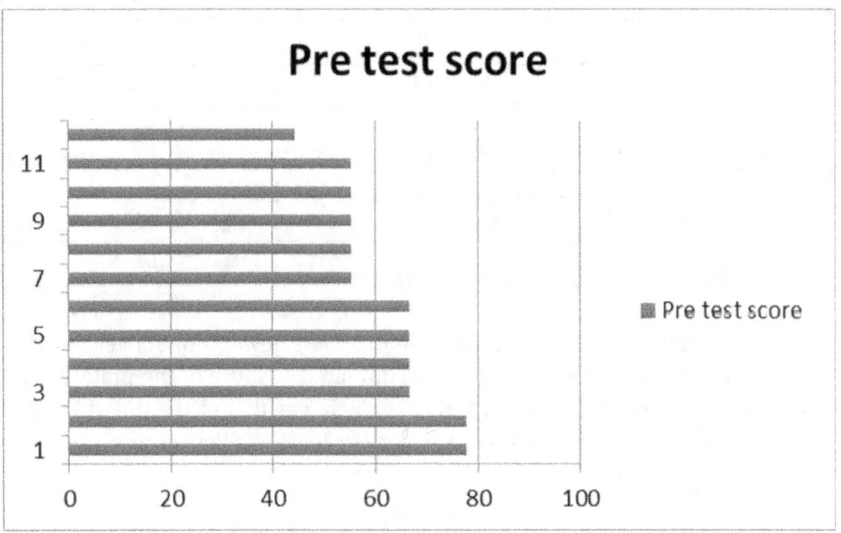

Figure 14.1 Global Correct Response (Pretest)

As displayed in Figure 14.1, no student had all the answers right. One student did not reach half of it. Next, we wanted to look at the experimental items and in particular about the correct response concerning the English dative alternation in each of the two groups who were separated into two groups at random.

6.1. Explicit Teaching Group

During the first hour in two class sessions, the teacher - who acted as the experimenter - made an explicit presentation of the DA phenomena through different materials and activities to expose and explain different examples. First, the students had to put together a set of cards containing words in English to make syntactically correct sentences, like those exemplified above (cf. 5-7). Later on, the students wrote the sentences on the board. Finally, sentences were explicitly discussed concerning their Spanish counterparts, as to whether or not they were correct.

Table 14.2 includes the percentage of correct response by those students that answered the experimental items concerning the DA condition in both the pretest and the post-test. Figure 14.2 depicts the contrasting results concerning both the pretest and the post-test.

Table 14.2 Explicit Teaching Group

Explicit	Pretest	Postest
1	**77,7**	88,8
7	55,5	77,7
8	55,5	66,6
10	55,5	77,7
11	55,5	88,8
12	44,4	66,6

By comparing students' response to both tests, relevant differences may be observed in the results of the post-test compared to those of the pretest. The average hit rate of the pretest was 57.37%, whereas that of the post-test was 77.7%. There has therefore been an increase in 20.33% of the success rate.

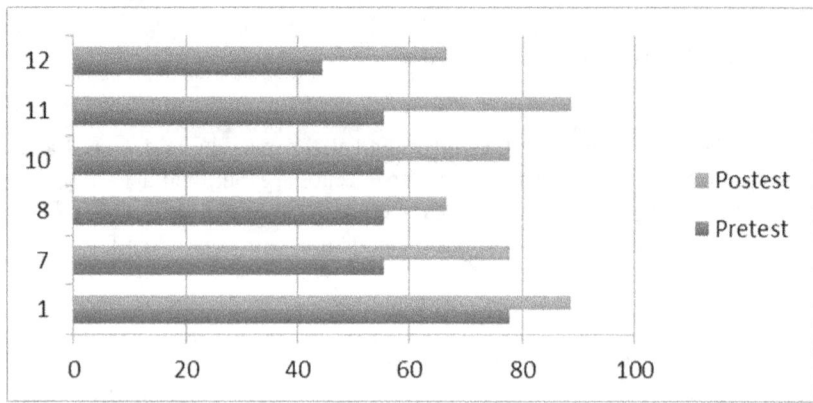

Figure 14.2 Correct Response (DA condition, Explicit Teaching)

6.2. Implicit Teaching Group

In the first session, the teacher-researcher designed a Role Play activity. For this purpose, students were given brief scripts in pairs with ditransitive verbs like the ones found in the DA alternation discussed above. Each script contained relevant contests for producing DA in the target language. Before the performance of each pair, the teacher asked the students to focus on the content of the dialogues without explaining the linguistic phenomena under study. Each pair then repeated their roles. When the role-play was played twice, the students listened to an average of eight examples of the Dative Alternation in context.

It is essential to point out that the communicative restoration situations that formed the basis of the implicit instruction different DA structures were involved so that students were aware of the presence of different participants in the action: agents, themes and recipients. Below are the table and the graph with the comparative results between the pre-test and the post-test of the group attending the implicit instruction.

Table 14.3 Implicit Teaching Group

	Pretest	Postest
2	77,7	66,6
3	66,6	77,7
4	66,6	66,6
5	66,6	33,3
6	66,6	66,6
7	55,5	77,7

Considering the results obtained in the pretest and the post-test by the students of the implicit instruction group we, however, do not observe much difference. The average success rate of the pretest was 66.6%, whereas that of the post-test was 64.75%. As we can see, not only is the correct response similar in both tests, the results in the post-test are significantly worse.

Considering both groups together, Table 14.4 below includes the best rates targeting the DA phenomenon per test.

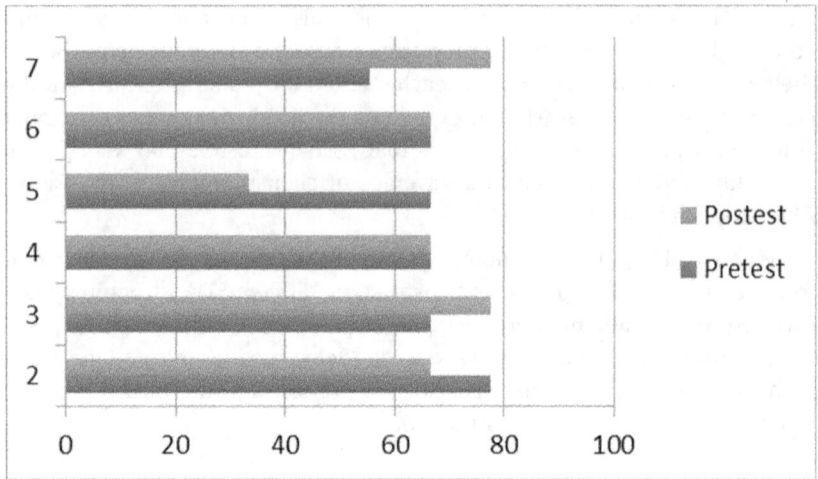

Figure 14.3 Correct Response (DA condition, Implicit Teaching)

Table 14.4 Correct response: Both groups collapsed

	Pretest	Post-test
Explicit instruction group	57,37%	77,70%
Implicit instruction group	66,60%	64,75%

Furthermore, Figure 14.4 depicts the development line in each group.

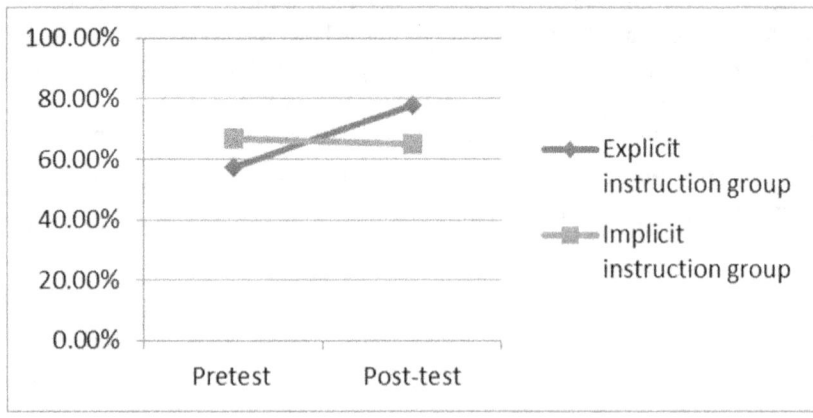

Figure 14.4 Development line per group

7. Discussion and concluding remarks

The data from the study reported below clearly suggest that those students whose contact with the **DA** was through explicit instruction obtained significantly better results than the other ones. Pupils under explicit instruction heard the targeted grammar structure exclusively, avoiding any communicative context. On the other hand, those students under implicit instruction have heard the grammar structure embedded in a meaningful context. Our finding that using an explicit methodology offers greater effectiveness in the learning and acquisition of grammatical structure compared to an implicit methodology through ESP content is supported by other studies, such as the one carried out by Scott (1990). In her study, the researcher provides empirical data on explicit and implicit strategies for teaching foreign language grammar. Among his conclusions, he states that students who receive an organized grammatical explanation gain more significant knowledge as it is easier for them to organize the different linguistic elements.

Among the possible explanations for the correct interpretation of our results, we can address several issues. We must consider the language transfer and that the similarities that may exist between the L1. The target language may cause the data of the analytical methods and studies to vary. In our specific case, the similarity between the English Prepositional phrase construction and the Spanish structure may be linked with the fact that some students are not aware of the validity of the double object structure in English. Those students who have not received a direct explanation of this issue are precisely the ones more likely to make mistakes when admitting the acceptability or otherwise of these constructions. In this sense, one of the advantages of explicit instruction is to provide systematic and organized teaching that allows the teacher to have greater control over the targeted structure and the student to avoid confusion when distinguishing between what is essential or not. The linguistic phenomenon of the DA has provided valuable information. In methodological terms, the choice of one type of instruction or another can determine success in achieving the proposed objectives. In the case of this research, the complexity of some structures chooses one type of instruction (explicit/implicit) crucial. As we have seen from the data obtained, the acquisition of AD is more effective when carried out through explicit instruction, since this is a rather intricate linguistic phenomena in the foreign language classroom (Escobar-Alvarez, 2016).

Pragmatics is the part of linguistics that studies the relationship of language with its users as well as their circumstances (context) where communication takes place. All this information provides valuable information on the implementation of CLIL methodology. The role of pragmatics regulates the social relations of the speaker and their ability to increase the opportunities to apply real language use. The teacher-researcher perceived an increase in the level of student motivation through the practical information provided by the contents and activities outcomes proposed. Unlike previous experiences in formal education, the students assumed the practical and functional nature of the ESP course that they completed.

The context in which the teaching-learning process takes place plays a critical role. Students in an ESP course are in a situation where they have to divide up work and study hours, which compromises their performance in class since combining work and study is an arduous task that requires much effort. As we pointed out earlier, the students of this ESP restoration course left their formal studies some time ago. In principle, this can cause their motivation to be affected by negative self-esteem and self-concept. Often these concepts are interrelated. Self-esteem is considered a personal appreciation in the different areas of social and personal relationships. The appreciation and self-evaluation of qualities and aptitudes result in a positive or negative value, a positive or negative self-image according to the self-evaluation that one makes of oneself and in comparison, to ideals that one values positively. It is, therefore, a complex constructor that indicates the social-emotional and affective value that one gives oneself in different vital aspects of personal and individual relationships – appreciation or contempt, which is attributed in essential aspects of life and of one's aptitudes. From our point of view, we understand that the design, preparation, and implementation of methodologies of any nature (explicit and implicit) should take care of motivation. For certain activities, this is one of the essential issues, among which we highlight learning as the cornerstone of our research interest. In the educational field, we can understand motivation as the will and effort of a student to learn a subject in a specific area of knowledge

Our study has been limited by the number of ESP students which is small compared to other areas of teaching. This issue has resulted in not being able to obtain a more significant number of responses in the pretest and the post-test for subsequent analysis of a higher number of data that shed more light on the question under study. Research has focused on ESP students, which suggests several considerations: ESP students have generally not had direct contact for a long time with the formal teaching of a language, in this case, English. The level of the students is another aspect to take into account since their level, having finished secondary school in Spain, is A2/B1, according to the CEFR.

Future research in this field should include studies with a more significant number of subjects and establish comparisons not only between members of the same group but also between different ESP courses with different levels (intermediate, proficiency) in order to compare and establish relationships between the different ways of teaching (explicit and implicit) and the students' learning styles. In this way and through the information obtained, it will be easier to design more effective teaching techniques in the field of ESP, taking into account the cross-linguistic contracts that take place and to give more effective responses to the problems that may arise.

References

Aguirre, I. A. (2015). The acquisition of dative alternation in English by Spanish learners. *Vigo International Journal of Applied Linguistics*, (12), pp. 65-66.

Archer, A. L., & Hughes, C. A. (2010). *Explicit instruction: Effective and efficient teaching*. Guilford Press

Benati, Alessandro and Angelovska, Tanja (2016) *Second Language Acquisition: A theoretical introduction to real world applications*. Bloomsbury, London, UK.

Bialystock, E. (1983). Some factors in the selection and implementation of communication strategies. In C. Faerch & G. Kasper (Eds.), Strategies in interlanguage communication London: Longman, pp. 20-60.

Bresnan, J., Cueni, A., Nikitina, T., & Baayen, R. H (2007). Predicting the dative alternation. In G. Bouma, I. Kraemer, &J. Zwarts (Eds.), *Cognitive foundations of interpretation* (pp-69-94). Amsterdam: KNAW.

Cohen, A., & Brooks-Carson, A. (2001). Research on direct versus translated writing: Students' strategies and their results. The Modern Language Journal, 85 (2), 169- 188.

Dalton-Puffer, C. (2007). *Discourse in content and language integrated learning (CLIL) classrooms* (Vol. 20). John Benjamins Publishing.

Demonte, Violeta. (1994). La ditransitividad en español: léxico y sintaxis. En V. Demonte, ed. Gramática del español, 431-470. México: El Colegio de México.

Demonte, Violeta. (1995). Dative alternation in Spanish. Probus 7.1: 5-30

Dudley-Evans, T., & St John, M. J. (1998). *Developments in ESP: A multidisciplinary approach* (No. 428.007 D849). Cambridge university press.

Ellis, N. C. (2002a). Frequency effects in language processing: A review with implications for theories of implicit and explicit language acquisition. *Studies in Second Language Acquisition*, 24, pp.143–188.

Escobar Alvarez, M.A (2016) L2 Acquisition of Spanish dative clitics by English and Dutch learners. Studies in Second Language Learning and Teaching, 7 (3), pp.517-534.

Fries, C.C. (1945). Teaching and Learning of English as a Foreign Language. Ann Avbor: University of Michigan Press

Gass, S. M. (2000). Fundamentals of second language acquisition. In J.W. Rosenthal (Ed.), Handbook of undergraduate second language education (pp. 29-46). Mahwah, New Jersey: Lawrence Erlbaum Associate, Inc., Publishers.

Green, G. (1974). Semantics and Syntactic Regularity. Bloomington: Indiana University Press.

Gropen, J., S. Pinker, M. Hollander, R. Goldberg, and R. Wilson. (1989). The learnability and acquisition of the dative alternation. Language 65 (2), pp 203–257.

Halliday, M. A. (1980). Three aspects of children's language development: Learning language, learning through language, learning about language. *Oral and written language development research*, 7-19.

Mackay, R., & Mountford, A. J. (1978). The teaching of English for special purposes: Theory and practice. *English for specific purposes*, pp. 2-20.

Morales, J. R. (2008). *Los dativos en el español* (Vol. 101). Arco Libros.

Oehrle, R. T. (1976). The grammar of the English dative alternation. Cambridge, MA: MIT Department of Linguistics and Philosophy Ph.D. dissertation.

Scott, V. M. (1990). Explicit and implicit grammar teaching strategies: New empirical data. *The French Review*, *63*(5), 779-789.

Wright, C. (1992). The benefits of ESP. *Cambridge language consultants*, 5.

Wolfe-Quintero, K. (1993). The dative alternation in English, pp. 91.

Appendix

Say if the following sentences are CORRECT, INCORRECT OR "I DON'T KNOW":

1. **I will give Peter a bicycle for his birthday.**
2. Their friends brought a new book for Harry.
3. Mary touched his foot.
4. A new song was created by Laura.
5. **Mike sent a package to Sylvia last week.**
6. Helen bought a new car for her son Alex.
7. Mary touched her head.
8. New comics were selected by Peter.
9. **Rita sold John a car.**
10. An award was given to Spielberg.
11. Mary raises her hand.
12. The car door was opened by Arthur.
13. **I gave a bicycle to Peter for your birthday.**
14. Their friends will bring a new book for Harry.
15. Mary washes her hand.
16. The project was finished by Lara.
17. Mike will sent a package to you last week.
18. Helen will buy a new car for her son Alex.

19. His motorbike will be washed by Jack.
20. **Rita sold a car to John yesterday.**
21. Joanne makes a cake to her friend Suzanne.
22. Mary draws her head.
23. The landscape is described by my father.
24. Mary´s dog died.
25. Their friends brings a new book for Harry.
26. Mary broke her leg.
27. Don Quixote was written by Cervantes.
28. **Mike will send Sylvia a package next week.**
29. Rita will sell John a car.
30. Joanne will make a cake to her friend Suzanne.
31. Mary touches Andrew´s nose.
32. The books were given to the student´s.
33. I gave you a bicycle for your birthday.
34. Joanne made a cake to her friend Suzanne.
35. Mary scratches her head.
36. Helen returned the wallet to his owner.

Contributors

Amina Gaye is an Applied Linguist teaching English at Fatima College of Health Sciences, Abu Dhabi, UAE. She holds a PhD. Her teaching and research areas include Academic Writing, Computational Linguistics, Curriculum Design and ESP Teacher Training. She is a member of the International ESP Teachers' Association (IESPTA).

Arzu Ekoç received her BA from Translation Studies from Boğaziçi University and her Master's in ELT from Istanbul University. She completed her PhD in ELT at Istanbul University. She has been working as an English lecturer at Yildiz Technical University in Istanbul, Turkey, since 2006. Her research interests are learner identity, higher education and continuing education, EAP, second-language writing.

Bárbara Malveira Orfanò is an Adjunct Professor at the Federal University of Minas Gerais, Brazil. Her main research interests are corpus-based studies within Applied Linguistics with a focus on learner corpora, specialised corpora and English for Academic Purposes.

Brian G. Rubrecht is a Professor in the School of Commerce's English Department at Meiji University in Tokyo, Japan. He earned his Masters degree in TESOL and Bilingual Education from Georgetown University in 2000 and graduated from The University of Texas at Austin in 2004 with a doctoral degree in Foreign Language Education. His professional and research interests include aspects of language learning motivation, second language writing, curriculum development, translation and interpretation, identity, phonetics, and cultural aspects that influence the learning of a foreign language.

Elena Bárcena Madera is a full professor in the Department of Modern Languages at UNED, the Spanish national distance learning university, where she is the founding coordinator of the Master in Information and Communication Technologies for Language Learning and Processing. She has also been the director of the ATLAS (Applying Technologies to Languages) research group since 1997. She is also an expert adviser for national and international institutions and a member of the editorial board of a number of specialized journals in this field. She is also currently working the boundaries between formal and non-formal language learning, particularly on Mobile Assisted Language Learning and Massive Open Online Courses.

Ian Michael Robinson is a language Researcher at the University of Calabria in Italy. He has taught in many different places, including Greece, Japan and the UK, as well as in Italy where he is particularly involved in ESP. He has also written articles on such topics as fairy tales and corpus linguistics, CLIL, and intercultural studies.

Iván Calleja Rituerto works as an English language teacher in primary and secondary schools and is currently a PhD candidate at UNED, Spain. He holds a MA in both Teaching Languages and European Literature and Gender, Identity, and Citizenship (Universidad de Huelva). His interests are teaching and learning of languages through content transversality and EAP.

Joanna Moraza Erausquin is a language teacher and a PhD candidate at UNED, Spain. She holds an MA in Applied Linguistics in Spanish as foreign language acquisition. Her interests are CLIL and ESP.

Leonardo Pereira Nunes is an Adjunct Professor of English for Academic Purposes (EAP) and a member of the Laboratory for Experimentation in Translation (LETRA) at the Federal University of Minas Gerais (UFMG), Brazil. His main research interests are corpus-based studies and machine-assisted human translation within academic writing.

Mohamed Abdelsalam Osman Mohamed Ahmed is an assistant professor who has worked for more than ten years in different institutions such as Sudan University of Science and Technology, Bahri Ahlia College, Gizera College of Technology, and Halfaya Vocational Training Center. He holds a PhD from Sudan University. He is a member of the International ESP Teachers' Association. His interests are in all branches of linguistics specifically in ESP, Semantics, Syntax, and discourse analysis.

Mohammad Amerian holds a Ph.D. in Teaching English as a Foreign Language (TEFL) from Allameh Tabataba'i University (ATU), Iran. He has taught English at various levels and is currently a lecturer in the university, Business English tutor and interpreter. His research interests include ESP, content knowledge, content-based instruction and curriculum development.

Omar I. S. Alomoush is an Assistant Professor of English linguistics at Tafila Technical University, Jordan, where he is currently Head of English Department. He holds a PhD in Sociolinguistics from the University of Liverpool, UK. His research interests include sociolinguistics, English and globalisation, language policy and planning, linguistic landscape, Arabic semantics and pragmatics. He published several papers in sociolinguistics and linguistic landscape in prestigious journals such as English Today.

Sonia Sharmin completed her Ph.D. in TESOL from the University of Georgia in 2018 where she was also a Fulbright Foreign Language Teaching Assistant. She has taught in Bangladesh and the U.S. for more than 13 years. Her areas of interest are second language writing, digital literacy, and composition studies.

Svetlana Rubtsova is an associate professor and the head of ESP department, Dean of the Faculty of Modern languages at St. Petersburg State University (SPbSU. She holds a PhD in Philology (St. Petersburg State University, 1983), with an extensive experience in teaching GE/EAP/ESP, teacher training, translation studies, intercultural communication studies, course development and syllabus design, language and assessment (examiner of BULATS 2016-2017), ELT and translation studies management in St. Petersburg University, supervisor of the educational programme "Translation in the sphere of professional communication"

Takeshi Kamijo is currently a professor at the College of Business Administration, Ritsumeikan University, Japan. His research interests include English for Academic Purposes, reading and writing strategies, socio-cultural theory and learner development, classroom research and language testing and assessment.

Tarek Assassi is an associate professor at Biskra University, Algeria. He holds a doctorate degree in English Language and Education, and he has taught several courses and supervised a number of master's dissertations. He is a certified assessor of aviation English (EALTS) by Bournemouth University experts, and he is currently the pedagogical coordinator of the Centre for Intensive Language Teaching at the same university.

Tatiana E. Dobrova has been teaching General English and ESP for International Relation and Law Bachelor students of Saint Petersburg State

University since 1998, an author some textbooks, educational aids and teaching devices. She is currently Academic Secretary of the Faculty of Modern Languages. The sphere of her academic interests includes the general issues of ESP methodology, integrating digital technologies in ESP, the issues of intercultural communication and intercultural competence, teaching ESP for Chinese students.

Index

A

absolute and variable characteristics, 80
Abstract writing, 200
academic and professional settings, 119
academic English, 108, 163
academic language, 59, 122
academic skills, 83, 222
academic texts, 164, 176
academic writing, 151, 160, 163, 176, 179-192, 197-198, 207, 209
adopting, 3, 129, 131
aeronautics, 3
Alvermann, D., 68
American Psychological Association (APA), 180
Anthony, L., 80
Arabicised English, 15
Arab region, 18
Assignment, 153
Authenticity, 133
aviation English, 3-13

B

background information, 32, 128
Basturkmen, H., 7, 35, 36,
Belcher, D., 47, 57, 117
Bhatia, V. K., 115
bilingual teaching, 80
Blackboard system, 111
blended learning, 103, 107
Bologna Process, 82
boosters, 195-202, 209
Borowska, A., 9-10

business English, 47-48, 58, 121, 135

C

Cary, S., 72
Chen, L. N., 28
Chi-Square, 38
China, 153
classroom language policy, 127
code-mixing, 15
coding category, 152
Coffey, B., 119
cognitive function, 132
cognitive reading model, 149
cognitive theories, 222
collective activity, 99
commodification, 28
Common European Framework of Reference (CEFR), 52, 168
communicative competence, 11, 12, 104, 118
communicative language approach, 80
communicative needs, 5, 7, 16, 48
competency based training system, 32
complexity, 71, 229
constraints, 83, 216
constructive process, 150
content based academic reading, 160
content-based instruction, 129
content knowledge, 58
context-first, 122
contextual cues, 150
Corpus Query Tool, 170
corpus-driven, 164, 168

corrective feedback, 155-157
Council of Europe, 117
course design, 46, 115, 120
critical and evaluative reading, 152
critical reading, 155
critical thinking, 100, 121, 207
Croft, W., 6
cultural differences, 77, 99
cultural texts, 75
cultural practices, 67
curriculum, 68, 104, 216

D

dative alternation, 215
Davis, K., 71
deductive, 51
dialogues, 84, 227
dictation, 82
digital literacy, 65-69, 98-101
discontextualized task, 76
discourse analysis, 119
discursive approach, 18
discursive sphere, 192
distance learning, 98, 107
ditransitive verbs, 215, 223-226
diversity, 56, 218
domains, 182, 188
Douglas, D., 5, 179
drawbacks, 97, 103
Dudley-Evans, 46, 80, 116, 216
dynamic notions, 56

E

EAP experts, 52, 56
educational mobility, 104
educational platform, 103
E-learning, 97, 103
Ellis, N. C., 6, 131, 222
Ellis's terms, 222
empirical studies, 103

English for general purposes, 5, 33, 40, 80
English language syllabus, 39
Erasmus, 83
ESP course design, 46
ESP course, 230
ESP curriculum, 216
ESP material, 83
ESP practitioners, 121
ESP teachers, 80, 115, 122
evaluative reading strategies, 149, 151, 157
ESP theory, 116

F

feedback, 34, 55, 87, 92, 108, 153, 157
five-minute fillers, 82
Flowerdew, J., 164, 191,
Flowerdew, L., 47-48, 59, 122
follow-up exercise, 84, 87
formulaicity, 10-12
frequency of hedging, 208

G

general language policy, 83
genres, 79, 81, 116, 121-123
genre analysis, 115, 119-121
Giner, D., 197-198
globalisation, 98, 103
glocalisation, 17
Google forms, 169
Gorter, D., 16, 18, 22
Grammar Translation Method, 216
Gunnarsson, 180

H

Hallidayan Systemic Functional Linguistics, 176

hangouts, 102
Harmer, J., 82
hedges, 198, 204
higher education, 98, 101
Hutchinson, T., 35, 46, 117-118, 120, 123
Hyland, K., 46, 164, 195-199, 201, 203-204
Hyon, S., 81, 119

I

identity, 72, 107, 183
idiomatic expressions, 84
iMessage, 71
immigrants, 47, 68, 83
impersonalization strategies, 201
implementation of, 98, 223
implicit learning, 215, 222
innovation, 20, 100
interactive, 88, 91, 103
interdisciplinary, 130, 216
interlanguage, 164, 215, 221
International Civil Aviation Organisation, 3, 5
international communication, 130
interpersonal, 48
intertextual awareness, 154, 160

J

Japanese university, 127
Jordan, R. R., 80, 118
Jordanian linguistic landscape, 16, 28
journals, 168, 184, 201

K

Kaplan, R., 179
Karen refugee, 65
Karlander, D., 18

Kasanga, L. A., 18
Kenny, N., 138
Knobel, M., 67, 101
Korean soap operas, 68, 73, 76
Kress, G., 66,

L

language and culture, 82
language for specific purpose, 5, 116, 129, 180, 192
language-centred approach, 118, 120
language program, 128-129, 138
language system, 117
learning needs, 118
learning objectives, 80, 92
lexical sphere, 192
lifelong learning, 97, 217
Life Sciences, 169
Likert scale, 52
Lingua Franca, 163
linguistic landscape, 16, 18
linguistic knowledge, 82
listening skills, 79
literacy practices, 65-72

M

massive open online courses (MOOCs), 102-103
Maleki, A., 121
McCulloch, S., 149, 151-152, 154, 160
metacognitive strategies, 150, 160
metadiscourse, 195-209
material development, 81
methodological methods, 128
monolingual, 16, 22, 27, 66, 131, 151
Moodle system, 105-107, 111
Moussaoui's study, 207

multilingual, 16, 67
multilingual identities, 78
multimodality, 68
Munby, J., 118
Murphey, T., 82

N

native-like proficiency, 4, 81
needs analysis, 31, 36, 80, 117, 120
networking, 17, 69
non-native speakers, 6, 119
novice writers, 197, 199, 207

O

occupational needs, 54, 80
occupational English, 83
Omerbašic, D., 66
online ESP teaching, 97

P

paradigm, 98, 100
passive that-clause, 163
pedagogical practices, 128, 130, 142
peer-assessment, 51
phraseology, 6-9
Plakans, L., 151
Pope, R., 83
Post Graduate Qualified Exam, 107
postgraduate students, 109
practical applications, 45
pragmatics, 229
Prepositional Construction, 220
Prinzo, O. V., 9
problematic areas, 52, 54, 56
productive skills, 55, 58
professional English tasks, 52
proficiency level, 50, 153
psychology-related texts, 185

psychology discipline, 182
Public Speaking course, 195-196, 201

Q

qualitative data, 49, 54, 56
quantitative data, 28, 47
quantitative phase, 191

R

Reeves, C., 180
refugee, 65, 67, 72
reinforcement, 150
Rhetorical Structure Theory, 192
Richterich, R., 117
Robinson, R. S., 199,

S

Scollon, R., 18
Second language acquisition, 82, 155
Self-assessment, 51
Shen, C., 82
Simpson, A. J., 82, 91
Sketch Engine, 169-170
social interaction, 72
Social Policy, 79, 82, 91
sociocultural approach, 67
sociolinguistics, 15-18
software, 99
songs, 69, 79
Spanish structure, 229
specific reading strategies, 151
specific vocabulary, 180, 191, 224
Spolsky, B., 17
Saint Petersburg State University, 97, 99, 111
Starfield, S., 47
study skills, 79, 121

sub-corpora, 167
subject knowledge and content, 120
subject-matter experts, 52
surveys, 81
sustainable, 98
Swales, J., 81, 115, 119-120, 149, 151, 164
syllabus design, 35, 48

T

target needs, 118
target situation analysis, 46
taxonomy, 197
team teaching model, 130
technical vocabulary, 31, 38, 41, 47
technology use, 74
tentative assessment, 196
textbooks, 35, 180, 181
text-first, 122
textual sphere, 192
that-clauses, 163-176
themes, 153, 227
think-aloud, 149-156
Tomlinson's principals, 81
topic introduction, 79
TRANSITIVITY, 163-176
Trilingual, 23, 26,
Turkish ELT, 197
types of ESP, 117

U

undergraduate students, 163, 195, 199
underlying methodology, 116
Upton, T., 150
utterances, 3, 133

V

Van Dijk, A., 160, 192
Varnosfadrani, A. D., 36
varieties of English, 115
Vazquez, I., 197-198
verbal processes, 167, 173
Virtual University, 101
vocabulary and, 57, 118, 220
vocational training, 31, 33, 46
vocationalism, 48

W

Weschler, R., 133
West, R., 36
Weyers, J. R., 18
Woodrow, L., 80-81, 88, 91-92
work of ESP, 79
workplace, 45-59
Wood, A., 180
World Englishes, 81
Wright, C., 216
writing tasks, 87, 149, 151

Y

YouTube, 70
Yagiz, O., 198, 208

Z

Zhang, Y., 102